The Tower of London
in the History of England

Frontispiece: The White Tower, the central keep,
built by William the Conqueror

A. L. ROWSE

THE TOWER OF LONDON
IN THE HISTORY OF ENGLAND

G. P. PUTNAM'S SONS
New York

© A. L. Rowse 1972

Library of Congress Catalog Card Number: 72-80681
SBN 399-11040-2

Designed by John Wallis

Printed in England

Designed by John Wallis for
George Weidenfeld & Nicolson Limited

To Elizabeth Jenkins
admirable writer
and most constant friend

Contents

1 Building and Medieval Background 9

2 Yorkists: Richard III and the Murder of the Princes 19

3 Henry VIII and Sir Thomas More 35

4 Reformation Chops and Changes 57

5 Protestants and Catholics 77

6 Sir Walter Ralegh and Essex 107

7 Gunpowder Plot: the Wizard Earl and Ralegh 123

8 Arbella Stuart; the Murder of Sir Thomas Overbury 143

9 Victims, Royal and Parliamentary 155

10 The Tower in Civil War and Revolution 173

11 The Restoration: Whig and Tory Antics 187

12 Stuart Sequel: the '15 and '45 Rebellions 217

13 Georgian Amenities: Eccentrics, Americans, Spies, Traitors 235

14 Victoriana – Epilogue 249

Chronology 261

Plan of the Tower 267

Genealogical trees 268

Acknowledgments 273

Index 275

I

Building and
Medieval Background

THE Tower of London is probably the most familiar, as it is a unique, symbol of the English state – of its power, and also of a good deal of its history. Its very shape is compelling both to the memory and the imagination: the strong, sturdy, square mass of the central keep, the White Tower, with its pepper-pot turrets at the four corners, appropriately finished off by one of the strongest of English kings, Henry VIII. There it stands four-square amid its surrounding grey walls, bastions, lesser towers, the moat on three sides of it, the Thames with the Tower Wharf on the fourth: the dominating spectacle to greet anyone approaching London up the river, and to say farewell to anyone leaving it, going down and out to sea, the big flag flying in the breeze – the fortress never captured.

To the historic imagination it presents an image of power and resolution; to the informed mind the appropriate emotion is perhaps a mixture of foreboding and pride. In earlier times its bulk must have been even more impressive, bullying the small houses and roof-levels of the City coming up to its gates. And indeed that was one of its prime purposes, to overawe London, as its other purpose was to defend the approach to the nerve-centre of the kingdom.

For we must remember that the Tower is the visible expression of a conquest, the Norman Conquest of England. After the organisation of a powerful state out of the haphazard heptarchy of the Anglo-Saxons, by those men of iron the Normans, the island was never again conquered – though it might have been subverted, as recently as in 1940. The Tower was built by that great man, William the Conqueror, with stone largely brought across from Caen.

It may be that the English did not wholly relish the memory, for they liked to think that the Tower went back to the Romans and was founded by Julius Caesar. This was the folklore: it is expressed by William Dunbar in the fifteenth century, in his poem in praise of London:

> By Julius Caesar thy Tower founded of old
> May be the house of Mars victorial,
> Whose artillery with tongue may not be told . . .

9

Henry III, the artist king who rebuilt the Great Hall
and made other improvements to the Tower

While Shakespeare, who is a great one for expressing folklore, refers in *Richard II* to 'Julius Caesar's ill-erected tower' – meaning not that it was ill-built but that it was built for ill.

In fact it was not built by the Romans, though some parts of the complex rest on Roman foundations. The Conqueror built his first fortress in the south-east angle of the existing Roman wall around the city; subsequently the Wardrobe Tower was erected on the base of a Roman bastion; and traces of the Roman wall can be seen within. So there are those elements of continuity with Roman power and civilisation to satisfy the imagination; but the essential is that William I brought over a Norman expert, Gundulf, as his artificer and he designed the White Tower.

The Tower was not only a fortress, it became a royal palace; indeed it came to serve several purposes at once: a state prison for the loftiest and most eminent, those considered dangerous to the state, those accused of treason. It was also the home of the Mint; the treasury for the Crown Jewels and regalia; a record office for state papers, with a line of scholarly Keepers; and an observatory. Since the lion was a royal animal, and thus a suitable present to kings, one tower, the Lion Tower which formerly existed at the present main entrance, was a menagerie. As other awkward presents of animals accumulated, leopards, bears, wolves, lynxes, the Tower formed until 1834 the original Zoo.

After it received its girdle of walls and subsidiary towers, and was surrounded by a deep moat by Richard Cœur-de-lion, the general appearance of the vast complex was much as we see it today. But, within, there have been significant changes. In front of the White Tower, i.e. on the south side facing the river, there grew up a royal palace, with great hall and private lodgings. Medieval kings occasionally resided, or took refuge, here – and here many historic events took place, stately and ceremonial, pathetic or dreadful, such as the murder of the princes, Edward IV's sons. It was the custom for the kings and queens to spend the night, or a few days, before their coronation in these apartments, and from them the coronation processions set out on their way to Westminster. Charles II's was the last; after that the royal lodgings lapsed into desuetude and were ultimately swept away, to leave the White Tower in splendid isolation.

Still, altogether the complex of buildings known collectively as the Tower of London offers a unique combination historically: a trinity of fortress, palace, and prison. Other countries have had their Bastilles, or their fortress of St Peter and St Paul for a state prison; the Escorial was both royal palace and monastery; even the Popes had their Castel St Angelo to take refuge in in time of trouble. The Tower of London combined all these functions – and, in addition, we have it in almost complete preservation. As a fortress alone the Royal Commission on Historical Monuments describes it sedately as 'the most valuable monument of medieval military architecture surviving in this country'. But in its buildings we can read much of the history of England – it is that aspect which will engage our attention in this book.

Today, in the decline of the British state, we think of it more as a venerable relic of the past, with the attractive Tudor costumes, crimson and gold, halberds and all, the ancient ceremonies of delivering the key at night to the Governor, giving the password, etc., pickled and preserved. The English have come to look upon it not only with pride but something of affection. The historian, however, may still feel something of a *frisson* as evening descends upon the grey walls and stony corridors, and the populace is shut out; the tide laps the wharf outside Traitors' Gate, a mist from the river wraps the scene in a shroud, and as night comes on, with the cheerless lights in the alley-ways, the ghosts with their memories clamour for release.

The Tower as zoo: Henry III's elephant

The Tower of London

After the Conqueror the medieval king who left most mark upon the Tower was the extravagant aesthete, Henry III, to whom we owe Westminster Abbey. He was a man of taste, who preferred things of beauty to fighting – no wonder he was always in trouble for money and was not popular with his bellicose barons. By 1236 he had rebuilt the Great Hall; he built the Wakefield Tower, next to the royal lodgings, the archway to the Bloody Tower (now so-called), and the main angle towers along the wall. Very devout, he had the Norman chapel of St John in the White Tower re-decorated – now stripped unliturgically bare, by the Reformation, of its screens and stalls. He completely refurbished the church of St Peter-ad-vincula, having the royal stalls painted, the images and figures coloured, a new statue of the Virgin set up in the north aisle; panels painted before the two altars; a marble font sculpted. His own chamber in the royal lodgings was frescoed with the story of Antiochus – we can derive an idea from the contemporary frescoed room in the papal palace at Avignon. Henry III was anxious to keep up with his French relations – but then he was a Frenchman, like all our kings till the end of the Middle Ages.

Unfortunately Henry had trouble in making a direct waterway entrance from the Thames into the Tower: once and again the foundations of the wharf gave way. Not until an oratory was built to the blissful martyr St Thomas were the foundations ensured. Becket was a favourite with the citizens of London – had he not been born one? And the fight he put up against a monarch appealed to their citizenry. In Tudor times the Water Gate beneath St Thomas's Tower – the saint deposed by Henry VIII – became better known as Traitors' Gate: a nice epitome of the times. Henry III's militant son, Edward I, contented himself with finishing this tower and St Peter's fabric – for the rest, he was more interested in conquering Scotland, which achieved nothing but a waste of money and energy. The Tower may be said to have reached its final medieval form. All that remained for Henry VIII to add were two large mounts for the improved cannon of his day – with his personal interest in artillery – the King's House or Lieutenant's Lodging in the south-west corner, considerable repairs and, of course, the angle-turrets on the White Tower so prominent today.

Several individual episodes reveal in a lurid light the general history of those times. In 1244 Griffith, son of Llewelyn the last independent Prince of Wales, attempted an escape: he made a rope from his bedclothes, but it broke, the Prince fell to his death, head crushed between shoulders – it might be taken as a symbol of the crushing of Welsh resistance. At the expulsion of the Jews from England in 1278, some hundreds were temporarily rounded up in the Tower –

12

Opposite above: Evening shadows at the Tower; St Thomas's Tower seen from Tower Wharf. Beneath the Tower is Traitors' Gate
Below: Traitors' Gate. Henry III breached the wall so that a channel could be cut from the river to the Wakefield Tower up which barges could come into the Tower

a sufficiently barbarous measure, but nothing compared with what our own enlightened time exhibited, at the hands of the Germans, nearly seven hundred years later. In 1337–8 we see the Tower in full activity as an arsenal: there Edward III made many of his preparations for the French war that began with the naval victory of Sluys and ended up as the Hundred Years' War.

The Tower was the stage of some of the significant events of Richard II's unfortunate reign, from his coronation procession to his abdication. For the former the boy-King was clad all in white – a colour also chosen for the equally unfortunate Charles I: henceforth regarded as unlucky, and not favoured again. At the outbreak of the Peasants' Revolt in the high summer of 1381, Richard, his Court and ministers took refuge in the Tower, while London burned beyond the walls – his uncle, John of Gaunt's splendid palace of the Savoy, with all its treasures, went up in flames. From the vantage-point in the Tower Richard could see the fires, and no one knew what to do. The young King took the initiative and got out a message to Mayor Walworth to meet him, with the citizens armed, at Mile End on the morrow. Protected by the aura of sacro-sanctity that an anointed king enjoyed in the Middle Ages, Richard rode forth to his revolting subjects.

The Tower was strongly garrisoned by men-at-arms and archers, and the Court should have been safe. Within were the King's mother, the beautiful Joan of Kent (widow of the Black Prince), the Archbishop of Canterbury, Treasurer Hales – responsible for the poll-tax that had so angered the peasants – with other lords and ministers. While the King was away at Mile End there was collusion from inside, as often in revolutionary circumstances, and the mob burst in in familiar rough humour, 'pulling the beards of the Guard and inviting them to join their *societas* [company], invading the royal bed-chambers and attempting familiarities with the Princess of Wales, while not one of her knights ventured to intervene'. It reminds one of the French Revolution mob bursting into the Tuileries to insult Louis XVI and Marie Antoinette. The Archbishop and the Treasurer were dragged out from the Chapel, where they had taken refuge, and with two others were executed on Tower Hill – a small number for such an upheaval: the mob was more merciful than the governing class, when it recovered its nerve. The King's mother was smuggled out of the Tower to Baynard's Castle, while her son regained the initiative with Mayor Walworth's killing of the leader, Wat Tyler, and the dispersal of the peasants.

In happier circumstances in 1390 Richard held a grand jousting, described by Froissart: a splendid cavalcade issued out of the Tower, three score coursers apparelled for the joust, mounted by esquires; three score ladies riding side-saddle on palfreys, each lady leading a knight with a silver chain: so through the streets to Smithfield. Such was (one side of) medieval chivalry. Six years later Richard's child-bride, Isabel of France, was conducted thence on her coronation procession. The pace quickened, with the last neurotic years of Richard's rule.

When Richard had the ill judgment to absent himself in Ireland, after keeping his cousin Bolingbroke out of his rightful succession to his father, John of Gaunt, as Duke of Lancaster, the King left the coast clear for his enemies to overthrow him. Psychotic and unstable, he had made a hopeless king, and the ruling class, with the Church, turned against him. In Bolingbroke, who was the next heir in the male line, they had a much better candidate for the job. In 1399 the Tower witnessed Richard's enforced abdication: he did not resign the Crown voluntarily, as was put about, and he did not resign it to his cousin, but to God. The two Chief Justices were deputed to make formal renunciation of homage and allegiance to the dethroned monarch in his chamber there.

The chronicler Adam of Usk gives us a pen-portrait of poor Richard in his

Left: The Peasants' Revolt; King Richard II speaks to the mob, and Wat Tyler, their leader, is killed by the Lord Mayor of London
Right: Richard II enthroned, from the fourteenth-century portrait in Westminster Abbey

altered circumstances – it is rare to have such a close-up from the Middle Ages. During dinner Richard discoursed woefully:

'My God! a wonderful land is this, and a fickle: which has exiled, slain, destroyed or ruined so many kings, rulers and great men, and is ever tainted with strife and variance and envy.' Then he recounted the histories and names of sufferers from the earliest habitation of the kingdom. Perceiving the trouble of his mind and that none of his own men nor such as were wont to serve him, but strangers who were but spies upon him were appointed to his service – and, musing on his ancient and wonted glory and on the fickle fortune of the world, I departed thence much moved at heart.

We see that Shakespeare's rendering of Richard is not far from the historic truth, and also already forming, in the womb of time, the melancholy procession of monarchs who fell down on their job: before Richard, Edward II; after him, Henry VI, Charles I and James II; in our day, Edward VIII.

Medieval monarchy was a tough struggle for survival. Richard's cousin survived it, but only just. Though called to the throne by the will of Church and Parliament, he bore a double burden through the circumstances of his accession – some were bound to look on him as a usurper. Only a few days after this scene in the Tower, he set out on the usual coronation procession to Westminster, attended by the leaders of the nation, himself on a white charger and bare-headed according to custom – and so to a life of anxiety and trouble as Henry IV.

After *his* son, Henry v's, victory at Agincourt the Tower was for a time crowded with the French nobles captured there. The grandest of these was Charles, Duke of Orleans, the French King's nephew, worth a prince's ransom. For a short time he had been held at Dover on his way to the Tower, where he had leisure to compose the verse that made him one of the foremost poets of the age:

> En regardant vers le pays de France
> Un jour m'avint, à Douvres sur la mer,
> Qu'il me souvint de la douce plaisance
> Que je souloye où dit pays trouver.
> Si commençai de cœur à souspirer
> Combien certes que grand bien me faisoit
> De voire France que mon cœur amer doit . . .

> *Envoi*
> Paix est trésor qu'on ne peut trop louer :
> Je hais guerre, point ne la doit priser ;
> Détourbé m'a longtemps, soit tort ou droit,
> De voire France que mon cœur amer doit.*

After some years of imprisonment, the rumour was that he was dead:

> Nouvelles ont couru en France
> Par maints lieux que j'étais mort . . .†

But his greatest grief, understandable for a Frenchman, was the deprivation of female company, in particular of a lady-love in France:

> Là! Je suis seul sans compagnie!
> Adieu, ma Dame, ma liesse!‡

Not till 1440, after twenty-five years, and further spells at Windsor and Pontefract, was he released for a sum of fifty thousand *livres* – in time to beget a son who became king of France as Louis XII and married Henry VIII's sister.

---

*In looking towards the land of France, one day it happened, at Dover on the sea, that I recalled the sweet pleasure which I used to find in that country. I began to sigh at heart at how much it affected me to see France, to which my sad heart is bound.
Envoi
Peace is a treasure one cannot too much praise. I hate war, which no one ought to prize. Right or wrong, it grieved me long to see France, to which my sad heart is bound.
†Rumours have spread in many places in France that I was dead.
‡Alas, I am alone without companion. Farewell my lady, my joy.

17

Richard abdicates in the Tower to his cousin, Bolingbroke, who became King Henry IV

2
Yorkists: Richard III and the Murder of the Princes

ENRY IV would probably not have attained the throne – though he was the heir in the male line – if it had not been for the incapacity of Richard II as ruler. Similarly the Lancastrian house would not have lost the throne, to which the will of the nation – expressed by Parliament and Church – had called it, if it had not been for the imbecility of Henry VI. The Wars of the Roses, to use a misnomer, were the consequence. In these London was of perhaps decisive importance: what the trading classes of London wanted above all things was efficient government, which poor King Henry VI, saintly and slightly daft, could never provide.

The country at large, the Church, the bulk of the peerage, were mainly with the accredited royal house. Even with all Henry's debility, the issue would hardly have been decided in favour of the Yorkists, if it had not been for the military ability of young Edward IV, never once defeated. In the turns and twists of these dramatic events, of which the decisive peaks were reached in 1459–61, 1470–1 and 1483–5, the Tower was very much to the fore as military strong point, refuge in distress, prison changing hands and inmates, stage-setting for historical melodrama, a hive of death-cells.

In 1450 Jack Cade's rebellion, a popular rising with surreptitious Yorkist support, challenged the royal government which, for a time, faltered. Once more an archbishop of Canterbury took refuge with other councillors in the Tower. The pacific Henry – in contrast to spirited young Richard – retired to Kenilworth. Though the rebels made a fruitless attempt upon the Tower, the predatory Treasurer, Lord Say, was surrendered and murdered by them in Cheapside. Not a good omen for government: after that the citizens took their own defence in hand and expelled the Kentish rebels over London Bridge.

Out of the dizzy changes of 1459–61 young Edward of York emerged victor with the battle of Towton, fought on Palm Sunday in a snowstorm fatal for the Lancastrians: there was a great killing of their leaders, though the indomitable Queen Margaret carried Henry and their son, the Prince of Wales, into Scotland for the time. Edward came south for his coronation on Sunday,

Richard III by an unknown artist; last of the Yorkists, he lost his crown to Henry Tudor at Bosworth Field in 1485

29 June 1461. A couple of days before, he was conducted to the Tower by the mayor, aldermen and citizens, enthusiastic for the winning side and the prospect of peace and order. Edward feasted his Yorkist lords and partisans, and created thirty-two Knights of the Bath, who rode before him in blue gowns with white silk in the customary procession to Westminster.

Edward IV used the Tower as a residence more than any king before him: partly for its military convenience – he was very much of a soldier; partly on account of the instability of his throne during his first decade; perhaps also for its proximity to the City, where he was always careful to cultivate popularity. He several times kept his Court there with much splendour. Ceremonies and celebrations were particularly grand in 1465, when Edward made public his love-match with Elizabeth Woodville (a Lancastrian widow): the new Queen took up formal residence previous to her coronation, more Knights of the Bath, another procession to please the populace.

That same year Henry VI, who had been in hiding in the fells of Lancashire for many months, was at last betrayed and brought a prisoner to the Tower. He was conveyed there by the powerful Earl of Warwick, who became known as the King-maker, legs bound beneath the horse that carried him up Cheapside and Cornhill, a straw hat on his head, hooted by the mob. There, behind the walls for the next five years, he disappeared from view – but not entirely. Perhaps he was happier than he had been as a king; he certainly was glad to be rid of any pretence at ruling – he should have been a monk. He had a chaplain to say the daily offices before him – the chief nourishment that held him to life at all. We have notes of payments to the Yorkist retainers who had charge of him. For example 'to Robert Ratcliffe ... for expenses of Henry of Windsor, late in deed, but not of right, king of England: 40 s'.

So much for the cant of politics. Though sunk in lassitude and physically frail, Henry knew his rights. According to his contemporary biographer, he said to a detractor of them, with simple dignity: 'My father was king of England, and peacefully possessed the Crown for the whole of his life. His father, my grandfather, was king before him. And I, a boy, crowned almost in my cradle, was accepted as king by the whole realm, and wore the Crown for nearly forty years, every lord swearing homage and fealty to me, as they had done to my forefathers.'

There were conflicting reports of Henry's treatment. The Yorkists said that he was treated with humanity and reverence, and certainly he was allowed visitors. The Lancastrians said that he was insufficiently cared for and occasion-

Henry VI praying at the Shrine of St Edmund from a fifteenth-century miniature

Edward IV with his Queen, Elizabeth Woodville, family and courtiers, from the frontispiece to *Sayings of the Philosophers* by Elizabeth's brother, Lord Rivers

ally ill-treated. 'Forsooth and forsooth,' he would say – his strongest oath – 'ye do foully to smite a king anointed thus.' But as long as his son and heir was alive and out of their clutches, it was to the interest of the Yorkists to keep Henry alive.

Suddenly, in 1470, there was a swift turn in the political kaleidoscope. Warwick had been offended by Edward's marriage and was resentful of the young King's independence of him. With typical Yorkist overconfidence Edward was caught napping and had to fly the country; Edward's brother, Clarence – 'false perjured Clarence' – deserted him and went over to the enemy. Warwick's new line was to make it up with Queen Margaret in alliance with France, and to restore Henry VI in form, with himself in control.

On 5 October 1470 Warwick's brother, Archbishop of York, and old Bishop Waynflete – remembered as the founder of Magdalen College, Oxford – went down to the Tower, where they found Henry 'not so worshipfully arrayed nor so cieanly kept as should seem such a prince'. The poor King was trotted out into the light of day, freshly arrayed, and conducted to West-minster. A shadow of himself, he was made to wear the crown in public, and to preside over a Parliament.

Warwick's new deal foundered on the unpopularity of any alliance with France. Edward had fled for support to the Netherlands, England's natural ally and commercial partner. In March he landed in the North, at first judiciously recognising Henry to gain acceptance, but shortly claimed the kingdom and made for London where he was welcomed. He went straight to Henry, who greeted him: 'My cousin of York, you are welcome. My life will be safe in your hands.'

On Easter Day Edward marched out against Warwick, taking Henry with him, to the battle of Barnet, fought in a thick fog. The Lancastrian cause had its usual ill-luck – one part of their forces mistook another for the enemy in the confusion: they were overwhelmed and Warwick was killed. Clarence had ratted once more to his brother's side, in time to enjoy the fruits of victory. Henry, whom Edward had placed in the thick of the battle, went unharmed and was taken back to the Tower.

On the same day Margaret landed, too late, in the West Country. Though supported by contingents raised by loyal western nobility and gentry, and cannon contributed by Bristol, they were no match for Edward's speed and efficiency. The field of Tewkesbury saw another slaughter of Lancastrian leaders, almost fatal to the cause, for among them was the Prince of Wales, hope

of the dynasty. Once he was out of the way King Henry was in mortal danger: a clean sweep could be made.

On 21 May Edward entered London from his final victory. That night Henry was put to death in the Tower. It was given out that he died 'of pure displeasure and melancholy', but nobody believed that; for it was common knowledge that he died between eleven o'clock and midnight, 'the Duke of Gloucester being then at the Tower and many others'. So says the contemporary chronicler, Warkworth. The Croyland chronicler, at a safe distance, even specifies that Henry was 'strykked with a dagger by the hands of the Duke of Gloucester' – one need not put it past him: Richard was quite capable of it at nineteen.

We have the accounts of the expenses for laying Henry out, linen cloth and spices, the torches when he was carried to St Paul's where the body was exposed to view. Unfortunately it bled, and again at Chertsey Abbey, where he was first buried. Shortly Henry was venerated by the people for the saint he was, patient and long-suffering, humane and kind in a brutal time:

> A prince thou wert, meek and benign,
> Patient in adversity,
> Wherefore thou hast a crown condign,
> In bliss of all felicity,
> Where joy hath perpetuity.

When Richard usurped his brother's son's throne and made himself king, he had Henry's body removed for more honourable burial at Windsor: an act of propitiation, like others of Richard's later, sufficiently suggestive to anyone of any psychological perception.

Henry VI's memory is one of the more sympathetic shades that haunt the Tower. The tradition there – and there is usually something in a long-standing tradition – is that Henry was done to death in the oratory within the vaulted upper chamber of the Wakefield Tower. It is likely enough, for this led directly to the now vanished royal apartments. At any rate, of all the Tower victims, Henry's memory is the one regularly observed: on 21 May, with a ceremony and a sheaf of flowers from his two foundations, white lilies from Eton, white roses from King's College, Cambridge.

The next grand victim of the Yorkists was within their own family: Edward IV's own next brother, Clarence. Handsome and of a winning charm, especially to women – he was the favourite of his mother, the Duchess of York, and of his sister Margaret – he was yet unreliable to the point of treachery. He was possessed of an insane jealousy of his magnificent brother the King: he had betrayed him once and gone over to the enemy, and was ready to do so again, a perpetual source of trouble. Edward was himself a *faux-bonhomme*, but a good fellow if not provoked. At length provoked beyond endurance, he determined to bring Clarence to book: he personally denounced him for treason to the Parliament of 1478: he would not answer for the peace of the realm if he were pardoned. This was enough: the Commons received their cue and petitioned that justice be carried out. To this politic pressure Edward yielded, and the execution was secretly wrought within the Tower on 18 February 1478. There is no reason to doubt that he was drowned in a malmsey-butt – contemporary chroniclers agree upon that. He was appropriately buried at Tewkesbury.

It is said that Edward afterwards suffered remorse for this fratricide; certainly Richard gained greatly by it, and he was a step nearer the throne, if anything should happen to Edward's children. A modern historian comments, 'Edward IV might well have taught his brother a severe lesson, and stopped short of fratricide. . . . He forgot that there had once been four Yorkist brothers, then three, and now there were to be only two.' It set a regrettable precedent within the family.

The tragic event in the Tower that has most impressed the popular mind is the murder of the two princes, Edward IV's sons, the young King Edward V and his brother: two boys of twelve and a half, and ten. And the popular instinct is quite right; for, apart from the horror of the deed, there is this consideration: in the bloody record of the Wars of the Roses the killing of one's opponents, grown men, came to be accepted – but one did not kill women or children. It was this that turned the stomach of the country against the perpetrator, who had usurped his nephew's throne and then ordered the killing of both boys to make sure: it alienated his own party, so that many of them went over to the Lancastrian pretender abroad; at the battle of Bosworth Richard, desperate, was deserted by his own side. The unknown Henry of Richmond – who had not been in the country since he was spirited away, after Tewkesbury, at fourteen – would never have got the throne if Richard had done his duty by his brother's sons.

The affair was managed with the utmost secrecy; though everybody at the time suspected what had happened, it was dangerous to speak. Once Richard, as Protector upon his brother's death, had got both boys in his possession in the Tower they were never seen outside it again. The autumn after their disappearance, in 1483, there were spontaneous risings in every county in the South for their deliverance – the people did not yet know what had happened to them. But at New Year 1484 Richard was accused, before the public opinion of Europe, by the Speaker of the French States General, with the making away of his brother's sons – if only he could have produced them he would have been on velvet. After Bosworth next year, the Act of Attainder passed by Parliament carried an unprecedented clause, condemning him for the shedding of infants' blood – it was not necessary to specify what infants: everybody knew.

But we should never have known the facts if it had not been for the trouble Sir Thomas More took to investigate and record what he found out – and he was not only the most scrupulous and truth-telling of men but one of the most eminent of lawyers, especially skilled at dealing with evidence. And he was in a good position to find out, for he was personally acquainted with a number of those closest to events in London at the time. There was the Archbishop of Canterbury, Cardinal Morton, who knew more than anyone; More was twenty-two or twenty-three when Morton died, and had been his page at Lambeth. More was a friend of the Bishop of London, Richard Fitzjames, who had been a chaplain to Edward IV; he was friendly with the second Duke of Norfolk, the son of Richard's crony, who had been present on the decisive day in the Tower, 20 June 1483, when Richard had Lord Hastings summarily executed without trial; after which there was no turning back. More knew several others who had been close to those events: Bishop Foxe, Sir Thomas Lovell, and Sir John Cutte, Richard III's servant whom More later succeeded as Under-Treasurer. One telling detail More informs us he got from his father, Judge More – who was sympathetic enough to Edward IV to bequeath prayers for him in his will. More himself was notably favourable to Edward IV; he had no pro-Tudor bias whatever, and indeed was ultimately martyred by one of them.

We are indeed fortunate to have these dark events illuminated for us by one of the most conscientious of men, as well as one of the sharpest of minds. More is very careful to tell us, 'I shall rehearse to you the dolorous end of those babes, not after every way that I have heard, but after that way that I have so heard – by such men and by such means – as methinketh it were hard but it should be true.' He had carefully sifted the evidence and its credibility.

The general background is widely known. On Edward's death Richard became, quite properly, Protector of the young King, Edward V, and of his realm – though there were people who expected that he would try to make himself king. Nor was the idea absurd: everybody knew the dangers of a minority, a mere boy as king, and the circumstances were those of crisis, the probability of renewed war with France. Everything depended on how it was done: it was the murders that alienated the country and lost Richard the throne when he had got it.

On the young King's way to London, with inadequate escort, at Stony Stratford he fell into his uncle's power, who knelt to him as King – and packed off his guardians, Sir Richard Vaughan and Earl Rivers, his maternal uncle, and his half-brother, Lord Richard Grey, to Pontefract. There they were all summarily executed the moment Richard got the throne. At this Edward's widow, sensing danger, took herself, her younger son and daughters, into sanctuary at Westminster Abbey. Richard conducted the elder boy to the Tower, acclaimed as King passing through the City – all quite regular and customary in preparation for his coronation on Sunday, 22 June 1483. Preparations for this went forward at the Tower – we have the signature of young Edward as acknowledged King on administrative documents along with Richard's, his Protector.

The point was to get the other boy into his power. There was a good argument for this: at Westminster he might be made the focus of intrigue by the Queen's party. But a stronger argument was put to the mother – that his brother needed the solace of his company. The Queen yielded the boy up – and the two were last seen shouting and playing in the Tower grounds that month.

Meanwhile, Richard suspiciously divided the Council: while formal business was transacted at the Tower, his own plans went forward at Crosby Place where he was residing. Canny Lord Stanley, husband of Lady Margaret Beaufort, mistrusted this and warned Lord Hastings: 'While we talk of one matter in the one place, little wot we whereof they talk in the other place.' Hastings had been the bosom-friend of Edward IV, and was confident of Richard – but Richard had found out that Hastings would not go along with him in his plans.

The decisive moment was reached on Friday 20 June with a meeting of the full Council at the Tower, to make final arrangements for the coronation. There followed the famous scene of the *coup d'état*, of which Shakespeare did not fail to make full use – he well understood the inner tensions of Richard's personality. The night before, Stanley had a fearful dream presaging Hastings' fall and sent an urgent messenger suggesting that they leave London. Over-confident, Hastings would take no notice. Richard arrived at the Council late, apologising courteously for oversleeping. He said to Bishop Morton – from whom More could have had it: 'My lord, you have very good strawberries at your garden in Holborn: I require you, let us have a mess of them.' He excused himself while waiting for them, but did not return for an hour.

It was a very different Protector who returned, acting a part, lowering countenance, biting his lips, as he was apt to do in moments of tension. He burst out with a charge of conspiracy – such as we have become accustomed to in our time in Russia and Germany – and bared his left arm for the evidence of sorcery upon it: showing a 'werish withered arm and small, as it was never other. And thereupon every man's mind sore misgave them, well perceiving that this matter was but a quarrel.' Banging his fist on the table, the pre-arranged signal, Richard filled the room with his armed men. One of them wounded Stanley, who might have been killed had he not shrunk back; Archbishop Rotherham of York and Bishop Morton were arrested. Hastings was taken out for

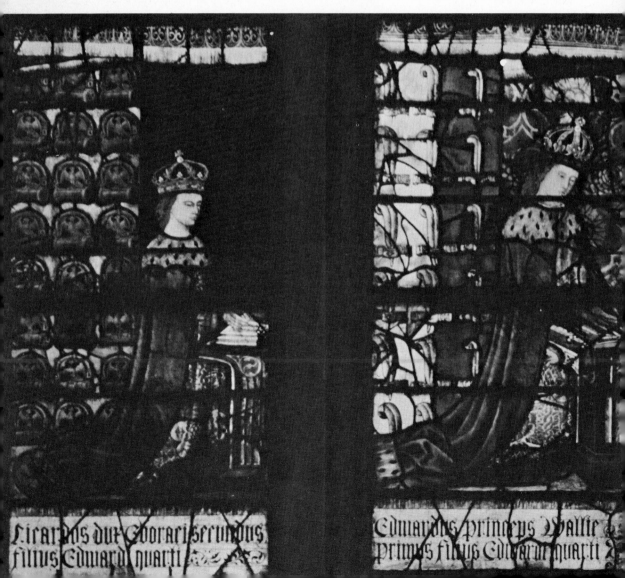

immediate execution: Richard swore he would not go to dinner till his head was off. Edward IV's boon-companion in his amours was allowed a priest to shrive him, by the disapproving, moralistic Richard (it does not require a Freud to understand his sexual jealousy of his brothers and of Hastings). Hastings was speedily dispatched upon a log timber waiting upon Tower Green for repairs.

This was the turning-point – no legality whatever in Hastings's execution, no trial: this was a *coup d'état* in the contemporary Italian style. Everybody was terrorised, in an atmosphere of crisis, by the speed of events. Edward IV's children were declared illegitimate, and Edward IV too, for good measure – to the scandal of their pious mother, Cecily, Duchess of York. The preparations which had been made for the boy-King's coronation were now available for his adult, military uncle – merely postponed for a fortnight, to bring up large forces from the North to make all secure.

In our time More's story has been completely corroborated by the discovery of the account of an Italian diplomat in London at the time, Mancini. He knew Dr Argentine, the last attendant of the young King, who told Mancini that after Hastings' decapitation, 'all the attendants who had waited upon the King were debarred access to him. He and his brother were withdrawn into the inner apartments of the Tower proper, till at last they ceased to appear. The young King, like a victim prepared for sacrifice, sought remission of his sins by daily confession and penance, because he believed that death was facing him.'

It was not until London emptied after the coronation and Richard betook himself on progress that the decision to put the boys out of the way went forth. More tells us that Richard sent John Green to Sir Robert Brackenbury, Constable of the Tower, with a letter of credence to do the job. 'This John Green did his errand unto Brackenbury, kneeling before Our Lady in the Tower, who plainly answered that he would never put them to death, to die therefore.' This answer, which greatly discontented Richard, he received at Warwick – and we know independently that Richard was at Warwick for the week 7 to 15 August 1483.

Sir James Tyrrell, ambitious to rise in Richard's favour, came to his help and took the matter in hand. Richard sent the command to Brackenbury to hand over the keys of the Tower for one night. Tyrrell entrusted the deed to two fellows: 'Miles Forest, one of the four that kept them [i.e. looked after the princes], a fellow fleshed in murder beforetime. To him he joined one Dighton, his own horsekeeper, a big broad square strong knave.' These two stout fellows

The Two Princes, Edward, Prince of Wales, and Richard, Duke of York, from a window in Canterbury Cathedral smothered the boys in their bed together, and after took the bodies out naked 'to bury them at the stair foot, meetly deep in the ground under a great heap of stones'.

In that very place, when repairs were being made at the Tower in 1674, their bones were discovered, tumbled in one upon the other face to face, Edward on his back, young Richard face downwards upon his brother. The bones were reverently taken to Westminster Abbey, where they were re-buried in an urn designed by Sir Christopher Wren. In our time they have been authoritatively re-examined and reported on: the bones of two boys, about thirteen and ten respectively. These men, Tyrrell, Forest, John Green, received their rewards from Richard, pinpointed in the grants for that year. More, like the moralist he was, tells us how they were rewarded otherwise. He says that 'Miles Forest, at St Martin's, piecemeal rotted away'; it is corroborated that he died not long after the deed. 'Dighton indeed yet walketh on live in good possibility to be hanged ere he die.' No one could bring the crime home to Tyrrell, but Henry VII got him in the end for treason against himself, and he was beheaded on Tower Hill. More tells us that while in the Tower 'both Dighton and he were examined and confessed the murder in manner above written, but whether the bodies were removed they could nothing tell'. (Richard had intended to remove them, as he did remove Henry VI's, for they were of royal blood.) 'And thus as I have learned of them that much knew and little cause had to lie.' Nor had More the slightest cause to lie in his account of the matter.

It was not until two full years later that Bosworth was fought, 22 August 1485, and Henry VII won the throne – which he would never have done but for Richard's 'heinous crime': this is the Elizabethan Lord Henry Howard's phrase, revealing the private tradition within the Howard family which had owed its dukedom to Richard. In 1484 Richard had sent Clarence's son and heir the young Earl of Warwick to close confinement at Sheriff Hutton; now Henry had him brought to the Tower. Two years later there was a rumour that he was dead, and Lambert Simnel, a good-looking Oxford lad, was brought forward to impersonate him – actually crowned king by the Irish in Dublin. At this Henry had the real Warwick paraded through the streets of the City to Mass in St Paul's, where he was much 'wondered upon' and recognised by the lords present – as Richard had not been able to produce the two princes. Then back the poor boy went to the Tower, for his dangerous royal blood.

Elizabeth of York, eldest daughter of Edward IV,
whose marriage to Henry VII united the rival houses

He was not much of a danger himself, being unable 'to discern a goose from a capon'; but, as the last direct male Yorkist, he could be made use of for others' designs. The designing Margaret, Edward's sister now the widowed Duchess of Burgundy, having nothing better to do, sent two thousand mercenaries to support the impostor, Simnel, and made Henry fight for his throne again at the battle of Stoke, 16 June 1487. This settled the issue for good.

In accordance with his solemn promise, Henry had married Edward IV's eldest daughter, Elizabeth, to unite the rival houses. In 1486 she had borne him a son and heir, Arthur. But it was not until 25 November 1487 that Henry had her crowned, to make it clear that he did not occupy the throne by any other right than his own. The day before, he received her at the Tower, attended by his mother, the austere and politic Lady Margaret, through whom his title

came, for she was the undoubted heiress-general of the Lancastrian line, great-granddaughter of John of Gaunt. There, in the royal apartments, Henry and his Yorkist Queen kept 'open household and frank resort' for all the Court. On the morrow, according to custom, she proceeded from the Tower in state, apparelled in white cloth of gold, her fair hair flowing loose about her shoulders: she was rising twenty-three.

After the exposure of Simnel, Duchess Margaret transferred her support to Perkin Warbeck, who was welcomed by Henry's enemies in Scotland and (of course) Ireland; for six years he was a source of anxiety, if not of danger. In 1497 Warbeck was lodged in the Tower, then released and allowed his freedom, under observation, at Court. Next year he attempted an escape, and went back to the Tower. The year after, a man of spirit, he attempted to corrupt his keepers and involved the innocent Warwick – now twenty-four – in a plot. This may have been a frame-up, for Henry was under the strongest pressure from the Catholic Kings, Ferdinand and Isabella, to get rid of the last Yorkist claimant, before they would consent to the marriage of their daughter to Henry's heir. Certainly Catherine of Aragon regarded her repudiation by Henry VIII as a judgment for her marriage having been 'made in blood'. Warwick was innocent enough to plead guilty and was beheaded on Tower Hill, Warbeck hanged at Tyburn.

Henry's Queen commanded the popularity that he himself never could, for all his success as a ruler and his transcendent services to the state. During her last pregnancy the Queen was in delicate health, and in childbirth she died, 11 February 1503: it was her thirty-eighth birthday. The young Thomas More wrote his *Lamentation* for her:

> O ye that put your trust and confidence
>   In worldly joy and frail prosperity,
> That so live here as ye should never hence:
>   Remember death and look here upon me . . .
> Was I not born of old worthy lineage?
>   Was not my mother queen, my father king?
> Was I not a king's fere [wife] in marriage?
>   Had I not plenty of every pleasant thing?
> Merciful God, this is a strange reckoning:
>   Riches, honour, wealth and ancestry
>   Hath me forsaken, and lo now here I lie.

One way or another, the Tower was fatal to Yorkists.

After his capture by Bolingbroke, Richard II is taken into the Tower

3
Henry VIII and
Sir Thomas More

THE clue to Henry VIII is that he was a Yorkist: he did not in the least take after the Lancastrian line (after his Tudor father or his Beaufort grandmother), which was apt to be austere and chaste, introvert and not outgoing, hence with no gift of popularity; with no undue confidence in the outer world, prudent, not given to making mistakes through rashness. Henry VIII was recognisably like his grandfather Edward IV: large-limbed, over-sized, running to fat; a gourmandiser, with an appetite also for women; an out-of-doors man, keen on sport; of exceptional vitality, with a wide response to life; capricious and cruel, yet always able to command popularity.

Henry VIII made less use of the Tower as a residence than his predecessors had done, but he made much more use of it for putting people into it. Never so many or such eminent persons lost their lives there as in his reign: two of his queens, two famous saints – Thomas More and John Fisher, without counting the Carthusian and Protestant martyrs, many leading peers, knights and gentlemen, a foremost statesman in Thomas Cromwell, a poet of genius in the Earl of Surrey.

We are apt to be impressed by the cruelty of it all. But, to get a contemporary perspective, we must remember the hazards of life at the time anyway, the high rate of mortality, the visitations of plague and other epidemics, the continual presence of disease, the familiar acquaintance with death. We should also bear something else in mind: this was the sixteenth century, four un-enlightened centuries ago, and yet Henry VIII's cruelties were nothing com-pared with Hitler's and Stalin's. The progressive, enlightened twentieth century has been much worse – elsewhere, if not in Britain.

Henry VIII began his reign with joyousness, in conscious reaction to his dour and careful father, with a splendid coronation for himself and Catherine of Aragon on Midsummer Sunday, 1509. He was within a week of his eighteenth birthday, a magnificent physical specimen admired by everybody – especially

35

The Tower in the Middle Ages from the poems of Charles, Duke of Orleans

by the sensitive Erasmus, always susceptible to male good looks; Catherine was five or six years older – which meant much more then – and always a plain body. However, they were grandly dressed for their parts: Henry, riding bareheaded according to custom, in crimson velvet and gold; Catherine in white satin, in a litter drawn by two white palfreys. So they emerged from the Tower, Henry attended by the twenty-four Knights of the Bath he had created the day before.

A perhaps more revealing pointer to the future was Henry's throwing his father's financial agents, Empson and Dudley, to the wolves in the interests of popularity. These men had incurred much odium in the course of piling up Henry VII's immense surplus in the treasury, which his son, like an outgoing man, was to spend. Both men were committed to the Tower, where Dudley wrote his political treatise, *The Tree of Commonwealth*, an interesting contribution to the literature composed there. It was to have its successors, in the next century, in the political tracts written there by the Parliamentary leader, Sir John Eliot; but those were of a very different persuasion, arguing for limitation upon monarchical power, where Dudley was influenced by his fear of social disruption. Unable to reach his young sovereign, Dudley attempted to escape with his brother Peter: this settled his and Empson's fate, who were executed on Tower Hill. Several members of Dudley's remarkable family were to be acquainted with the inside of the Tower in the next generations, two of them fatally: his son, the Duke of Northumberland, and grandson, Lord Guildford Dudley, husband of Lady Jane Grey.

Meanwhile, the rounding up of Yorkists in the female line became a fairly constant Tudor activity, for they were a prolific stock where the Tudors were poor at proliferating. Henry VII had been kind to Richard III's nephew and heir, Suffolk, and restored him to Court; but twice he absconded from the country, the second time taking his brother Richard over to Henry's enemies abroad. This underlined the danger of the White Rose – as Suffolk was known abroad – to the Red. Henry reacted by sending the third brother, Lord William de la Pole, and Lord Courtenay, who had married Edward IV's daughter Catherine, to the Tower.

One feels sorriest for young Lord William, who was not only extremely handsome but sensible. He had made a promising start, out of the disaster to his family, by marrying a rich elderly widow who was besotted on him. This enabled him to cut a gay figure at Court, until his brother brought trouble upon them all. William lived out his life in the Tower, almost the whole reign

Henry VIII, who had two of his wives and many
of his opponents executed in the Tower

of Henry VIII, who provided generously for him, rich gowns furred with the skins of animals, velvet doublets, silks and satins. After all, was he not of the blood royal?

So were the Courtenays, and this brought them into danger at the time of the Pilgrimage of Grace. The King's eminent enemy abroad, Cardinal Pole, brought disaster upon his family by holding Henry's divorce proceedings up to obloquy before the public opinion of Europe and condemning his breach with Rome. The long strain of the King's 'great matter' over the six years, 1527–33, caught as he was in an almost inextricable tangle, told upon Henry. A bull-like man, bent on his own way, he was held up, frustrated, maddened; an obsessive egoist with an exceptional self-esteem, he was exposed to ridicule before all the Courts of Europe and to criticism even at home. The odd thing is that he was as patient as he was during all those years of strain, caught between two women, too: one as obstinate as a Spanish mule, the other a brazen heartless woman with whom he was passionately in love, but who did not care for him and exacted the highest price for her 'favours'. The explanation is that Henry was determined on a male heir who should be recognised to be legitimate – and this was difficult.

The divorce indeed divided Henry's reign in two parts, and the experience deeply affected his character. Before it he had been sufficiently bonhomous and good-natured; the note of the youthful reign was enjoyment, encouraged by Wolsey in control. After it Henry became harder and more capricious; opposition of any sort made him see red. The reign darkened, the tone of the Court became fearful, a kind of terror ruled around him: the *bonhomme* became a *faux-bonhomme*. When Sir Thomas More resigned office, he advised Cromwell always to tell the King 'what he ought to do, but never tell him what he is able to do. . . . For, if the lion knew his own strength, hard were it for any man to rule him.' Both More and Cromwell were to experience the truth of this in their own bones. When More fell into danger for his opposition to the Supremacy, the Duke of Norfolk warned him with the old Latin tag, *Indignatio principis mors est* (The anger of the prince is death). Henry seems to have taken this as an imperative rather than an indicative, and he was often angry.

Henry once told the French ambassador, Marillac, that he had long made up his mind to extirpate the house of the White Rose. The Pilgrimage of Grace, which infuriated him, gave him his opportunity. The Courtenays and Poles were opposition-minded: conservative and catholic aristocrats, they hated the new deal; they were in correspondence with Cardinal Pole abroad, and they talked among themselves at home. They were betrayed by a light-headed member of the family, Sir Geoffrey Pole. The head of the Courtenays, the Marquis of Exeter, his wife, and only son, Edward, were sent to the Tower. So was their friend Sir Nicholas Carew, Master of the Horse, formerly a favourite with Henry; so, too, the head of the Pole family, Lord Montagu, and others of the group.

We have a rare glimpse of what was thought of all this among the lower classes in the knowing talk between a London goldsmith and a Tower attendant in a boat at Paul's Wharf in November 1538. The warder said, sagely: 'We have great pain in watching of these naughty men lately brought into the Tower. Would to God every man would know their duties to God and their Prince!' Upon which the goldsmith asked this well-informed person, what news of 'that naughty fellow, Pole, beyond sea?' The warder said he was made Bishop of Rome. 'How know you that?' said the goldsmith. 'I have heard it of great men.' 'Of whom?' inquired the craftsman. 'Of some of my Lord Privy Seal's [Cromwell's] house.' A third man broke in: 'I have heard as much as this, for the Council doth know this thing well enough.' 'I pray you,' said the goldsmith, 'how do you know they know it?' 'By the ambassadors and others.' Pole did not become Pope; but the Tower warder knew that Michael Throckmorton had been sent abroad with offers to Pole (or rather to report home on him), and that he had opted to remain in the Cardinal's service.

This gives us a rare insight into the mind of the people at the time. Not a town or a country cat mewed at the beheading of an aristocrat; what is important is that Henry was more in touch with the mind of the country, if that is the word for it. He could go forward with impunity to extirpate the rest of the party.

We learn of a kindly action on the part of a Keeper, Thomas Phillips, who lent Sir Nicholas Carew an English Bible in his last months; so that on Tower Hill he was able to make confession of both 'his folly and superstitious faith', thanking God 'that ever he came in the Tower, where he first savoured the life and sweetness of God's most holy Word'. Certainly the Tower was a school of education in more senses than one. Young Edward Courtenay spent most of his life, and received his education, there. On the accession of Edward VI he translated an Italian tract of a Reforming flavour, *The Benefit of Christ's Death*. His mother, the Marchioness, was an intimate friend of Princess Mary; on her accession Courtenay was restored to the earldom of Devon, but did not know how to behave himself. After his life in prison he went wild and entered into conspiracy against the Queen: back he went into the Tower, which must have seemed like home, before he was sent into exile, where he died.

There remained the indomitable old Countess of Salisbury, Clarence's daughter, of truly royal courage. Nothing could be extracted from her, though examined from morning till night: 'We have dealt with such a one as men have not dealt withal before us: we may call her rather a strong and constant man than a woman.' In the absence of evidence she was condemned by act of attainder and held two years in the Tower, 'where she maketh great moan for that she wanteth necessary apparel both for to change and also to keep her warm'. She was now nearing seventy, a good age for the time. The Council sent her 'a night-gown furred, a kirtle of worsted and petticoat furred, another night-gown of say [soft serge], lined with satin of Cyprus and faced with satin, a bonnet with a frontlet, four pairs of hose, four pairs of shoes and a pair of slippers'. People expected that she would be pardoned. But an idiotic rising by a Neville in Yorkshire settled her fate. Informed of it, she answered that no crime had been imputed to her, and walked with resolution across Tower Green where a low block awaited her, with the Lord Mayor and a small company to witness the old lady being very inexpertly handled by a novice in the art.

If this was the treatment Henry meted out to his Yorkist cousins he was hardly more gentle with his (errant) wives. At the beginning Anne Boleyn was given a magnificent send-off of a coronation, for her years of waiting. Setting out from Greenwich in pomp, she was received at the Tower by Henry and peals of ordnance, 29 May 1533. The next night a number of Knights of the Bath 'were bathed and shriven according to the old usage of England'. Next day, the eve of Whitsun, Anne was accorded a procession grander even than Henry and Catherine's twenty-four years before. The French ambassador had a place of honour, and his gentlemen headed the show – not only had Anne had her training at the French Court but her coronation was as pleasing to Francis I as it was displeasing to the Emperor Charles V, Catherine's nephew. Descriptions of the event omit to notice that Elizabeth I was present, as a six-months' formed child in her mother's womb – Henry cannot but have been pleased to make public this evidence of his potency.

Only three years later – so brief a spell of dizzy glory – Anne came to her doom within these walls. No one to this day knows whether she was guilty of the adultery and incest with her brother with which she was charged, but

Above left: The Countess of Salisbury, executed in 1541 at the age of seventy
Right: Anne Boleyn, Henry's second wife, who was condemned for her adultery

there was no one to defend her. In her giddy exaltation she had been arrogant to everyone, including Henry, and harsh to Catherine and her daughter Mary. No one has noticed the bitter irony that in the end her life came to depend on her hated rival's: the moment Catherine was dead (January 1536) Henry could make a clean sweep, begin again with an unchallenged marriage, hope for an unquestioned heir. At the end of that month Anne produced a still-born boy. She may have thought that Henry was incapable of siring a healthy heir – she and her brother certainly derided him as a performer – and tried others, since her position depended on producing a son. The inwardness of the matter was really political. Of course, Tudor people thought in terms of moral absolutes, but the real danger was that, if there were any doubt as to the genuineness of an heir to the throne, it could give rise to civil war.

Certainly Anne was brazen enough to behave with undue familiarity with men in public – and this was observed in her daughter, Elizabeth's, conduct later, with whom it was an obvious sign of innocence. Henry had become

41

disgusted with Anne and been watching her conduct for some time, like a great cat, who suddenly pounced. Several gentlemen of her privy chamber were arraigned and confessions, of sorts, extracted; Henry Norris, however, stoutly denied anything of the kind – and for this, later, Elizabeth rewarded his son and all the Norrises with her constant favour: the only way in which she could express her belief in her mother's innocence.

On May Day 1536 there was a tournament at Greenwich, at which the Queen was said to have dropped a handkerchief for one of her supposed lovers; but Henry was convinced that he already had evidence. Next day she was escorted to the Tower by the Lord Chancellor (successor to More, whom she had encouraged Henry to kill), and her uncle, the Duke of Norfolk. On entering the gate, she fell on her knees protesting her innocence; throughout the agony of those May days she never wavered in declaring to the Constable of the Tower, Sir William Kingston, that she had had no criminal intercourse with any man whatsoever. A kindly man, he came to believe her. But, once within the Tower, there was no hope for her. Her case was prejudged by the condemnation of her alleged lovers, including her brother Lord Rochford, traduced by his horrible wife. Tried before a tribunal of peers presided over by her uncle, and including her father, she was condemned without a dissentient voice: everybody knew his duty to the King.

Her marriage was conveniently annulled by her only friend, Archbishop Cranmer, on the ground of a pre-contract with the Earl of Northumberland – who denied its existence on the sacrament. There is a strange account from her daughter's reign, of a Protestant who was with Cranmer in the garden at Lambeth the night before her execution, and spoke of the Queen's agony on the morrow. For a moment, the mask of the great ecclesiastic dropped, and Cranmer in tears said that tomorrow there would be a queen in heaven. He had heard her confession. We do not know whether the story is true.

The Queen herself displayed the courage which went along with her hardihood. Deserted by everyone, she came to welcome death. The good Constable wrote, 'This lady has much joy and pleasure in death.' When brought out to the scaffold on the Green, she spoke briefly to the select company, nobles, mayor and aldermen: she expressed perfect submission to the law, accused no one of her death, but never acknowledged the crimes with which she had been charged. Her head was struck off at one blow with a sword – 'so little a neck', she had said, putting her hands around it – by an expert executioner specially brought over from Calais as a kindness to her.

The Queen's House built in the 1530s. Anne Boleyn was confined there for the eighteen days before her execution

Hardly six years later her cousin, Catherine Howard, Henry's fifth queen, followed her on precisely the same spot. There was no doubt about her guilt – or, rather, improprieties – but before marriage. After the ludicrous fiasco of Anne of Cleves, the 'great Flanders mare' whom Henry could not stomach, he was inveigled into marriage, by the Catholic party at Court – Norfolk and Bishop Gardiner – with this plump girl who had nothing in her head. She did her best to accommodate the eldering pasha, who, on All Saints Day 1541, ordered his confessor, the Bishop of Lincoln, to thank God for him for the good time he was having and hoped to have, 'after sundry troubles of mind which had happened to him by marriages'. Next day, at Mass, the blow fell upon him: Archbishop Cranmer put into his hand a paper of evidence as to the Queen's misconduct. Henry, at first, was unable to believe the news and, on its corroboration, gave way to an exhibition of self-pity: bitter tears before the Privy Council, 'which was strange in a man of his courage', it was observed. Once and again he complained that, for all the wives he had had, not one of them had put herself out to be a comfort to him.

Actually, young Catherine had – for an unattractive old hulk of a man, obese and monstrous. But she had accommodated others before marriage, as a prudish Mary Lascelles witnessed, and one of the men in this case confessed. She had been badly brought up in the household of the old Duchess of Norfolk – Norfolk's step-mother – and, even after becoming Queen, Lady Rochford had

admitted the young men up her back staircase for stolen interviews. But there was no certain evidence of subsequent intercourse, merely 'vehement presumption', and Henry promised her a pardon. While the Queen remained at Syon House in custody, Lady Rochford went off her head with terror.

This was to leave matters in an impossibly untidy state, and Parliament came to Henry's aid with an act of attainder of the two women. A deputation waited upon him, beseeching him not to take his misfortune too heavily, for the sake of the realm which depended upon him for its weal; and suggesting that he might give his assent by commission to the proposed procedure, without any ceremony or words to renew his pain. This offered a convenient way of going back on his promise to pardon the silly girl.

So she was conveyed down the river from Syon to the Tower, and on Sunday evening, 12 February 1542, was told that she was to die the following day. She merely asked for the block to be brought to the apartment, so that she might rehearse the scene, not to falter or appear nervous. Nor did she, before the whole Council present as witnesses – her cousin, the poet Surrey, among the rest. Lady Rochford displayed no such queen-like courage: she went frantic to the block – retribution, perhaps, for her betrayal of her husband before.

As for Henry, his self-esteem had received such an unkind blow that it was months before he could pluck up his spirits to marry again. The detached reader, after the lapse of centuries, may well wonder how these women could take such risks with such a man.

A portrait believed to be of Catherine Howard, Henry's fifth wife, whose misconduct brought her to the block

Henry VIII and Sir Thomas More

The Tower's most endearing memory is that of Sir Thomas More – everything about him is endearing, except his high morality, and his persecution of others for their (opposite) faith. In our time he has been sanctified, but even the not particularly believing Dean Swift considered him 'the person of the greatest virtue that this kingdom hath ever produced'. As the most eminent Englishman of his day, everything about him was also news: he was the subject of one of the earliest English biographies, by his son-in-law Roper, of that faithful family. The result is that his life in the Tower is exceptionally well known to us, and several of the incidents and conversations are famous.

When More consented to succeed Wolsey and serve Henry as Lord Chancellor, the King gave him an undertaking that he would not put a strain upon More's conscience by forcing his private opinions. Upon this understanding More took his part in helping the Divorce proceedings, though he well knew what kind of man he was dealing with. When Henry married Anne, More recognised the right of Parliament to regulate the succession and was ready to accept Anne's progeny as legitimate heirs to the throne, but he would not swear the oath. Before the Commissioners at Lambeth, Cranmer tried to save More by a quibble; but refusing the proffered gloss upon the oath, More was committed to the Tower, 17 April 1534. On his admission and throughout his time there, he joked on the gravest subjects – for he understood the duplicity of things – in a way that scandalised the dull and conventional but lit up the sad scene with a wintry smile, to form part of the folklore of the English people.

More was wearing a rich gold chain, as he did in public. Sir Richard Cromwell was conducting him and, with the worldly concern of that family, advised More to send it back for the benefit of his. Not a bit, said More: if he were captured in battle, he hoped that his enemies might fare somewhat the better by him. Received by the Lieutenant at the gate, the porter demanded his upper garment, according to custom. More offered him his cap, apologising that it was no better; the porter was forced to explain that he meant Sir Thomas's gown, a more valuable item. All this is in keeping with the rather grim Tudor sense of humour. When the Lieutenant expressed his concern whether his 'poor cheer' contented his eminent prisoner, Sir Thomas courteously thanked him: 'I do not mislike my cheer; but whensoever I so do, then thrust me out of your doors.'

His favourite daughter, Margaret, the only one who knew of the hair-shirt he wore beneath the magnificence of the Chancellor, made suit to visit him. She found him well content with his lot, except for the pain he was giving to

his family: 'If it had not been for my wife and you that be my children, I would not have failed, long ere this, to have closed myself in as strait a room, and straiter too.' He meant the Carthusian cell he had tried as a young man, and would have settled for, but for the flesh. This talk was not to the mind of his sensible wife, when she got leave to see him. She marvelled at his being such a fool – and he taken for a wise man – as to be content to be shut up among mice and rats, when he could be at liberty and in favour with King and Council. All the bishops and best learned in the realm had agreed – why couldn't he, and be at home at Chelsea with her and the children, his books and the garden?

I have always had much sympathy with plain Dame Alice's – the woman's – common sense point of view. What good did More's high-principled resistance do anyone? We know that it caused a great deal of suffering to many. All that her husband could say to explain to her was: 'Is not this house as nigh heaven as mine own?' To which Dame Alice, not liking such talk, gave her usual 'Tilly vally, tilly vally'.

When his daughter came, who was closer to him and understood him better, they regularly said the seven penitential psalms and the litany together, before they talked of worldly matters. He told her that he was contented as if he were at home: 'Methinketh God maketh me a wanton, and setteth me on

46

Left: Sir Thomas More with his family in a painting believed to be by Holbein. His favourite daughter Margaret is seated second from the right of the picture

Right: A drawing by Holbein of Bishop Fisher, who was executed shortly before Sir Thomas More

his lap and dandleth me.' One day he happened to ask how Queen Anne did; and Meg said, 'In faith, father, never better.' To which More said sadly, 'Never better? Alas, alas, it pitieth me to remember me in what misery she, poor soul, shortly shall come.'

More was troubled in mind only when his best-beloved daughter pleaded with him to reconsider his stand. Of all the threats to him, 'surely they all touched me never so near, nor were so grievous unto me, as to see you, my well-beloved child, in such piteous manner labour to persuade me unto the thing wherein I have, of pure necessity for respect unto mine own soul, so often given you so precise answer before'. The suggestion that More's resistance was inspired by Bishop Fisher, the only member of the bench to refuse the oath, irked More's pride – so that we can diagnose an element of intellectual pride in his obstinacy. 'Verily, daughter, I never intend to pin my soul at another man's back, not even the best man that I know this day living. There is no man living, of whom while he liveth, I may make myself sure.'

Fisher had been the confessor of Henry's sainted grandmother, the Lady Margaret, her adviser in her foundations – St John's and Christ's at Cambridge. Nothing availed with the grandson when the old family friend opposed him and refused the oath, while Paul III's conferring on him a cardinal's hat roused

47

Henry to fury. He swore that Fisher's head should be off before his hat was on, and Fisher went forward with More to their martyrdom. Not precisely step by step however. The Act of Supremacy was passed in November 1534; when the oath was presented to Fisher he refused it outright: there was no difficulty about him. It was more difficult to catch the most brilliant brain in England, who had been Lord Chancellor.

Thomas Cromwell with other Councillors came down to the Tower to get a definite answer to the Supremacy: yes or no. They courteously asked More to sit with them, like the fellow-Councillor he had been – 'which in no wise I would'. He told them that he trusted in the King's good faith that no such question would ever be demanded of him. Nor could they get an answer out of him. More knew as well as they did that his duty was obedience, and he would dispute neither with kings' titles nor popes': he had ceased to meddle with the things of this world. Cromwell went right to the heart of the matter: More's attitude was encouraging the resistance of others. This was true: a number of the London Carthusians were now in the Tower for refusing to acknowledge the Royal Supremacy. More replied, truly, that he had given no man counsel on the matter, one way or another. He added that his poor body was at the king's pleasure: 'Would God my death might do him good.'

This touched Cromwell, who said 'full gently', More reported to Margaret, that no advantage should be taken against him of anything he had said. In any case, it was not Cromwell who was More's enemy, but Henry, urged on by Anne. All the worst side of Henry's character was coming out under the strain upon him: he was becoming more and more tyrannical – and Erasmus had noticed earlier More's peculiar loathing of tyranny.

It happened that Margaret was in the Tower with him that day early in May – perhaps it was designed – when the Carthusians were marched out on their trek to hanging, disembowelling and quartering at Tyburn. Watching them from the window together, More said that they were 'as cheerfully going to their deaths as bridegrooms to their marriage. . . . What a great difference there is between such as have spent all their days in a strait, hard, penitential and painful life religiously [i.e. in religion], and such as have in this world, as thy poor father hath done, consumed all their time in pleasure and ease licentiously.' More had long wished for the Carthusian life and death to the body; here was his death-wish: it cannot have consoled Margaret and those who loved him.

After the agony of the Carthusians Cromwell was sent again with a message from the King that Henry 'minded not with any matter, wherein he should have any cause of scruple, from henceforth to trouble his conscience'. This may have represented a genuine vacillation on Henry's part, but it is more likely to have been part of the process of 'softening-up' the prisoner, with which we are so familiar in our day. But there was no softening up a prisoner who already wished for death. And shortly the reverse side of the technique was set in motion: More's books were taken from him, pen and ink taken away – there could be no greater hardship for such a man.

In 1534 More wrote his *Dialogue of Comfort against Tribulation* – one of the most eminent, and appropriate, works of Tower literature. Its purpose was to comfort those he was leaving, though for himself he wished 'with God's will to be hence and longed to be with him in heaven'. It must have been inspired by Boethius's *Consolation of Philosophy*, written in similar circumstances, for More begins with a chapter 'That the comfort devised by the old pagan philosophers were insufficient' – the only possible foundation was faith. An analysis of the book would be out of place here; we need say only that it gives a complete conspectus of the good effects tribulation may have, to draw men to God, to persuade them to penance, etc. All this is quite allergic to a modern mind, but More saw very well the way the world was going. At the time the Turks were making deep inroads into Christian Europe, and More uses the Turkish advance to mean the progress of the Reformation. 'We fear that thing sore now which, few years past, feared it not at all. . . . No small part of our own folk are, as we fear, falling to him, or already confederated with him.' More saw Catholic Christianity in peril, and 'there is no born Turk so cruel to Christian folk as is the false Christian that falleth from the faith'. True enough in regard to tolerance within the Turkish Empire, the history of the century was to show Catholicism far more intolerant and cruel in persecuting than the Protestants were.

All his life a reading and writing man, having finished the *Dialogue* More now began his *Treatise upon the Passion*. He called it a 'treatise historical', for it was based on the accounts in the four Gospels, as if they were historical, and the commentary of the great scholastic doctor Gerson – for More was as much of a medieval as he. Before he had quite finished, pens and paper were taken away again; even the Introduction got no further than, 'when we come once there, dwell there we shall and inhabit there for ever'. More's mind was full of the next world, as to which he was very certain. Everything he wrote was treasured by his family – to whom he might have been more considerate; so we have a number of his prayers and meditations also: 'Give me thy grace, good Lord, to set the world at nought.' 'With a coal, for ink then had he none,' he wrote a verse to conclude a poem he had written on *Fortune* thirty years before:

> Aye, flattering Fortune, look you never so fair,
> Nor never so pleasantly begin to smile,
> As though thou wouldst my ruins all repair,
> During my life thou shalt not me beguile.
> Trust I shall, God, to enter in a while
> Thy haven of heaven sure and uniform:
> Ever after thy calm look I for no storm.

More was now shortly to have his wish: the problem for the government was how to entrap him into an overt expression of opposition. This job fell to the new Solicitor General, Sir Richard Rich. While More's books were being trussed up Rich engaged him in an argument designed to lead him into a trap. Knowing More's traditional reverence for Parliamentary authority, Rich put the case, for sake of argument, suppose Parliament passed an act that the realm should take him for king: wouldn't More accept that? More agreed. Then, suppose Parliament passed an act that the realm take him for Pope; wouldn't More accept that? More was not to be so easily caught. He came back with, suppose Parliament passed an act that God should not be God – would Rich accept that? No, he would not, since no Parliament could make such a law. To this, Rich gave evidence that More added, 'No more could the Parliament make the King supreme head of the Church.'

This addition was a lie; but upon it More was condemned at his trial in Westminster. Rich repeated it upon oath – upon which More gave him the greatest snub that anyone can ever have received in a court of law. More pinned it down as the perjury it was, and went on:

We long dwelled both in one parish together, where – as yourself can tell – you were esteemed very light of your tongue, a great dicer, and not of commendable fame [i.e. in morals]. And so in your house at the Temple were you likewise accounted. Can it therefore seem likely unto your lordships, that I would, in so weighty a case, trust Master Rich – a man of me always reputed for one of so little truth – so far above my sovereign lord the King, or any of his noble councillors, that I would unto him utter the secrets of my conscience touching the King's Supremacy, the special point and only mark at my hands so long sought for? A thing which I never did, nor ever would, after the Statute thereof, reveal.

Upon this, Sir Richard Southwell and Mr Palmer, who had been present at the conversation in the Tower, refused to perjure themselves by witnessing to

Sir Thomas More, a most famous prisoner of the Tower, who was executed on Tower Hill on 6 July 1535

Rich's declaration. The Solicitor-General held to his story: he knew his duty as a Tudor official. In course of time he became Lord Chancellor, made an enormous fortune, and died in the odour of sanctity – as a Catholic, in Elizabeth's reign – at Felsted, where one sees him upon his tomb, hard by his religious foundations.

Before the Lord Chancellor gave judgment, More came into the open and condemned himself: he declared himself against the royal assumption of head-ship of the Church. The Lord Chancellor expressed again his wonder that Sir Thomas should stick out alone against 'all the bishops, universities, and best learned men of the Realm'. It was indeed a case of intellectual, if not spiritual, pride: ordinary people wondered, like More's wife, whether he was not 'the foolishest wise man, or the wisest foolish man' in the kingdom. On his way now to desired martyrdom, More was very sure that the greater part of the saints in heaven were of his mind and parted with their lordships praying that 'we may yet hereafter in heaven merrily all meet together to our everlasting salvation'. He was too sure about heaven.

After his condemnation, the axe turned towards him, More was conducted back to the Tower by the kindly Constable, 'a tall, strong and comely knight, his very dear friend', who broke down in tears: More had to comfort him. Margaret, afraid that she would never see her father again, was waiting on the Tower Wharf with other bystanders. When she saw him, she broke through the throng and the guards with their halberds about him and – contrary to Tudor etiquette – 'hastily ran to him and openly in the sight of them all embraced and took him about the neck and kissed him'. More gave her his fatherly blessing; then, once again, she broke the ranks to say a last farewell. The crowd was reduced to tears. During his last week in the Tower – the government still hoping he might relent – More wrote, in charcoal, to her, sending her his penitential hair-shirt: 'I never liked your manner toward me better than when you kissed me last: for I love when daughterly love and dear charity hath no leisure to look to worldly courtesy. Farewell, my dear child, and pray for me, and I shall for you and all your friends, that we may merrily meet in heaven.'

There followed the last scenes, with More's sayings and quips that are so famous.

Thomas Pope – who made a fortune as an officer of the Court of Augmenta-tions which dealt with monastic property, remained a good Catholic, and founded Trinity College, Oxford – was sent with the warning that the King

Lady Jane Grey, another victim of being born too close
to the crown. After Northumberland had attempted
to make her Queen, she was executed by Queen Mary

did not wish More to speak much at his execution. More expressed himself grateful for the warning, otherwise he might have spoken out; he asked merely that Margaret might be present at his burial. Henry gave leave for all the family to be present. 'O, how much beholden I am to his Grace that unto my poor burial vouchsafeth to have so gracious consideration.' Saying farewell, Master Pope, to whom More had been kind when he was a young Master in Chancery, could not refrain from weeping.

On the morrow, Sir Thomas arrayed himself in his best, like a bridegroom for the feast. The Lieutenant of the Tower remonstrated with him: by custom the apparel fell to the executioner, who was 'but a worthless fellow'. More returned that he could not think him a worthless fellow who was going to do him 'so a singular a benefit', and cited St Cyprian, who had given his executioner thirty pieces of gold. So, of the little money More had left he gave him a gold angel instead.

On the Lieutenant's persuasions More came forth from the Tower, on the morning of 6 July, in a garment of coarse frieze; he had a long, straggling beard – not the More we know from his portraits, with that amused and amusing look; he was haggard from long imprisonment, and was carrying his cross. As he passed, a woman offered him a cup of wine. He had not put by his old playful humour. The scaffold rigged up for him was so weak it was ready to fall; as More mounted it, 'I pray you, I pray you, Master Lieutenant, see me safe up, and for my coming down let me shift for myself.' He made his speech short, as he had been bidden; but it concluded with the significant sentence – the excuse for all this suffering – that he died 'the King's good servant, but God's first'. The poor executioner was hard put to it to do his duty; More cheered him up, 'Pluck up thy spirits, man, and be not afraid to do thine office: my neck is very short.'

Dreary Protestants disapproved of such jokes in More's situation. But what good did his martyrdom do? It made not the slightest difference to the course of events. More had been so very certain of the next world – he was a man of intense imagination and of undoubted sanctity. But what if it all were an illusion, as we now think?

Sir Thomas More's cell in the Tower

4
Reformation
Chops and Changes

T HE execution of Thomas Cromwell was the most inexcusable thing that Henry VIII ever did. Sir Thomas More was, after all, the King's most eminent opponent on a crucial matter of policy in a time of revolution. But Cromwell was entirely the King's creature – and the ablest administrator he ever had, as Henry admitted after he had gone (like Edward IV's regret for killing Clarence). Cromwell had made Henry rich by the dissolution of the monasteries; he had carried through one half, but only a half, of the English Reformation. It is fascinating to speculate what his future might have been, had he been suffered to live.

He had not outlived his usefulness when he made two fatal mistakes with Henry: the combination killed him. Most ministers are competent, if at all, at either home or foreign affairs, but hardly ever at both. When England appeared to be threatened by a *rapprochement* between Francis I and the Emperor Charles V, Cromwell pushed Henry into an alliance with the inferior Protestant princes of Germany. The threat was averted and Henry's better judgment of the foreign situation proved right. But Cromwell had also stuck his neck out in the more dangerous area where Henry's self-esteem was affected. He brought about the marriage with Anne of Cleves, an unappetising German *frau* whom Henry could not stomach.

When the alliance proved unnecessary, Henry resolved to get rid of his encumbrance – and of Cromwell for encumbering him. The minister was generally hated, so getting rid of him was popular. Cromwell's enemies such as Norfolk and Bishop Gardiner – conservative and Catholic (except for Papal Supremacy) – moved in for the kill, and they had a more appealing morsel waiting in Catherine Howard. No one spoke up for Cromwell, except Cranmer. On the afternoon of 10 June 1540 Cromwell was arrested at a full Council, Norfolk stripping the George from his neck, the Lord Admiral, not to be behind, the Garter from his leg. He was taken from Whitehall to the Tower by water.

Holbein's portrait of Thomas Cromwell, Henry VIII's able minister

He was kept there only long enough to supply Henry with the evidence he needed to quash the marriage on the ground of nullity. This he was willing enough to do. From the Tower he deposed as follows: Henry had said to him, '"Surely, my lord, as ye know I liked her before not well, but now I like her much worse. For," quoth your Highness, "I have felt her belly and her breasts, and thereby, as I can judge, she should be no maid. Which struck me so to the heart, when I felt them, that I had neither will nor courage to proceed any further in other matters."' After Candlemas and before Shrovetide Henry had imparted the confidence that 'your heart could never consent to meddle with her, notwithstanding your Highness alleged that ye used to lie with her nightly or every second night'. Henry had assured him that 'your greatest grief was that ye should surely never have any more children for the comfort of this realm if ye should so continue'. This was the important point.

Cromwell wrote from the Tower, 'with the heavy heart and trembling hand of your Highness' most heavy and most miserable prisoner and poor slave. Most gracious prince, I cry for mercy, mercy, mercy.' Henry was well content with the 'evidence' he had extracted – and Anne of Cleves was well advised to agree. There was no need to keep Cromwell officiously alive. It was a matter of some months only before Henry, his anger appeased, was complaining how much he missed Cromwell's services.

In the latter part of Henry's reign, 'tyranny had become an ordinary fact of life'. This was not entirely due to Henry: it was legalised by Parliament, by the Treasons Act of 1534, and many people in the circumstances of revolution approved of it. Lord Chancellor Wriothesley for one: 'Rather than I would have consented in my heart to any party, tumult or faction in the realm, if I had had a thousand lives I would have lost them all one after another.' Others disagreed: the more tolerant Seymour – Prince Edward's uncle – regarded the treason laws as 'almost iniquitous in their severity'. When he became Protector he had them repealed – and was rewarded by the outbreak of two dangerous rebellions, and other uprisings, a loss of control which eventually lost him his head. More in keeping with the facts of contemporary society was the judgment of a low-born Fellow of All Souls, who knew what people were really like: Sir John Mason thought the repeal of the treason laws 'the worst act that ever was done in our time'.

So Henry, whom some thought 'the most dangerous and cruel man in the world', had contemporary opinion with him. Sometimes he intervened to save someone – Cranmer, for instance, from the fate Norfolk and Bishop Gardiner intended for him. They thought that they had enough evidence of his heterodoxy to get him inside the Tower. Cranmer was politically so naive that he put up no struggle. Henry was astonished at such innocence, and said didn't he realise that, once they had got him inside, he wouldn't get out again? Henry came to the rescue of his favourite ecclesiastic, to the humiliation of Norfolk and Gardiner.

Though the French ambassador reported that 'when a man is prisoner in the Tower none dare meddle with his affairs, unless to speak ill of him, for fear of being suspected of the same crime', some prisoners got off and out. Many were pardoned; it is probable that the great majority were not executed; some few made their escape. On the other hand, there was the use of torture, the rack and thumb-screws. One unexpected pardon in these years came to an important prisoner, an illegitimate son of Edward IV, Arthur Plantagenet, Lord Lisle. He had made an incompetent governor of Calais and, when a former chaplain plotted to betray the place, Lisle was inculpated. Sent to the Tower in May 1540 – joined there, so briefly, by Cromwell – Lisle was held till January 1542. Henry then declared that he had erred through ignorance rather than ill-will, had his Garter restored to him and sent him a diamond ring as a token of favour. It is said that Lisle died of joy at the news of his release; I do not believe it, but certain it is that he died shortly after.

Catholics were not the only martyrs for their religious beliefs, there were Protestants too. The summer of 1540 saw the martyrdom of Dr Barnes – there is a flavour of heterodoxy about the name – and his two Cambridge companions, who were seduced by the doctrine of Justification by Faith. Whatever that means, they went from the Tower to the fires of Smithfield for its sake.

Six years later Anne Askew gave more trouble, for she was a lady of family; the persecuting conservatives in the Council – Gardiner, Wriothesley, Norfolk – hoped that, through her, they might get at the circle of reforming ladies around Queen Catherine Parr (Henry's last), the Duchess of Suffolk (mother of Lady Jane Grey), and the wife of Prince Edward's uncle, who was to become Protector. It was the last throw of the conservatives in the game to control the succession. Anne Askew was a tiresome woman, puffed up with theological conceit, and a liability to her friends. By her own account she was much superior to all the clergy she met in argument: they could not even convince her that there was a miracle in the Mass.

It is likely that conservative politicians were more interested in her contacts than her theological views, and Lord Chancellor Wriothesley was in a position to put the screw on her when, after previous escapes, she at last got herself into the Tower. Wriothesley and the gallant Sir Richard Rich 'did put me on the rack, because I confessed no ladies or gentlemen to be of my opinion, and thereon they kept me a long time'. This is what they wanted to elicit, not the privilege of her views on non-sense questions. But 'because I lay still and did not cry, my Lord Chancellor and Master Rich took pains to rack me with their own hands till I was nigh dead'. This, however, must be an exaggeration; for, after the ordeal, she was able to sit 'two long hours reasoning with my Lord Chancellor upon the bare floor'. Since nothing could persuade her, she was sent, with three other Protestant fanatics, to the flames at Smithfield. Even here she interrupted the preacher to inform him that he spoke without the Book. Offered Henry's pardon if she would recant, she refused to look at the offer: she 'came not there to deny her Master'.

She was as adamant as Sir Thomas More – but on the opposite side. One wonders what good such people do, with their (mutually exclusive) convictions?

What really mattered was the struggle for power, for the control of young Edward when he should become king on the demise of his father. But Henry remained wilful and determined to keep control to the last. Norfolk and his son Surrey saw that they were losing to Edward's uncle – at this time, Earl of

Left: A seventeenth-century print of the burning of Anne Askew at Smithfield

Right: The portrait of Henry Howard, Earl of Surrey, at Arundel Castle. This poet of genius was executed in the last month of Henry VIII's reign

Hertford – and his allies, John Dudley (to become Duke of Northumberland), and Secretary Paget. Hertford was even able to force his brother, Thomas Seymour, as a member of the Privy Council upon the old King. (Hertford would have reason to regret this: Henry's judgment was vindicated.)

As against this combination of *parvenus* the Howards had only their own family power, their immense estates, their royal lineage – though proximity to the throne was dangerous, as we have seen. There was also Norfolk's remarkable talent for survival, at whatever cost of pride or dignity. He had helped to ruin both Wolsey and Cromwell; he had crawled out from under the ruin of two nieces whom he had forwarded to Henry's bed and throne.

Now all was put in jeopardy by his son, who was a flagrant liability. Surrey's mother was the daughter of the Duke of Buckingham whom Henry had sent to the block. This descent gave Surrey a near claim to the throne, and there were people ready to treat him as a prince. With his genius as a poet there went a temperament of neurotic instability and megalomaniac pride – one can see it

all in the splendid Renaissance portrait of himself he had painted, at Arundel Castle. Henry had once and again saved him from the consequences of his follies, had in fact put up with a lot from him, which he would not have tolerated in anyone else. In the King's last months, when he was ill and then would temporarily recover, Surrey came out with armorial bearings which proclaimed his royal descent, and announced what he would do with his opponents when the time came. Where Norfolk was preparing to come to terms by a series of marriages with the Seymours, Surrey refused to countenance the upstarts. He advised his sister, widow of Henry's illegitimate son, Richmond, to promote herself to the King's bed as his mistress and govern him as Madame d'Etampes did the King of France. But Henry was not a doddering Francis I; he used his last energies to look into what Surrey was up to. He confessed himself 'much perplexed'. But there was no doubt about the gist of the matter: Surrey was planning to control the succession, perhaps by a *coup de main*: 'If the King die, who should have the rule of the Prince but my father, or I?'

Both Norfolk and his son went to the Tower. Here the Duke made the best possible move to survive: he wrote to Henry that all his estates and offices should be reserved for the young Prince. This was a welcome suggestion and gave Henry something to comfort him in his last days. Surrey, like the brilliant ass he was, sealed his fate by a bungled attempt at escape. His apartment in the Tower had a privy which communicated with Thames water coming up to it at full tide. The Earl arranged to have a boat brought round one midnight when the tide was out. He was caught half way down the privy shaft: a humiliating posture for one of his magnificence. Nor did his insolence at his trial help his case: he dared to express the home-truth that 'they always find the fallen guilty'.

Surrey was taken out to execution on Tower Hill on 21 January 1547. It was a great waste: in him there was extinguished the one poet of genius until we come to Philip Sidney thirty years later. The Duke of Norfolk's attainder was passed by both Houses of Parliament on 27 January. It was too late for Henry's assent, who, 'loth to hear any mention of death', died on the 28th. Norfolk survived by a hair's breadth – and remained safe in the Tower throughout the more emollient reign of Edward VI.

Never was the Tower more a key-point in the nation's affairs than in the decade following Henry's death – there were so many swift turns and about-turns, many of them taking place within its walls, the Tower itself almost an active participant, as fortress or royal residence, prison or arsenal. After Henry's great carcase was out of the way, the Council met there to erect the fabric of Edward's government. At once the disadvantages of a royal minority became apparent, with the reptiles gorging themselves upon the Crown's, i.e. the nation's, wealth. Hertford was made Duke of Somerset and Protector, Dudley, Earl of Warwick, more peerages for others. Mere titles were not what mattered – there was a large hand-out of estates and revenues to support these new 'honours'. The foundations of a number of historic families go back to that funeral feast.

The young King was knighted by his uncle; the Protector's brother was made Lord Admiral. A chapter of the Garter was held, to which the younger Seymour was promoted. The day before the coronation the procession set out for Westminster with the usual pomps and pageants. All seemed set fair; the Protector was determined to set a new model of lenity and humaneness after the late tyranny.

But he had counted without his brother – and indeed the Protector did not have much understanding of human beings. From the beginning brother Seymour was jealous of his senior and wanted to share his ascendancy; defeated in this, he intrigued for the Princess Elizabeth's hand, and then against the

The Coronation procession of Edward VI leaving the Tower on its way through the City to Westminster Abbey

government. Somerset was forced to bring him to book, who should have been his chief support; but the Treasons Act having been swept away, it was difficult to get the Lord Admiral framed. Parliament condemned him, however; his career was concisely summed up by that sage girl of sixteen, the Princess Elizabeth: 'This day hath perished a man of much wit [i.e. cleverness], and very little judgment.'

That same year, 1549, the Protector's personal rule crumbled in ruins. His combination of arrogance towards his equals and sentimentality towards the people undid him. They rewarded him with two dangerous rebellions, one in the West Country, the other in East Anglia, with movements in the southern Midlands thrown in – and ruined him. The majority in the Council turned against him, both conservatives and less moderate Reformers, and ganged up under the alternative as leader, Warwick. The City rallied in support, they secured the Tower, and Somerset found himself inside it – with his old opponents, Norfolk and Bishop Gardiner. Here he had the leisure to read, as Gardiner had to compose, polemical religious works, on opposite sides of the fence.

Like his brother he did not know when he was best off: released next year, 1551, he could not refrain from intriguing for restoration to power, and he had a party in his support. Warwick managed to hold his majority together and to send Somerset, with his leading supporters, back to the Tower. Here he remained for some weeks while the evidence was put together against him. His humane repeal of the Treasons Act created difficulties for the government, and he could only be condemned for felony, to hanging. When the people saw 'the axe of the Tower put down', symbolically, they thought that he had been acquitted and, on his way back to the Tower, cried 'God save him' along the streets. There was a great crowd for his execution on Tower Hill; at the last moment a cry of 'Pardon' went up from the crowd, though Somerset knew better. Popular with the mob, some of them pressed forward to dip handkerchiefs in the blood of their martyr.

Henry Machyn (Makins), the merchant tailor, tells us in his Diary of a curious experience on the Hill that morning – as it might have been an earthquake:

> There was a sudden rumbling a little afore he died, as it had been guns shooting and great horses coming. A thousand fell to the ground for fear; for they that were at the one side thought no other but that one was killing the other, that they fell down to the ground upon one another with their halberds. . . . Some fell into the ditch of the Tower and other places, and some ran away for fear.

It helps us to understand better the mercurial nature of people at the time, the sudden shifts of temper and sympathy – the ups and downs of fortune, the sense of melodrama – as it is authentically depicted in Shakespeare's historical plays.

Citizens' diaries of the time enable one to glimpse a more commonplace aspect of Tower activities. An accident with gunpowder lights up its rôle as the leading arsenal. In 1552 seven men were burned and eight maimed, 'like to die, and all was by taking ill heed, beating gunpowder in a mortar and striking of fire, that a spark fell into the powder'. Carts of ammunition and ordnance are continually being brought in and out: the Tower such a busy place, executions but a minor part of its activities. At the height of Wyatt's rebellion, in 1554, the rebels on the southern bank discharged their pieces at a boat belonging to the Lieutenant of the Tower and by chance killed a waterman of Tower Stairs. The Lieutenant was so enraged that he trained seven pieces of ordnance against Southwark, full against the bridge and the steeples of St Tooley's (St Olave's) and St Mary Overy (now Southwark Cathedral); 'besides all the pieces on the White Tower, one culverin on the Devil's Tower, and three falconets over the Water Gate, all being bent towards Southwark'. This threat so alarmed the inhabitants that they besought Wyatt to move away: which he did.

Machyn also describes for us an official visit that Elizabeth made as Queen to the Mint, where she was given specimens of the fine new gold coinage, after the restoration of the value of sterling. That year, 1561, there was a fire in the Tower, beyond the White Tower; fortunately not within it, for there were kept the rolls and state papers. At the end of her reign she made the admirable antiquarian William Lambarde, Keeper of the Records, of which he presented her with a manuscript account, *Pandecta Rotulorum*. Then, too, there were the religious activities at both chapels, so much to the fore under pious Queen Mary.

Edward's early death presented a fearful problem for the government, the new deal of the Reformation, and the country. If he had lived out a full span of years, there would have been an Edwardian, instead of an Elizabethan, Age. No one expected the hiatus, the reaction, of Mary's reign – a woman out of touch with government and affairs for twenty years, who thought it the will of God to put the clock back.

Everyone has blamed Northumberland for the attempt to fiddle the succession and place Lady Jane Grey on the throne, but Edward was at least as responsible. Dying of consumption at sixteen, he yet had a masterful Tudor will: he forced the Council to swear to his Device for the succession and the exclusion of his half-sisters: they were only of 'the half-blood and therefore not his heirs'. Each had already once been declared illegitimate by Henry; both could not be legitimate, while there was no doubt about the legitimacy of Henry's three Grey nieces, daughters of the Duke of Suffolk. Lady Jane was the eldest; not yet sixteen, she was a remarkable young woman, well educated, self-possessed, but reluctant to assume the dangerous elevation she was forced into.

The brief episode of her reign was passed within the walls of the Tower. Brought thither by water from Syon House, 10 July 1553, she was received in state, a procession through the Great Hall formed, her mother bearing her train, and thence with her young husband – Northumberland's son – to the royal apartments. At St Paul's the Bishop of London, Nicholas Ridley, preached her in. Mary had already written to the Council declaring herself Queen, twenty-one councillors united to reply that Jane was Queen. The Lord Treasurer surrendered to her the Crown Jewels; she signed state papers as 'Jane the Queen', and made appointments. Her husband, Lord Guildford Dudley, wanted the title of king; but, though fond of him, she was too much of a Tudor to allow that.

The Council wished to send her father into East Anglia to bring in Mary; Jane would not allow it, but insisted that Northumberland should go. Reluctantly he made his preparations, expressing mistrust of his mission and of the Lords who had gone all the way with him and Edward in putting Jane forward. 'After dinner the Duke went in to the Queen, where his commission was by that time sealed for his Lieutenantship of the army, and there he took his leave of her; and so did certain other lords also.' The Catholic Earl of Arundel, who meant to betray him, 'prayed God be with his Grace: he was very sorry it was not his chance to go with him and bear him company, in whose presence he could find in his heart to spend his blood, even at his foot'. Arundel took the Duke's page by the hand: 'Farewell, gentle Thomas, with all my heart.'

While the Duke was away, news came to the Council in the Tower that Mary was being proclaimed Queen, that the tenants of the nobility refused to serve against her, and that the ships stationed to keep watch at Yarmouth had gone over to her. The country wanted Henry VIII's children, not his niece. As soon as the news reached the Tower 'each man then began to pluck in his horns'; the Earl of Pembroke and the Lord Warden (Cheney) tried to rat, but were not allowed to get away. One evening, after Lord Treasurer Winchester had gone home to his house, the gates were suddenly locked and the keys carried up to Queen Jane, no one knew why. It appears that she feared he would abscond, and at midnight he was fetched back into the Tower.

There was a landslide in the country, which swept the ground from under the Council's feet. On the last day there was a grand christening in the church on Tower Hill, of a child related to the Protestant Throckmortons, with Suffolk, Pembroke and Queen Jane as gossips. Lady Throckmorton had to stand deputy for Queen Jane. Immediately after the christening, Queen Mary was proclaimed at Cheapside; Suffolk himself proclaimed her at the Tower Gate. When Lady Throckmorton entered, Queen Jane's cloth of estate was already taken down, herself held prisoner by her father. At Cambridge Northumberland had proclaimed Queen Mary, and was under arrest by his friend Arundel.

Mary made a triumphant entry into London – all the more popular for the trials she had undergone – attended by Princess Elizabeth, and those figures from the past the Duchess of Norfolk and the Marchioness of Exeter. At the Tower she greeted those others – Norfolk, Gardiner, and Courtenay: 'These be my prisoners', and kissed them. All were restored, and the Queen held Court at the Tower until Edward vi's funeral at Westminster, by Protestant rites in accordance with the law of the land. These were anathema to Mary, more of a

Queen Mary I
who set out to
reverse the
changes made
during the
reigns of
Henry VIII and
Edward VI and
restore the
position of the
Church of
Rome

dévote than a politician. Law or no law, she had a requiem Mass for Edward in the Tower; the Council had to attend it, and Gardiner performed it, the mitre once more on his head.

Gardiner was the leading survivor of the Henrician régime. He had been as much involved as any in every one of Henry's decisive steps – the divorce of Mary's mother, the breach with Rome, the King's Headship of the Church, of which he had been the principal defender. But Henry had left him out of the circle that he designed to govern his son's minority.

Whether subdued by this, or realising his exposed position, Gardiner had gone along with Somerset's new deal for more than a year. He did not even disapprove the doctrine of Cranmer's First Prayer Book of 1549: he said that it was capable of Catholic interpretation and the Communion Service was orthodox. But there were other things he misliked: the marriage of priests, and freedom to speak against the Mass. He was greatly surprised when he was laid by the heels in June 1548 and escorted to the Tower, but the predatory nobles of Edward's Council intended to get their hands on the possessions of the richest see in England. Northampton, Catherine Parr's brother, got Winchester House; Pembroke got some of the revenues of Winchester Cathedral.

Gardiner remained in the Tower for the next five years, his energy finding outlet in a large body of polemical writing – possibly the most voluminous contribution to Tower literature, with the exception of Sir Walter Ralegh's, who was there longer. We say nothing as to its worth: it consisted mostly of disputes with the Protestants Cranmer, Hooper, Peter Martyr and Bucer as to the true nature of the Sacrament, and other non-sense questions. Six volumes of theological controversy! – the intellectual level of which we may discern from Gardiner's reply to Hooper, who had made much of the 'fact' that Christ's body was in heaven, *therefore* it could not be in the Sacrament. Gardiner's answer was that with 'God' nothing was impossible: the question was not whether Christ's body could be in two places at once, but whether God willed it to be so. At that time, and for long after, men would kill each other over such rational considerations.

More appealingly, at odd moments Gardiner made extracts from the Latin poets or collected Latin proverbs. He was comfortably waited on by two servants of his household and was allowed visitors; but he enjoyed complaining to the Council, 'I have continued here in this miserable prison now one year, one quarter, and one month . . . with want of air to relieve my body, want of books to relieve my mind, want of good company, the only solace of this world, and finally want of a just cause why I should have come hither at all.' The Council took this 'in good part, and laughed very merrily thereat' – they knew their Gardiner. Next year Somerset, on his release and return to the Council, wanted Gardiner released – he might make a useful ally in the struggle with Warwick. Gardiner was so confident that he gave a farewell feast to the Lieutenant and Marshal, with their ladies and friends, with a present of satin for the ladies, and a message to his servants to prepare Winchester House for his return.

But this did not suit Warwick's book, who visited Gardiner with further articles to subscribe. Warwick, in his familiar manner of *bonhomie*, 'while I should write, would have me sit down by him . . . he pulled me nearer him, and said we had ere this sat together, and trusted we should do so again'. Gardiner found that he could not condemn himself by subscribing the articles and, instead of release, was put on trial. The uncompromising Bishop Ridley, who was pushing Cranmer from behind, told Gardiner that 'it was the hand of God that I was thus in prison, because I had so troubled other men in my time'. Gardiner could now be deprived, the overlarge possessions of the see pared down, and a good Protestant, Ponet, placed in pastoral charge of the nucleus that remained – quite sufficient for a self-respecting pastor of his sheep.

Warwick double-crossed the Catholic faction that supported him against Somerset, and threw in his lot with the left-wing Protestants. This had the advantage that Church lands and properties could be more generously used to provide for one's supporters. So Gardiner remained in the Tower until released by Mary. He at once sent orders to the Marchioness of Northampton to get out of Winchester House, and required Pembroke to surrender the cathedral revenues he had acquired.

Made the head of Mary's government as Lord Chancellor, Gardiner was now in a position to get his own back. Cranmer, Ridley, and Latimer took his place in the Tower, *en route* to being burned at Oxford. Latimer had been in the Tower before; when brought in, he said in his familiar way to a warder: 'What, my old friend, how do you? I am now come to be your neighbour again.'

Now Gardiner had the task of liquidating the Edwardian régime, making a complete about-turn in accordance with the Queen's hopeless views, out of touch and out of date – pro-Spanish, a Spanish marriage, submission to Rome. Only the first part of this programme was easy, for the house had fallen about Northumberland's ears. The Duke's execution was postponed that he might make an exemplary submission to the Church. In the Tower 'the altar in the chapel was arrayed', and Northumberland was fetched, with Northampton and others of his party, 'to Mass, which was said both with elevation over the head, the pax giving, blessing and crossing on the crown, breathing, turning about, and all the other rites and accidents of old time'. Before receiving the sacrament he confessed before all the people that this was the true way, out of which people had been seduced for the past sixteen years: hence all the plagues and troubles of the country. Kneeling down, with the Duke of Somerset's sons looking on, he asked all men's forgiveness.

Out of her window Lady Jane saw the party on their way to be reconciled. It was also the forty-fourth anniversary of the Duke's father's beheading. Next day the Duke's eldest son, Warwick, and Sir Thomas Gates made their submission at another Mass: 'This is the true religion' – at least it had temporarily turned up trumps. Gates asked Courtenay's forgiveness for being party to keeping him in prison. Somerset's sons again stood by. When Northumberland came to the scaffold on Tower Hill 'he put off his gown of crane-coloured damask' and once more, looking towards the Tower, repeated his confession of Catholic faith.

The Lady Jane's convictions were of firmer stuff. She was lodged in the Lieutenant's house, where one of the officers of the Tower dined at her board one day. She commanded the menfolk to replace their caps, and drank to their welcome. She asked for news of affairs. They regretted to say that Mass was restored in some places. 'It is not so strange,' she said, 'as the sudden conversion of the late Duke: who would have thought he would have so done?' Someone suggested that it was in hope of pardon. 'Pardon! woe worth him! He hath brought me and our stock in most miserable calamity and misery by his exceeding ambition. . . . Should I, who am young, forsake my faith for the love of life?' Evidently it did not occur to her that this was a reason for doing so. 'Much more he should not, whose fatal course, although he had lived his just number of years, could not have long continued. . . . Who was judge that he should hope for pardon, whose life was odious to all men? Like as his life was wicked and full of dissimulation, so was his end thereafter.' Thus the Lady Jane. She thought that Queen Mary was a merciful princess. But that remained to be seen.

Before Mary's coronation, Cranmer was brought into the Tower and lodged in Northumberland's room against the Water Gate (now Traitors' Gate). Licence was given for Northumberland's sons to be visited by their wives. Northampton, Huntingdon and Ridley had licence to come to chapel to Mass: Ridley would have refused, and Huntingdon – a cousin of Cardinal Pole – became an upright Puritan.

Mary spent the last three days of September at the Tower, arriving by water with her sister Elizabeth and her ladies, their arrival heralded by a peal of ordnance. Gardiner's chief rival, Paget, bore the sword before the Queen. For her coronation procession she was arrayed in blue velvet, furred with powdered ermine; on her head a caul of tinsel with gold circlet so heavy that the little woman 'was fain to bear up her head with her hands'. She rode alone in a chariot drawn by six horses with trappings of red velvet. After this came a chariot covered with cloth of silver, in which Elizabeth rode with her face forward, Anne of Cleves facing her. And so through the City with all its pageants to Westminster, where the crowning was performed – though it was Cranmer's right as Archbishop – by Gardiner.

No doubt at the beginning Mary wished to rule mercifully enough, but her determination to carry through the Spanish marriage and bring in a foreign king roused intense opposition and brought about the Wyatt rebellion which nearly unseated her. Wyatt's contacts were much wider than the Kentish forces he brought to the gates of the city. Courtenay, restored to the earldom of Devon and disappointed of his hope of marrying Mary, failed his West Country following prepared to rise on his behalf. The project was to marry him to Elizabeth, who was aware of what was on foot but too wary to commit herself. From Whitehall the Queen moved back to the Tower for safety.

Wyatt approached as near as London Bridge with two thousand Kentishmen, and occupied Southwark. As soon as they were sighted 'there was shot off out of the White Tower six or eight shot, but missed them, sometimes shooting over, and sometimes shooting short'. Mary forbade the bombardment of Southwark, when it was suggested by an ordnance-officer of the Tower. With proper royal courage she went to the Guildhall to appeal to the loyalty of the citizens, and they decided the issue.

The failure of so widespread a challenge put all the Protestant leaders in jeopardy, and gave the signal for an almighty revenge. Gardiner urged it forward both in preaching before the Queen and in Council. The Tower was filled with important prisoners, beginning with the Duke of Suffolk, who had foolishly incriminated all his family again. The first victims were Lady Jane and her husband, who were innocent. Young Lord Guildford Dudley was led out to execution upon Tower Hill: his wife watched him both going and coming, his body brought back into the chapel within the Tower. The Marquis of Northampton watched the execution from the leads of the Devil's Tower.

The Lady Jane was brought forth by the Lieutenant and, though she passed the dead carcase of her husband being carted into the chapel, she would allow no sign of fear and shed no tears. A scaffold had been erected for her upon the Green within the Tower, not to raise sympathy among the populace outside. She walked steadily forward, her eyes upon the prayer-book she carried, her waiting-women dissolved in tears. From the scaffold she spoke to the point, confessing her offence in consenting to take the Crown, 'but touching the procurement and desire thereof by me or on my behalf, I do wash my hands thereof in innocency before God' – and she wrung her hands. After saying the psalm *Miserere mei Deus* in English, she handed over gloves and prayer-book, and sought to untie her gown. The hangman made the mistake of offering to help her: she forbade him, and turned to her women. There followed the pathetic scene, which became so famous. When they tied the handkerchief about her eyes, she could not find the block; feeling for it, 'What shall I do? Where is it?' One of the standers-by guided her to it: 'Lord, into thy hands I commend my spirit.'

The same day Courtenay was sent back to what had been his home most of his life: he now occupied a room in the Bell Tower, from which he watched Lady Jane's father 'both outward and inward', to and from his execution. The space before the altar in St Peter-ad-vincula – Macaulay's 'saddest spot in Christendom' – was rapidly filling up with headless bodies: Anne Boleyn, her brother and his wife; her cousin, Catherine Howard, and the Countess of Salisbury; Somerset and Northumberland side by side in the fellowship of death; now Lady Jane, her husband and her father. The Tower was crammed with prisoners, London a sickening shambles with executions and hangings. Such were the Dead Sea fruits of the Spanish marriage, yet Mary persisted; the country was already turning against her, and it was yet early days; the burnings were yet to begin. Among those lost to their country was its most brilliant Italian scholar, William Thomas;* before his execution he had 'almost slain himself, with thrusting under the paps with a knife'. This reminds us that there was this way of delivering oneself out of durance, too. Sir William St Loe came in 'with a wonderful stout courage, nothing at all abashed'. He had carried a message from Wyatt to Princess Elizabeth: he survived to marry

*For him cf. my *The Elizabethan Renaissance: The Life of Society*, 17 foll.

The Tower's most famous prisoner: Elizabeth I as Princess. Her half-sister Mary imprisoned her there for two months

Bess of Hardwick, another proof of courage. Sir Nicholas Throckmorton made a celebrated defence at his trial, which, for the exceptional importance of his acquittal, has entered the law-books. The verdict made Mary ill with chagrin for several days; henceforth she had the City against her.

The problem was how to incriminate Elizabeth, who would certainly have been catapulted onto Mary's throne had the rebellion succeeded. The prospect looked black indeed for her: at this stage both Mary and Charles v's ambassador wanted to get rid of her; Gardiner was hostile, though protecting Courtenay – he evidently had him in mind for the succession. A letter from Elizabeth was found among the French ambassador's dispatches; when summoned up to Court she was ill – all very suspicious. When she arrived under guard, she was ordered to the Tower. It sent her into a fever of anxiety – few of her dangerous eminence emerged again: she remembered her mother and her cousins – and perhaps, at this moment, Thomas Seymour.

For, begging for time to write a personal appeal to the Queen, she began with what may well be a reference to him: 'I have heard in my time of many cast away only for want of coming to the presence of their Prince.' She prayed to be allowed to answer the accusations before her sister herself, not to 'be condemned in all men's sight afore my desert known'; above all not to be sent to the Tower, 'a place more wonted for a false traitor than a true subject'. While she wrote her letter – one can still see her beautiful Italian script in the Public Record Office – the tide in the river turned and London Bridge could not safely be shot. However, next morning she was sent off down the river, escorted by the Lord Treasurer and the Earl of Sussex. It was Palm Sunday, and a dismal day, raining hard. Thus the Tower received its most famous prisoner.

The girl of twenty was distraught, yet both put up a resistance and did not fail to make a bid for sympathy from the onlookers. Arrived at Traitors' Gate, she would not go in, saying that she was no traitor. The water was lapping up the steps and, she said, would go over her shoes. The lords had already landed; one of them came back for her, but she would not come. At that the Lord Treasurer said it was not for her to choose and, because it was raining, offered her his cloak. This she rejected, putting it by with her hand. Then, with one foot on the Tower stairs, she paused to say out loud, 'Here landeth the truest subject being a prisoner, that ever landed at these stairs.'

There was the Constable of the Tower, Sir John Gage, to receive her, and a crowd of officers and warders standing in order. 'What needeth all this?' she said, and addressed them all, looking up to heaven, 'O Lord, I never thought to have come in here as prisoner. I pray you all, good friends and fellows, bear me witness that I come in no traitor, but as true a woman to the Queen's Majesty as any now living. And thereon will I take my death.' When they had got her inside, and the lords took extra precautions to lock all doors strictly, she protested that such a show of force was hardly necessary for a weak woman. Sussex was reduced to tears, and took her side: 'What will ye do, my lords? What mean ye therein? She was a king's daughter, and is the Queen's sister: go no further than your commission: I know what it is.'

Thus Elizabeth disappeared inside the Tower for the next two months, where she made a troublesome prisoner, having made it as difficult as she could for her sister to kill her. Every effort was made to incriminate her; Wyatt and his accomplices were examined again and again for evidence against her. It is said that Edmund Tremayne was racked on her account and Sir James Croft 'marvellously tossed and examined', but gave away nothing. 'As for the traitor Wyatt,' she said, 'he might peradventure write me a letter, but on my faith I never received any from him.' Nothing could be found out from her. When Wyatt was at length brought to the scaffold, he completely exonerated Elizabeth and Courtenay from any part in the conspiracy. So far as Courtenay was concerned this was untrue, but Gardiner suppressed the evidence against him. At the end of May he was sent to Fotheringhay, whence he was allowed abroad – after the Queen was safely, unpopularly married – where he died. A week before, Elizabeth had been released, on her way to confinement at Woodstock.

But it had been a very near thing.

Princess
Elizabeth's walk
along the
battlements
overlooking
the river

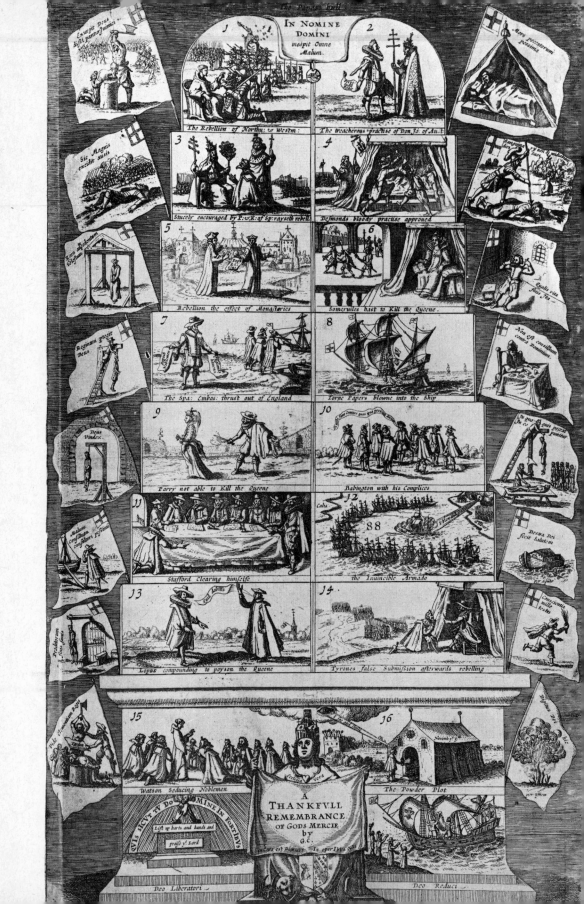

The Popish Plott

IN NOMINE DOMINI incipit Omne Malum.

1 · The Rebellion of Northu: & Westm:

2 · The treacherous practise of Don Ia: of Au:

3 · Stucely encouraged by P: & K: of Sp: rayseth rebell:

4 · Desmonds bloody practise approued

5 · Rebellion the effect of Monasteries

6 · Someruiles hast to Kill the Queene.

7 · The Spa: Embas: thrust out of England

8 · Torne Papers blowne into the Ship

9 · Parry not able to Kill the Queene

10 · Babington with his Complices

11 · Stafford clearing himselfe

12 · 88 · the Inuincible Armado

13 · Lopus compounding to poyson the Queene

14 · Tyrones false Submission afterwards rebelling

15 · Watson Seducing Noblemen

16 · The Powder Plot

A THANKFVLL REMEMBRANCE OF GODS MERCIE by G. C.

Lift up harts and hands and praise yᵉ Lord

Deo Liberatori

Deo Reduci

5
Protestants and Catholics

AFTER this experience it is hardly surprising that, as Queen, Elizabeth I used the Tower as a residence very little. Also, she preferred a Renaissance to a medieval background, and spent her time in a round of pleasant palaces and surroundings, Greenwich, Whitehall and Richmond, Oatlands and Nonsuch in Surrey. The reaction to the sour failure, the bitter events, of Mary's reign swept Elizabeth in with a popularity she always cultivated and which never failed her – and also carried her further on to the Protestant side than she could have wished.

The new Queen made her customary return to the Tower before her coronation in very different circumstances from her last appearance. She was accompanied on the river by 'the Mayor and aldermen in their barge, and all the crafts in their barges, decked and trimmed with the targets and banners of their mysteries'. Thus she entered, 'with great and pleasant melody of instruments, which played in most sweet and heavenly manner', received by all the chief officers of state. Winchester, who bent before every change 'like the willow, not the oak', still survived as Lord Treasurer, Sussex was Chief Sewer for the coronation. Northumberland's remaining sons – only two out of that promising brood of five – were there: Ambrose as Chief Pantler, Robert just made Master of the Horse. They must all have had interesting reflections.

After only two days' residence – and Elizabeth never held her Court there again – the coronation procession through the City took place on 14 January 1559. Magnificent as ever, it was notable as a triumph of propaganda. The Protestant City hailed her as a 'Deborah, the judge and restorer of the house of Israel'; one of the City pageants exhibited 'Ignorance' and 'Superstition' being trodden underfoot; another let down from heaven, by the hand of a child representing Truth, an English Bible. Such were the keynotes of the City's reception; there was no doubt which way the tide was flowing. Before leaving the Tower, Elizabeth had given thanks to God 'that he had been so merciful unto her as to spare her to see that joyful day'; she compared herself with the

An early seventeenth-century print giving thanks for the defeat of successive Catholic attempts to murder Queen Elizabeth and overthrow her régime prophet Daniel, 'delivered out of the den from the cruel and raging lions'. All the way along the new Queen responded, with gratitude to the fervent acclamations, the promise of a new age after the dark years. Many remembered, as she passed by: one recorded voice said, 'Remember old King Harry the eighth?'

After the popular rejoicings, back to the business of state. The new Queen always kept her eye on national unity. She would have liked to retain the services of the moderate Catholic bishops, those who had not burned; she would have had a celibate clergy, and kept the roods and ornaments of the churches, like the cultivated woman she was. It was not, however, found possible to be reasonable. The Catholic bishops would not serve her; the Protestant bishops would not serve with them, nor tolerate the roods and altars in the churches. Rejecting the return to Edwardian Protestantism, the Catholic bishops took the places of the Protestants, for a time, in the Tower. They were not burned, however; later, some of them were dumped, by an economical government, upon their Protestant successors to maintain.

More grievous was the unnecessary destruction. In the course of the Reformation, at one time or another, St John's Chapel was stripped of its furniture. The rood-screen and images went, the royal stalls, pews and woodwork; Henry III's painted windows with the Virgin and Child of his devotion. All vanished. The stark chapel as we see it today exposes the masculine muscularity of its Norman architecture, but it is not as the Middle Ages saw it. Even so, it expresses the history it – and the country – have been through: the wind of the Reformation has blown through it.

With Elizabeth on the throne the question of the succession was more acute than ever – there was now no Elizabeth waiting in the wings – and the marriage of persons of royal blood was a matter of state, as always. By an act of Henry VIII it was treason for them to marry without the sovereign's consent. This Lady Jane Grey's next sister, Catherine, proceeded to do. Unable to wait for the unlikely event of Elizabeth's permission, the young woman secretly married Somerset's son and heir in November or December 1560. 'During the following summer,' as the chaste Victorian Professor Pollard put it, 'the Countess's condition laid her open to suspicion.' In August she was consigned to the Tower, but refused to confess; next month the young Earl followed, but to separate imprisonment. On 24 September a son was born, and the Queen was furious. An archiepiscopal commission investigated their 'infamous conversation' and 'pretended marriage'. No documentary evidence was forthcoming; the marriage was declared null, the progeny illegitimate.

Lady Catherine
Grey with her
son, whose birth
in the Tower
infuriated Elizabeth I

The kindly Tower officials allowed the offending couple to co-habit, and in February 1563 Lady Catherine offended again, with another son. This settled her hash with the Queen, though, when plague visited the Tower this summer, the offender was allowed into the country. In 1564 the claim of the Greys to the succession was agitated by some would-be friends, and back the couple went to the Tower. Lady Catherine was allowed occasionally to visit the country house of the Lieutenant, Sir Owen Hopton, Cockfield Hall. But her husband was never allowed at Cockfield, for all the promise of its name and her pathetic appeals, and there she died in 1568.

Meanwhile, her younger sister, profiting not at all from the elder's misfortune, had similarly misconducted herself. The event was ludicrous; for Lady Mary was practically a dwarf, and she fell in love with the Queen's serjeant-porter, Keys, a huge man who was twice her age and twice her size. The couple were married secretly, and were made to bear the brunt of it.

The question of the succession was at the heart of the prolonged crisis of 1569–72, the real watershed of Elizabeth's reign: after that there was to be no going back on the course shaped in Edward's. Elizabeth's first decade exhibited a humane moderation, of which she was justly proud, after the terrible events of the previous decade. This was too much for the aristocratic conservatives in her Council, who hated the new deal and Cecil who was urging it forward. Another body in the Council, led by Leicester, though Protestant, was inspired by jealousy of Cecil. Together they formed a majority, which would have overwhelmed him but for the steady support of the Queen and – it is sometimes overlooked – of the country, gentry and middle classes, as represented in Parliament. Here was his real support: he never lost touch with it.

The coalition ganging up against Cecil thought that they had found a platform and a candidate, which would solve the problem of the succession by marrying Mary Stuart, now under restraint in England, to the (fourth) Duke of Norfolk. He was all too willing: though Elizabeth's cousin, he boasted that 'before he lost that marriage he would lose his life'. Mary Stuart was willing, as ever; the fact that he was a Protestant was no objection in her Catholic eyes, and she assured him that she would never desert him 'for weal or woe'. The insuperable obstacle was Elizabeth, who – with the acute sense of preservation won in a hard school – said that within four months of such a marriage she herself would be in the Tower again.

She gave Norfolk sufficient warning 'to look to his pillow', with its reminder of what had happened to Darnley. But blinded, as so many had been and still were to be, by the glamour of a throne, Norfolk persisted. Matters reached a crisis with the open rebellion of the Catholic Earls in the North in 1569, followed by the Pope's excommunication of the Queen and deposition from the throne. Elizabeth swore her cousin upon his allegiance not to persist; he should have known what that warning meant: to go further would be treason. He gave his assurance, then broke his word and drifted into conspiracy.

The coalition had two wings; Leicester's instigator was Sir Nicholas Throckmorton. Though an advanced Protestant, he was always friendly to Mary Stuart, and jealous of Cecil. Throckmorton fetched up in the Tower again, and through him the plan came out: Cecil should be overwhelmed in Council, as Cromwell had been, and packed off to the Tower, where 'means to undo him would not be far to seek'. But they reckoned without Elizabeth, less capricious and more humane than her father, and who knew the value of a faithful servant. Actually, in all this period, practically the only grandees who never saw the inside of the Tower as prisoners were the Cecils – tribute to their sense of preservation as well as their honesty.

Throckmorton was not disloyal, was released and shortly died. But Norfolk, hardly realising the implications of what he was doing, involved himself with Ridolfi, the papal banker, to raise money for arms and with plans for foreign intervention. As the only remaining duke, and free with his money, he was popular, particularly in Norfolk: he was a danger to the country. His nerve failed him to come out into open rebellion, for which he was now too late, and in September 1571 he was 'quietly brought into the Tower without any trouble,

Visscher's panorama of Elizabethan London, showing the Tower in the distance save a number of idle, rascal people – women, men, boys and girls – running about him as the manner is, gazing at him'. He was the last duke in England for many a day.

Norfolk made a most incompetent conspirator: he had left ciphers and letters in plenty at the Charterhouse to bear witness against him. Shortly a haul of prisoners joined him in the Tower, including Mary Stuart's indiscreet ambassador, the Bishop of Ross. He proceeded to incriminate his mistress, so that even good Dr Wilson was shocked: 'Lord! what people these be: what a Queen, and what an ambassador!' Norfolk, not the most intelligent of men, seems to have realised that no defence was possible. Nor was there any doubt at his trial. Since the state of the tide made it impossible to pass London Bridge, he was taken through the City to the 'Three Cranes' at Vintry Wharf, and thence to Westminster.

On his return, a condemned man, a close watch was kept on his room

looking on to Sir Owen Hopton's garden: 'In the night the march goeth continually hard by that garden, and in the daytime the warders and their wives have a common course that way, so it is very unlikely for any to receive letters there.' Norfolk asked for the ministrations of Dean Nowell, of St Paul's, and 'longeth much for Mr Foxe [the martyrologist], his old schoolmaster, to whom he most desires to perform that faith which he first grounded him in'. The best thing about this unsatisfactory duke was the long letter of instructions for his children which he wrote in the Tower – a sympathetic addition to its literature.

Norfolk had been friendly with Cecil, until the fatal figure of Mary Stuart raised itself between them. He now obtained the Queen's permission for Cecil to be guardian to his children. For each of them he had a message, enjoining upon his eldest son, Philip, to obey his guardian, 'so friendly and vigilant a nobleman', and to 'make some satisfaction for your father's disobedience'.

The Queen, poor woman, had the greatest difficulty in doing her duty and signing the death-warrant of her cousin. From week to week, and month to month, she put it off; she drafted orders, then when she considered his 'nearness of blood, his superiority of honour, etc., she stayeth'. At last Parliament forced her hand, and petitioned that the sentence be carried out. At his execution the Duke made no trouble: he recognised his fault, and the government's leniency. 'For men to suffer death in this place is no new thing, though – since the beginning of our most gracious Queen's reign I am the first, and God grant I may be the last.' He confessed himself the Protestant he had always been (contrary to the mistaken view of many recent writers): 'I have not been popish from the time that I had any taste in religion, but have always been averse to the popish doctrine.' Foxe was with him to the end; the Duke's body went to join his cousins Anne Boleyn and Catherine Howard, before the altar of St Peter-ad-vincula.

In his testament he had warned his eldest son: 'Beware of pride, lechery, taunting, and sullenness, which vices nature doth somewhat kindle in you.' The brief career of Philip, Earl of Arundel, bore out the exactness of his father's diagnosis of his character: he proceeded to exemplify every one of those traits in a marked degree. We need not go into his early career of lechery and flagrant neglect of his wife; she, a Dacre heiress, was an uncompromising Catholic and, when her husband was disappointed in the results of paying court to the Queen, who disliked and mistrusted him, his wife at length got him under her thumb.

As the conflict with Spain approached, and the Armada was building, Arundel prepared to place himself at the disposal of his country's enemies. He made two attempts, from Arundel Castle, to get a ship across-Channel from the coast one can see from the keep there. The government was taking no risk with so leading an opponent, who could have been used as figure-head in case of invasion. Arundel confessed that 'he would have served in any place that Dr [Cardinal] Allen had judged fit for him, so that it had been for the Catholic cause'. This aristocrat very properly spent the rest of his life in the Tower. He confessed his affection towards King Philip of Spain, not only as his god-father but as the leader of European Catholicism. When the Armada was on the way he could think of nothing better than twenty-four hours a day intercessions in the Tower to speed it. They do not seem to have helped.

In the Beauchamp Tower where he resided, attended by his own servants, he repented of his former gay life by equally extreme measures of abstinence: three fast-days a week, hours on his knees in prayer, beginning at five in the morning. When, not unnaturally, he grew weak and could not get out of bed for his devotions, he had 'his beads almost always with him in his bed'. He had hoped for the glory of a martyr's death on Tower Hill, but the government disappointed him of his wish. He died in his bed, to the side of which the Lieutenant of the Tower came to ask his forgiveness. This was Sir Michael Blount, of that Catholic family, whom Arundel reproached thus: 'Master Lieutenant, you have showed both me and my men very hard measure. . . . Remember, good Master Lieutenant, that God can in the revolution of a few days bring you to be a prisoner also, and to be kept in the same place where now you keep others.'

Within a matter of weeks, Sir Michael Blount 'fell into great disgrace, lost his office, and was indeed kept close prisoner in the Tower where he had kept others; and another Lieutenant placed, who carried as hard a hand over him as he had done others'. Thus Arundel's Jesuit biographer; it showed that Philip was a saint – or perhaps he had some inkling of the 'lewd behaviour' for which Blount was dismissed. One sees the look of fixation on the extraordinary long-visaged, dark countenance of the Earl, even in his days of Court finery. He had his books with him in the Beauchamp Tower, and translated Johann Justus's *An Epistle of Jesus Christ to the Faithful Soul*. Three more manuscripts he left, treatises on 'The Excellence and Utility of Virtue'. Unfortunately, he paid insufficient attention to Aristotle's doctrine of the golden mean, first on one side and then on the other.

Arundel had leisure to carve over his fireplace, in good Italian hand: ,*Quanto plus afflictionis pro christo in hoc saeculo tanto plus gloriae cum christo in futuro* Arundel June 22, 1587' (By so much the more affliction for Christ in this world, so much the more glory with Christ in the future). This prophecy also has been fulfilled, for quite recently he has been constituted a saint. His descendant the present Duke of Norfolk writes, 'now my greatest ancestor is canonised and joins the Saints in Heaven'. From a more worldly point of view, the historian may regard Henry VIII's Duke as the greatest Howard, to whom the family owes its wealth and prosperity.

The Earl of Arundel's inscription in the Beauchamp Tower

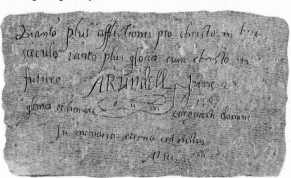

Another aristocratic family that found it difficult to accommodate itself to the new deal was the Percies – with more reason, for in the North they still held feudal state. Thomas Percy, seventh Earl of Northumberland, was executed after the Rebellion of 1569; his brother, a much abler man, helped to suppress it and stepped into his brother's earldom. 'Simple Thomas', men said, had but made way for 'Cruel Henry'. Henry Percy's was a working mind, and not content but he must join the grand intrigue on behalf of Mary Stuart; so he was one of those in the Tower in 1571–2. On release he was confined to his southern estate at Petworth. As if this were not enough he involved himself in the (Catholic) Throckmorton plot in 1582, and went back to the Tower (with Lord Henry Howard, Norfolk's brother) for a second spell. Still not content, he entered into further projects on Mary's behalf with the Pagets, and helped them to fly the country. Northumberland's agent in these unquiet proceedings was William Shelley, of that Sussex Catholic family. Shelley was racked in the Tower, and confessed; Northumberland returned for a third spell.

This was his last. Fearing attainder, he decided to cheat the 'bitch' – as he termed the Queen – of his estates, by committing suicide. He procured a pistol secretly, barred himself in his chamber and shot himself in the left breast. This

made a sensation and, of course, there were people who blamed the government. The coroner's inquest of the Tower Ward viewed the body and examined
his man that bought the pistol, as also the gunsmith who sold it. They brought
in a verdict of suicide. Of course the Catholics said that he had been made away
with – of which there was no evidence and no likelihood: the government
could always have sentenced him, and got his estates into the bargain. Nevertheless, Camden tells us, 'to satisfy the multitude, who are always prone to
believe the worst in such cases', the government felt obliged to publish its own
account of the matter, and the reasons for Northumberland's treatment.

These were dangerous years – open war with Spain, religious war declared
with the Papal release of Elizabeth's subjects from their obedience, and the
double Jesuit campaign of reconciling to Rome along with political conspiracy
and intrigue. Some were politicos, some not; Edmund Campion was not,
Father Parsons most certainly was. The effect was that of a Fifth Column
operating in time of war. Was the government not to defend itself on both
fronts? That would have been to neglect its prime duty. The victims were
caught in a conflict of loyalties, as so often with Communists in our day.
Ordinary loyal Catholics regarded themselves as the victims of Jesuit policy
they were.

These were years of plots to murder the Queen, and even if some of the
plotters were mad yet madmen have got away with such things in our time.
In this very year 1585 William Parry was in the Tower for such a plot. A
light-headed Welshman with a split personality, he had been a servant of the
Queen and a member of Parliament. As such he was the only member to
oppose severer legislation against the infiltrating Jesuits and seminaries. The
fact was that he had secretly become a convert. Having run through his wife's
estate, he was hard put to it to live; he went into exile and became a double-
agent. He seems to have got the Cardinal of Como to give a promised sanction
for Elizabeth's assassination. William the Silent had been assassinated the year
before, with Philip ii's approval, like other Protestant leaders, Coligny and the
Regent Murray; Henri iii and Henri iv were to die at the hand of Catholic
assassins. It would not have been impossible to get at Elizabeth – she was
singularly open in moving among her people, unlike Philip ii. Whether Parry
meant to carry out his project, or no, the government was quite right to take
no chances with such a type.

Somerville, two years before, had undoubtedly been mad. Camden says
that he had been distracted and seduced by reading the constant Catholic

attacks upon the Queen by Parsons and others, some of them very scandalous. Somerville had married an Arden, of the Warwickshire family to which Shakespeare's mother belonged; they were Catholics, and Somerville's mad march to London to kill the Queen incriminated the family. Arden had incurred the enmity of Leicester; the priest who lived with him as gardener betrayed him and gave evidence against him. Arden and Somerville were delivered over from the Tower to Newgate, where Somerville cheated the executioner by hanging himself in his cell.

There was nothing mad about Babington, except that he was mad about Mary Stuart; his conspiracy was a much more serious affair and involved a large number of people, chiefly hare-brained young men of good family. Babington himself came of ancient stock, rich and vain and handsome. Earlier he had been a page to Mary; later, his house was found to be full of Catholic polemical works against Elizabeth and prophecies of her downfall. The combination was too much for the young man's sense, let alone morals. From the arrival of the Jesuit mission in England, with Campion and Parsons, he formed a band of young gentlemen to support and sustain them. Brought up secretly a Catholic, there was not much secrecy around Babington – too many people were in the know, including Walsingham's intelligence service. George Gifford, another young Catholic of good family, was a double-agent who reported every stage in the development of Babington's plot, and at Chartley helped to lay the trap which eventually caught Mary red-handed, giving her assent to Elizabeth's assassination. Of course Mary denied all knowledge of Babington and his plot on the scaffold at Fotheringhay; but she was a consummate actress and congenital liar. Mendoza – formerly ambassador in London – reported to Philip that she was fully acquainted with the project, a letter which Philip annotated, in his usual manner, with no disapprobation.

The conspiracy which was intended to murder Elizabeth brought Mary to the block, and filled the Tower with prisoners. At his trial Babington did not deny his guilt, and declared all with 'a wonderful good grace'; but he put the blame on the priest Ballard for instigating the conspiracy and pressing him into action. This seems to have been true, though Ballard, when racked in the Tower, would give no details but acknowledged the general fact of the conspiracy. Ballard and Babington, with five of their companions, were dragged on hurdles from Tower Hill through the City to their hanging and disembowelling. On the scaffold Babington imparted the confidence that he honestly believed himself engaged in 'a deed lawful and meritorious'. One sees the dreadful effect that writings such as Parsons's could have – to which the poet Donne later bore witness.

Of the fourteen sprigs of good family who suffered for their criminal folly, one of them deserved a better fate, if only for his verses. Chidiock Tichborne, of that constant Catholic stock, wrote the most touching poem to have been written in the Tower:

> My tale was heard and yet it was not told,
>   My fruit is fallen and yet my leaves are green,
> My youth is spent and yet I am not old,
>   I saw the world and yet I was not seen;
>   My thread is cut and yet it is not spun,
>   And now I live, and now my life is done.
>
> I sought my death and found it in my womb,
>   I looked for life and saw it was a shade,
> I trod the earth and knew it was my tomb,
>   And now I die, and now I was but made;
>   My glass is full, and now my glass is run,
>   And now I live, and now my life is done.

This is the perspective in which to see the campaign against the Jesuits and seminary priests. Gone were the kindly days of the first decade of the reign, before the Papacy declared war: this was war against Spain, and against the Counter-Reformation, of which the Jesuits were the spearhead. The extraordinary success of the first Jesuit mission of Campion and Parsons in 1580 thoroughly alarmed the government: many among the governing-class, nobles and gentry, were reconciled to Rome – this was what was dangerous: it did not matter about the people. Campion was a saintly man and brilliant preacher, who converted scores; Parsons had the energy and gifts of an indefatigable politician. The government, near to panic, made every effort to catch them – and caught the wrong one: Parsons slipped through the net to the Continent and never set foot in England again. However, completely pro-Spanish, and lending himself to Philip's purposes at every point, he sent scores of priests to their deaths here.

Campion, with two more priests and several laymen, was taken through the City, a hooting mob around them, to the Tower. Sir Owen Hopton popped him into Little Ease, the cell where one could neither stand upright nor lie at full length. From thence, after a few days, he was conducted to Leicester's house to meet leading members of the Council, where he was treated with all courtesy. At Oxford Campion had been a brilliant student, taken notice of by the Queen for his promise, and for some years had found a patron in Leicester: he was a cruel disappointment. Every effort was made to make him see sense; but though he confessed himself loyal to the Queen – unlike Parsons – on the matter of religion, transcending sense, he was adamant.

Back he went to the Tower, where, refusing to give any information, he was three times racked. Actually, torture was not recognised by the Common Law of England, so authority had to be given by the executive, the Privy Council. The next attempt to break down his resistance was by way of a disputation in St John's Chapel with four Protestant divines, headed by the Dean of St Paul's. They were all prepared and loaded, Campion given no time or books. To the most gifted disputant in the Schools at Oxford this offered no problem: the upshot did no good to Campion, and had only a disturbing effect on his hearers – it is said that the Earl of Arundel was much affected, or, perhaps we should say, disaffected by it.

There was nothing to be done but to put Campion on trial, and even here the government was in a quandary: the best they could do was to arraign him and his companions under an old statute of Edward III against aiding and abetting the King's enemies. In pleading, Campion could not hold up his arm for the racking he had undergone; but at the death-sentence he and his fellows broke into a *Te Deum laudamus*. He and two companion priests were hanged at Tyburn, the youngest, Alexander Bryant, an extremely handsome West Countryman. What a waste!

Nor did the executions do the government much good among the credulous of those times. In the crowd watching was young Henry Walpole – of that family whose name in a later century became synonymous with secular good sense, but which in the sixteenth century almost extinguished itself by its faith and fanaticism. Some of the blood of the martyrs spurted upon Walpole's clothes; he took this for a sign from above that he was to carry on Campion's work. Already a convert, he became a Jesuit and joined Parsons in Spain. Returning to England, he was captured with two English soldiers who had served under Sir William Stanley, the traitor who surrendered Deventer to the Spaniards. Walpole was racked again and again in the Tower without any information being gained from him – he was still able to write, with some difficulty; he was sent back to York for trial and sentence.

Campion's sanctity and the courage with which he resisted torture – himself the most sensitive of men – inspired others and set a model for other priests to follow in the Tower. Everything that had belonged to him was venerated, in the credulous manner of the time; his girdle was preserved, and we find a somewhat improper use made of his thumb upon a woman later.★ And, of course, all this encouraged those who already had a death-wish, such as Robert Southwell expressed to the General of the Jesuits, before leaving Rome.

Father Southwell's father was the illegitimate son of Henry VIII's handsome Augmentations officer, Sir Richard Southwell, who came forward as the accuser of Surrey, his boyhood companion. The family remained Catholic, the poet's grandmother being one of the recusant Shelleys. On his return to England Southwell was lodged, comfortably enough, in the house of the stiff-necked Countess of Arundel, a North Country Dacre. Here he was able to follow his literary pursuits, putting forth consoling tracts for the aristocratic ladies, his patrons, with whom he had much success, even printing his perfervid, baroque, somewhat ultramontane, certainly not English, *Mary Magdalen's Funeral Tears*. In the house of a peer he was comparatively safe – for peers were not sued for recusancy; but one day in 1592 he was caught after saying Mass outside London, and captured by Topcliffe himself, the arch-persecutor of Catholics. (In the end the Queen laid him by the heels.)

Southwell was at first imprisoned in the Gatehouse at Westminster, which he found filthy and alive with vermin. His father petitioned that his son might be treated as a gentleman; he was transferred to the more salubrious Tower, where he was allowed books, clothes and necessaries. Here he remained for three years, several times tortured for information, but not by the rack: he must then have endured the thumb-screws. This did not prevent him from writing, though it is not known whether his poem *The Burning Babe* was composed there; if so, it might rank as the most famous to have emerged from those walls: it is in all the anthologies. But, indubitably, his surroundings are reflected in such a poem as *I die alive*:

> O life! what lets thee from a quick decease?
>   O death! what draws thee from a present prey?
> My feast is done, my soul would be at ease,
>   My grace is said: O death! come take away . . .
>
> Thus still I die, yet still I do revive,
>   My living death by dying life is fed;
> Grace more than nature keeps my heart alive,
>   Whose idle hopes and vain desires are dead.

★Cf. my *The Elizabethan Renaissance: The Life of Society*, pp. 268–9.

Or:

> Sith my life from life is parted,
>   Death, come take thy portion;
> Who survives when life is murdered,
>   Lives by mere extortion.

Again:

> Come, cruel death, why lingerest thou so long?
>   What doth withold thy dint from fatal stroke?
> Now pressed I am, alas, thou dost me wrong,
>   To let me live, more anger to provoke . . .

At length he petitioned that he might be brought to trial, and have his death-wish; and this, in 1595, was granted.

At just this time, William Shakespeare was expressing the ordinary Englishman's patriotic view by describing these people as

> the fools of time
> Which die for goodness who have lived for crime.

But, as we have seen, this was true only of some of them. The number of executions went up and down with the country's sense of danger, reaching a peak in 1588 and another in 1594. At that time the Queen protested that there had been enough bloodshed, and thereafter the rate of executions fell off notably.

Catholics were not the only people to enjoy the delights of the Tower for their stiff-necked opposition: there was the Left-wing fringe of forward Protestants who, if less dangerous, were more obstreperous. The Queen regarded the religious settlement and the succession to the throne as matters of prerogative not to be called in question by the House of Commons. A small group of MPs, with Peter Wentworth as their leader, were for ever interfering in these sacred matters, agitating opinion and, when called to account, stuck up for the liberties of Parliament: they were precursors of the later Parliamentarian leaders against Charles I. In consequence, several of them were sent to the Tower at one time or another: the Puritan controversialist Job Throckmorton, who was so rude about the bishops; Thomas Norton, no less vociferous; one Smalley, and even a follower of Burghley, Arthur Hall, for the tracts they published on these subjects.

Peter Wentworth was incorrigible; as someone said, 'Mr Wentworth will never acknowledge himself to make a fault, nor say that he is sorry for anything that he doth speak.' Nor did he. The result was several sojourns in the Tower; eventually he ended up there permanently and died there. He could always have

Protestants and Catholics

involved in Parry's plot to kill the Queen, and was spared for the evidence he gave. But he remained in the Tower until 1598; on his release he went to live in Flanders and lived to a good age, not dying until 1640. He has his monument in East Ham church today – he was the heir to the earldom but for his cousin's attainder.

Weston himself remained in the Tower through the excitement of Essex's rising in 1601. The warder, bringing in the supper, was accoutred in helmet and breastplate, in one hand a halberd, in the other a tray. Putting down the supper he rushed off in a great state of alarm. On James's accession the royal apartments were made ready for the customary visit before the coronation – after Elizabeth's long disuse of them they must have needed attention. At the same time an amnesty freed many prisoners. On the day of Weston's release his warder 'invited me to dinner, and did me the honour of seating me at his own table. He handed me 80 reals, and also obtained a room for me outside the walls, where my friends could come and see me.' This did not wholly atone for more disagreeable experiences. Weston had had leave to take the air, but there were 'frequent showers of stones thrown at me from above by heretics, the hissings and other expressions of hatred and contempt I came in for, as soon as they saw me pacing up and down'. Evidently, ordinary patriotic Englishmen regarded them as enemies of their country; and this further helps to explain the government's treatment of them.

The repertory of instruments of torture was small enough compared with what Continental state prisons could show, where breaking on the wheel was a favourite device. Nor was there anything to compare with the spectacle of

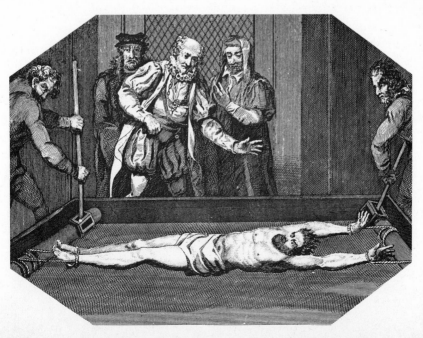

scores of condemned heretics or lapsed Jews consumed in *autos-da-fe*, graced by the presence of the royal family – as one can see in paintings of such events in the Plaza Major of Madrid well into the next century. The rack was used for Protestants under Henry VIII and Mary, for Catholics under Elizabeth, until her later years when it fell into some disuse. The first picture we have of the rack in operation is that of a Protestant, Cuthbert Simpson, in Mary's reign – stretching arms and legs with ropes turned upon rollers: the effect in crippling Simpson is given in an inset. In December 1557, when charged with heresy, the Lieutenant of the Tower and the Recorder of London 'did bind my two forefingers together and put a small arrow between them, and drew it through so fast that blood flowed and the arrow broke. Then they racked me twice.' It is to be hoped that this cured him of his heresy.

The Scavenger's Daughter, instead of elongating the person, contracted him within two iron hoops, which forced the body downwards until they met across the small of the back. From this torture blood spouted 'from nostrils, the mouth and the anus, and even on occasion from hands and feet'. We have observed the gauntlets or manacles in operation with Father Gerard, and the discomfort of Little Ease with Campion. Worse was the 'dungeon amongst the rats', below water-mark, for the tide came up to it bringing the Thames rats with it, and one could not sleep for fear of being eaten alive.

We must put these things in the perspective of the age, its ubiquitous cruelty: flogging and beating were frequent, schoolmasters believed in beating learning into their pupils' heads – the exemplary Lady Jane Grey was frequently beaten for her book. For scolds there were branks or gags across the mouth, spiked chastity-belts for unreliable wives, ducking stools for women who made nuisances of themselves.

These unsophisticated methods were hardly to be compared with the refinements of Belsen or Auschwitz – but that was Germany in the twentieth century. *Homo homini lupus*: of such are humans.

The sixteenth century was the golden age for inscriptions – a sententious age; people felt the need to inscribe moral sentiments in their houses and churches, to leave some visible memorials of themselves. Still more with prisoners in the Tower, who had plenty of time to occupy themselves with carving: some of their works – crests, coats of arms, symbols – are little works of art, all of them are of interest, telling the story of a life in name or initials, many of them with their own affecting pathos. For some reason most of them are in the Beauchamp

John Dudley, Earl of Warwick's inscription in the Beauchamp Tower

JOHN DVDLEY

...Y THAT THESE BEASTS DO WEL BEHOLD AND SE
...DEME WITH EASE WHEROF HERE MADE THEY BE
... BORDERS . . WHERIN . . .
...OTERS NAMES WHO LIST TO SERCH THE GROVND

Tower. One of the finest is an elaborate sculpture there executed by North-umberland's eldest son, John Dudley, Earl of Warwick, who was a good mathematician among other things. It portrays the bear and ragged staff of the Dudleys, surrounded by roses, sprigs of oak and acorns, with the lines:

> Yow that these beasts do wel behold and se
> May deme with ease wherfore here made they be
> With borders eke wherein [there may be found]
> 4 brothers names who list to serche the ground.

Thus were indicated all five of Northumberland's sons.

Moral sentiments are much to the fore – some of them, if heeded in time, would have saved their authors the trouble of inscribing them. Here, for instance, is Charles Bailly, an adherent of Mary Queen of Scots, 10 April 1571:

> I.H.S. Wise men ought circumspectly to se what they do; to examine before they speake; to prove before they take in hand; to beware whose compane they use; and, above al things, to whom they truste.

Later that autumn he carved a more elaborate memorial of himself with adages in English, French and Italian: *‚Tout vient apoient quy peult attendre.’* He did not have to wait long: he was shortly released. Not so the neighbouring Dr Story, who inscribed himself on the wall: ‘1570. Jhon Store. Doctor.’ He was a nasty man who made himself hated for burning Protestants under Mary. As an exile he got a good post in the customs at Antwerp, where he again made enemies. One day, when he boarded an English ship, the hatches were closed on him: he was kidnapped and taken to the Tower, to the joy of good Protestants.

A long inscription by Thomas Clarke in 1576 ends up with:

> Unhappie is that mane whose actes doth procuer
> The miseri of this hous in prison to induer.

A priest, he evidently thought better of it and recanted, preaching his recanta-tion sermon at Paul's Cross in 1593. Several of the last sprigs of Yorkist stock were rounded up before the French war of 1563, great-grandchildren of Clarence. Each of them left his inscription, Geoffrey, Edmund, and Arthur Pole, in 1562 and 1564. Arthur Pole was still there in 1568: ‘I.H.S. A passage perillus makethe a port pleasant. A° 1568. Arthur Poole. Aet. sue 37.’

Egremont Radcliffe, of that North Country stock, was of a turbulent spirit and could never be quiet. Quite young, he came out in the rebellion of 1569,

Hugh Draper's astronomical clock in the Salt Tower

and managed to get away to Spain, then led a wandering life in Flanders. When he came back to England without leave or pardon, the Queen herself advised this aristocratic hothead to slip away. Since he would not take the hint, he had a spell in the Tower, where he translated from French a book of *Politique Discourses*, dedicated to Walsingham and published in 1578. We find his inscription on a wall: 'Eagremond Radclyffe. 1576. Pour Parvenir.' Apparently he did succeed, and returned to Flanders, to be executed for conspiring the death of Don John, true or no.

The finest of all these monuments is the elaborate astronomical clock and calendar, surrounded by numerals, signs of the days, months, and symbols of the zodiac, in the Salt Tower. 'Hew Draper of Brystow made thys spheer the 30 daye of Maye anno 1561.' This confirms what little we know of him: he was a prosperous Bristol tavern-keeper, well up in astronomy, who was

accused of sorcery against Sir William St Loe and his redoubtable Bess. But Draper testified that he had long misliked his science and burned his books.

Perhaps the words that bring us closest to the state of mind of these men – women had the sense not to get into the Tower – are those of an unknown man, who has inscribed his cry from the heart: 'Close prisoner 8 monethes 32 wekes 224 dayes 5376 houres.'

Some of these monuments are so well executed and have such a similar idiom that it seems probable that a professional carver was employed upon them. Certainly works of professional sculptors remain in the sixteenth-century tombs in St Peter-ad-vincula. The finest of them is the late medieval Gothic tomb – with only a touch of the Renaissance in the twisted columns at the corners – of Sir Richard Cholmondeley and his wife. He was the Lieutenant to whom it fell to bear the axe before the haughty Duke of Buckingham whom Wolsey laid low. Two other monuments, designed as one, are later Elizabethan Renaissance, Corinthian columns of marble, dentil cornice, masks and swags of floral decoration. These are to Sir Richard and Sir Michael Blount. Though office was not hereditary, it was apt to run in families. On the eve of the Civil War Charles I appointed Mountjoy Blount, Earl of Newport, Constable of the Tower. The Constable was a grander person, apt to be a leading figure in the government, and more honorific than operative; the work was done by the Lieutenant.

The Lieutenant was a leading figure in the life of the Tower Ward and thereabouts; we find him frequently dining in the City with the Mayor and aldermen, or with the craft gilds in their halls. No less characteristically we find the Tower officials involved in disputes with the citizens. It was customary for the new Lord Mayor and Sheriffs to be presented to the Barons of the Exchequer at Westminster, or in their absence to the Constable at the Tower. Once in the 1580s when the Lord Mayor attended at Tower Gate, his sword borne before him within their sacred precincts, two of the warders attempted to hold it down. There followed one of the usual interminable conflicts about jurisdiction beloved by bores.

There were constant disputes as to the liberties, privileges and bounds of the Tower to enliven life in the vicinity. The Lieutenant annually perambulated his bounds, distributing a sheaf of arrows to the boys for remembrance. But the population explosion of Elizabethan London encroached upon the boundaries. The antiquary, John Stow, tells us that Tower Hill had become 'greatly straitened by encroachments for gardens and houses, some on the

The monument to Sir Richard Cholmondeley,
Lieutenant of the Tower under Henry VIII

bank of the Tower ditch, whereby the Tower ditch is marred'. Outside the
Tower Gate, where Mayor and sheriffs were sworn, a number of cobblers'
sheds were erected for the Gentleman Porter's profit. This led to rude
exchanges between the Lord Mayor and the Gentleman Porter; the Privy
Council had to intervene, astonished that the Gentleman Porter 'or any
under him should intermeddle in a matter not yet resolved'. Meanwhile tene-
ments were going up at the Postern Gate; and, to increase confusion, boundary
stones were removed. Every week the gunners of the Tower marched out for
artillery practice in Artillery Yard.

Overleaf: The memorial to the two Lieutenants, Sir Richard Blount,
who died in 1564, and his son Sir Michael Blount, who died in 1596

HEERE LYETH BVRIED S MICHAEL
BLOVNT KNIGHT SONNE HEYRE OF
S RICHARD BLOVNT KNIGHT WHO
SVCCEDED HIS FATHER IN Y OFFICE
OF LIEVTENANTCY OF Y TOWER OF
LONDON XII YEARES AFTER Y DEATH
OF HIS SAID FATHER & LEFT ISSVE BY
MARY HIS WIFE SISTER & ONE OF Y
COHEIRES OF THOMAS MOORE OF BYSS
RICHARD THOMAS & CHARLES CATHERIN
& FRANCIS RICHARD MARIED CECILY
YONGEST DAVGHTER OF S RICHARD
BAKER OF KENT KNIGHT CATHERINE
HIS ELDEST DAVGHTER MARIED TO IOHN
BLOVNT ALIAS CROKE OF STVDLEY IN
Y COVNTIE OF OXON ESQVIER SONNE &
HEYRE APPARANT TO IOHN BLOVNT
ALIAS CROKE OF CHILTON IN Y COVN
OF BVCKINGHEM ESQVIER & HATH
ISSVE IOHN HENRY & CHARLES AND
DAME MARY WIFE OF Y SAID
S ....

S. MICHAELL DIED ON SATER
DAYE BEING Y 23 DAYE OF
DECEMBER IN A° DO: 1592.
& SHE LIETH HERE BVRIED

Such were the amenities of life in the 1580s.

Stow sums up proudly the functions of the Tower:

A citadel to defend or command the City; a royal palace for assemblies and treaties; a prison of state for the most dangerous offenders; the only place of coinage for all England at this time; the armoury for warlike provision; the treasury of the ornaments and jewels of the Crown; and general conserver of the most records of the king's courts of justice at Westminster.

All this kept it very busy, a beehive of an establishment; and it was already a chief show-place for foreigners visiting London. We have several descriptions from them, which enable us to see what chiefly impressed them. The Duke of Württemberg – Shakespeare's comic Count Mompelgart, who left his bills unpaid – thought that the Armoury in 1592 compared less favourably with German armouries. No doubt, and 'although there are many fine cannon in it, they are full of dust and stand about in great disorder'. There was an enormous number of bows and arrows – with which the English and Welsh archers had won Crécy and Agincourt. After 1596 guns captured at Cadiz were on show.

A feature that attracted all eyes were mementos of the Queen's redoubtable father, who had been much interested in the development of artillery. On show were the two immense battering-rams that had helped to frighten Boulogne into surrender. There was Henry's outsize armour – which is still in existence – with helmet, breast-plate, and yellow gauntlets; a ten-span long barrel from which to shoot, the pistol which he carried on his saddle, and another breech-loading one, a new invention.

In 1598 and 1599 both Hentzner and Platter saw the royal apartments, for they noted the numerous tapestries, of silk, gold and silver thread; the rich bed-furniture, canopies and stuffs embroidered with seed-pearl; costly dresses, which roused the envious admiration of the impecunious Germans. Some of the furniture had belonged to Henry, a vast chair to hold his heavy frame; footstools and chairs, chests stuffed with materials, of the Queen, who kept clear of that coast. Everybody noticed the lions – one called Edward, a lioness called Elizabeth – the lean old wolf, and, by 1600, a tiger and a porcupine. Visitors were allowed to see the Lieutenant's apartments, where the axe was kept, and the dungeon which was the rack-room. At every stage, and for every section, a gratuity was expected; poor young Platter counted out eight in all. He came round to Traitors' Gate, and 'the grating through which criminals are led'; and adds, 'the Queen also was brought this way'.

So that significant passage of history was remembered to the end of her reign.

Henry VIII's armour in the Armoury of the Tower. It was made in 1540 in the royal workshops at Greenwich

6

Sir Walter Ralegh
and Essex

CATHOLICS were a minority of those in the Tower in Elizabeth's reign – and there were others who were close to her in blood, as we have seen, besides two who were much closer in favour. Sir John Perrot may have been her half-brother; he certainly said so himself. He was thought to be an illegitimate son of Henry VIII, since he was extraordinarily like him and his mother was about the Court at the time. A good marriage was found for her, and the son succeeded to considerable estates in West Wales. Much of his soldiering career was passed in Ireland, to which he was more fitted than to Court life, for he was a rough customer, uncontrolled in behaviour and speech.

He had enemies at Court, notably Sir Christopher Hatton, and he was sent back to Ireland as Lord Deputy at a time of crisis in 1584 – some said to get him out of the way, others said to give the Irish the kind of government they asked for. He ruled with severity and success; when he was recalled he left the distracted country at peace for a time. But the strain proved too much for his self-control. He could not endure the Queen's technique of alternate reproof and praise, which everyone had to put up with. After some sharp reprehension of him the Queen became apprehensive of a Spanish descent upon Ireland, and her tone altered with it to approval, a pat on the back. Bluff Sir John read her letters, and commented publicly in Dublin Castle, 'Lo, now she is ready to piss herself for fear of the Spaniard, I am again one of her white boys.'

This indelicate expression got round to the Queen, as conscious of her dignity as ever her father was; and it was accompanied by some very dubious behaviour. A treasonable letter was forged and laid against him; he was recalled, lodged in the Tower, and put on trial. On the false evidence he was condemned to death. Brought back to the Tower, he said angrily to the Lieutenant, Sir Owen Hopton, 'What, will the Queen suffer her brother to be offered up as a sacrifice to the envy of my frisking adversaries?' 'Frisking' was a contemptuous reference to Hatton, whose dancing had originally won him the

Robert Devereux, 2nd Earl of Essex, Elizabeth's last favourite,
who was executed for rebelling against her in 1601

Queen's notice. For her part, Elizabeth swore that Perrot was an honest man and that his condemnation had been procured by knaves. She would not sign the death-warrant. But the old man, while waiting for pardon, died in the Tower in September 1592. Perhaps Ireland had been too much for him.

At the very time Perrot was dying in the Tower Sir Walter Ralegh was released (15 September) from his five-weeks' confinement for his secret marriage with Elizabeth Throckmorton. He had to be let out to go down to the West Country to bring order into the unloading of the captured carrack, the *Madre de Dios*, which was being ransacked and spoiled at Dartmouth; otherwise he might have enjoyed the amenities of the Tower for a longer spell, for his offence was great. The marriage of grandees at Court was a matter for the attention, often permission, of the monarch; and the Queen was especially difficult about the marriage of intimates and favourites. When she was told of the secret marriage of Leicester to her cousin Lettice Knollys, Countess of Essex, she was furious and threatened to send him to the Tower. Even his enemy Sussex pleaded for him and said that no man could properly be sent to the Tower just for marrying.

With the Raleghs the case was different. He had seduced one of the Queen's maids-of-honour; he was also bound by his oath as Captain of the Guard, and by his honour to protect her ladies, to whose apartments he had the key. They had married secretly and a baby was born – about whom nothing was known until I brought to light the Diary of her brother, Sir Arthur Throckmorton★. Ralegh and his wife were a bold pair: they sought to brazen it out, and his wife went back to Court to wait on the Queen as Mistress Throckmorton. This was to put an affront upon the Queen and make a fool of her: it was never forgiven.

Such a secret could never have been kept for long: on 10 April the child was baptized, with Essex as a godfather. Before the end of July the news broke. A crony wrote to Francis Bacon's brother Anthony: 'if you have anything to do with Sir Walter Ralegh, or any love to make to Mistress Throckmorton, at the Tower tomorrow you may speak with them'. On 7 August, Arthur Throckmorton noted, his sister went to the Tower, as also Sir Walter; they were lodged separately, the marriage not recognised.

The Queen was leaving for her summer progress, on which Ralegh had before accompanied her in glory. Now he had leisure to reflect, within those walls, on all that he had lost, by falling into the trap of the other Elizabeth. He

★Cf. my *Ralegh and the Throckmortons.*

wrote to Cecil a letter in the vein of high poetic flattery, which was the tone of his relations with his Virgin Sovereign and had often done duty in the past.

My heart was never broken till this day that I hear the Queen goes far off, whom I have followed so many years with so great love and desire, in so many journeys, and am now left behind her, in a dark prison all alone . . . I that was wont to behold her riding like Alexander, hunting like Diana, walking like Venus, the gentle wind blowing her fair hair about her pure cheeks, like a nymph; sometime sitting in the shade like a goddess, sometime singing like an angel, sometime playing like Orpheus. Behold the sorrow of this world! Once amiss, hath bereaved me of all.

And so on. No answer was returned.

Sir Walter took to poetry in a grand way; he had had little enough leisure before. We have a rough sonnet from this time:

> My body in the walls captivèd
> Feels not the wounds of spiteful envy,
> But my thrallèd mind, of liberty deprivèd,
> Fast fettered in her ancient memory,
> Doth naught behold but sorrow's dying face.
> Such prison erst was so delightful
> As it desired no other dwelling place;
> But time's effects and destinies despiteful
> Have changèd both my keeper and my fare.
> Love's fire, and beauty's light I then had store;
> But now close kept, as captives wonted are,
> That food, that heat, that light I find no more.
>   Despair bolts up my doors, and I alone
>   Speak to dead walls, but those hear not my moan.

Here is a prison poem obviously. And Ralegh proceeded to embark upon the long poem *The Book of the Ocean* [Walter] *to Cynthia* [Queen Elizabeth], which, for all its unfinished state, constitutes his most important poem, his chief memorial as a poet to posterity. It is, in effect, the grandest poetic monument in Tower literature.

A great deal of heavy weather has been made about it by literary scholars, a lot of mystification where none need exist. Ralegh's relations with the Queen spanned twelve years; he therefore proposed to write their story in twelve books (as his friend Spenser was proposing to write twelve books of the *Faerie Queene*). Ralegh wrote the penultimate chapter, the most recent, of the story in an eleventh Book, of over five hundred lines, some of them unfinished, many of the verses in rough state, much of it unpolished. He began on a twelfth book, a kind of conclusion 'entreating of Sorrow', and wrote another twenty lines, breaking off in the middle of a line when he was freed to go down to the West Country.

That is all. There is no mystery about it, no great lost poem: there was no more than what we have got.

The images and phrases are very much like those of Ralegh's letters, the temper and complaints utterly characteristic of him, the story corroborated by the historic facts.

> Twelve years entire I wasted in this war,
> Twelve years of my most happy younger days;
> But I in them, and they, now wasted are:
> Of all which past the sorrow only stays . . .
>
> So many years those joys have dearly bought
> Of which, when our fond hopes do most assure,
> All is dissolved, our labours come to naught,
> Nor any mark thereof there doth endure.

Images of the Queen and his glory in his attendance on her haunt him close-kept in the Tower:

> Such force her angel-like appearance had
> To master distance, time, or cruelty,
> Such art to grieve, and after to make glad,

(compare her treatment of Perrot, her regular technique)

> Such fear in love, such love in majesty.
> Describe her now as she appears to thee,
> Not as she did appear in days foredone;
> In love those things that were no more may be,
> For fancy seldom ends where it begun.
>
> Thy days foredone have had their days' reward,
> So her hard heart, so her estrangèd mind,
> In which above the heavens I once reposed,
> So thy error have her ears inclined,
>
> And have forgotten all thy past deserving,
> Holding in mind but only thine offence,
> And only now affecteth thy depraving
> And think all vain that pleadeth thy defence.

A plan of the Tower at the end of Elizabeth's reign

Ralegh indeed made an 'error', as he said, in marrying Elizabeth Throckmorton: he had everything to lose, and nothing to gain – except the burdens
of a family. She had nothing much to lose, and everything to gain: she had got
her man – and what a man! – in the teeth of the Queen, her mistress. We can
detect the note of triumph in *her* letter from the Tower, underneath the
obscurity of her illiterate spelling:

I am dayly put in hope of my delivery I assur you treuly I never desiared nor never
wolde desiar my lebbarti with out the good likeking ne advising of Sur W.R.: hit tis
not this in prisonment if I bought it with my life that shulde make me thinkehit long
if hit shuld doo him harme to speke of my deliverey: but Sir R.S. [Cecil] was somwhat
deseved in his Jugment in that and hit may be hee findeth his eror: I pray you tell
your ladi I reseeved heer kind lettar from Cubham [Cobham]: when wee mit wee will
talke of hit: the towar standeth just in the way to Kent from Copt Hall: and who
knooeth what will be com of me when I am out: the plage is gretly sesid and ever hath
bin cliar heer a bout: and wee ar trew with in ourselfes I can asur you. Towar, even
asureedly yours in frinship. E.R.

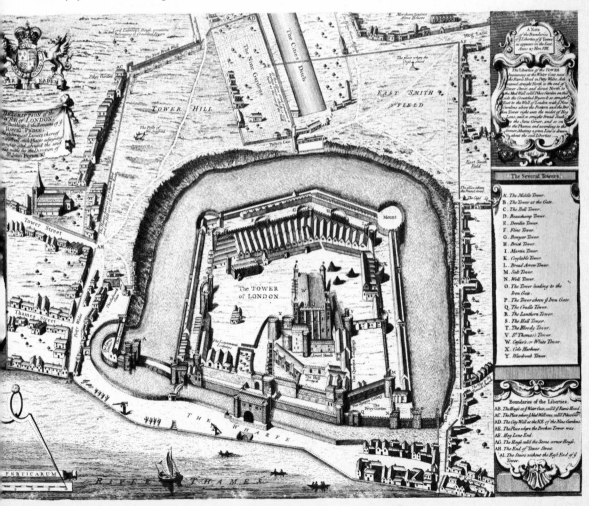

It was she, not Ralegh, who had attained the 'hopèd port': to be able to sub-scribe herself – like the other Elizabeth – E.R. This solitary letter gives us a pointer to the kind of woman she was, strong in her own self-confidence: for all Ralegh's arrogance, he came to stand in awe of her. The Queen kept her in the Tower for some months, not letting her out till a few days before Christmas.

Two years later, in 1594, the Queen's physician, Dr Lopez, was held on the charge of conspiring with Spain to poison her. These years were full of plots and counterplots, of espionage and betrayal, of informers, double-agents, busybodies in political intrigue. Lopez was one of the last class; from his posi-tion so close to the Queen and being a Jew, the case made a sensation, with an outburst of anti-Jewish feeling.

Lopez had been very successful as a physician; this made him enemies, and his elevation may have gone to his head. He made an implacable enemy of the favourite, Essex, now coming to the fore. Essex wanted to recruit Lopez to his intelligence service; Lopez, who had contacts in Spain and Portugal, refused. He added insult to injury by divulging that Essex was suffering from some venereal infection. This was fatal, not to the patient, but to the doctor.

For Lopez was in touch with Spanish agents in London, probably as a double-agent. He is said to have agreed to the death of Don Antonio, the Portuguese Pretender in London, upon 'the first illness that befell him'. He certainly accepted a magnificent jewel, with the promise of a large sum, from the Spaniards – it was said, if he would kill the Queen. But he presented the jewel to her, and she wore it to her dying day; as to the money, he said at his trial, that 'he had no other design in what he did but to deceive the Spaniard'.

Elizabeth never believed that he had any intention of poisoning her and told Essex that 'he was a rash and temerarious youth to enter into a matter against the poor man which he could not prove'. This made it a matter of 'honour' for Essex to bring the charge home; he got in touch with Don Antonio's attendants who were prepared to incriminate Lopez. In January 1594 he was sent to the Tower. All that winter there was talk of the threat to the Queen's life, the dark cloud shadowing her. In Elizabethan England if a man could not prove his innocence then he was held guilty. And Dr Lopez could not prove his innocence, when tried at the Guildhall in February by a court over which Essex presided.

He was condemned, but for three months the Queen held out and would not sign his death-warrant. The issue became one not only of Essex's prestige but a touchstone of the Queen's confidence in him; and, of course, popular feeling in London as always was with him. In the end she was made to give way, and the poor Jew was sacrificed to the 'honour' of the Earl. But she showed what she thought by exercising her prerogative to restore the doctor's forfeited estate to his family. Not until 7 June was his condemnation carried into effect, and himself carried from the Tower to Tyburn.

This is the episode referred to in the too-much discussed line in Shakespeare's Sonnet 107, where so many have been led astray without any conception of the importance of strict dating:

> The mortal moon hath her eclipse endured.

In Elizabethan English 'endured' means that she has come through, emerged from the shadow upon her. And this is made certain by the very next lines:

> Incertainties now crown themselves assured,
> And peace proclaims olives of endless age –

which is a clear reference to the end of the civil wars in France with the surrender of Paris to Henri IV in March 1594, and the expectation of general peace. The convergence of two topical events upon one point gives chronological certainty – to those who understand such things.

Just as, two years earlier, in Sonnet 25 Shakespeare had completely described Ralegh's fall from favour, which was the sensation of 1592:

> Great princes' favourites their fair leaves spread
> But as the marigold at the sun's eye,
> And in themselves their pride lies burièd,
> For at a frown they in their glory die.

> The painful warrior famousèd for fight,
> After a thousand victories once foiled,
> Is from the book of honour razèd quite,
> And all the rest forgot for which he toiled.

There we have the whole situation summed up: Ralegh's pride and well-known industriousness – 'he can toil terribly' were Sir Robert Cecil's very words of him at that juncture; the famour warrior 'once foiled' practically reflects his own words, 'once amiss' all his past toil and deserving forgot.

Essex's own turn came towards the end of Elizabeth's life, just before the accession of James which Essex had intended to dominate. The issue of the succession was as fatal to him as it had been to others meddling with the arcana of the state. This is what he had discussed with the great Irish rebel Tyrone, and it subsequently transpired that he considered bringing over contingents of the army to force his aims in England. He was on a dangerous course, himself unstable and irresolute. Returned to London, he appealed to all the discontented elements, military men, irresponsible young peers, both Puritans and Papists, against the Queen and the central pillars of the state. Summoning some three hundred of his followers to Essex House, he made a crazy outbreak into the City on 8 February 1601 and – finding no support – surrendered. The Queen described it contemptuously as *rebellio unius diei*.

That night Essex and his closest follower, Southampton, were taken prisoners to Lambeth, 'because the night was dark and the river not passable under bridge'. Shortly after they were carried to the Tower, followed by the young Earl of Rutland, Lords Sandys, Cromwell and Monteagle, Sir Charles Danvers and Sir Christopher Blount; the rest were crammed into the common prisons. On 19 February Essex and Southampton were tried before their peers at Westminster, and condemned to death. No defence was possible, though there were people who thought that their ill-considered outbreak was hardly a capital crime. On the other hand, it would be a danger to the state to leave Essex alive.

On his surrender Essex had stipulated that he might have the ministrations of his chaplain, the Puritan Abdy Ashton. The Council sent him the Dean of Norwich to urge him to acknowledge his guilt. Where the good Dean failed to melt the sinner's hardness of heart, the Reverend Mr Ashton unloosed an avalanche of repentance. Essex not only accused himself but turned to accusing others. Neurotically unstable as ever, he was so troubled in mind that he was persuaded of damnation to Hell if he did not make a clean breast of everything, including his friends and confederates. He asked particularly to see his principal opponent, Secretary Cecil, who came to the Tower with the Constable, Lord Thomas Howard and Lord Admiral Howard – the Cecil–Howard axis of the next reign already thus adumbrated.

Essex found that most of the conspirators had yielded up what they knew, but he inculpated Sir Henry Neville, who, instead of proceeding as ambassador to France, found himself in the Tower. Lord Mountjoy, who had sided with Essex in the earlier stages, was now in Ireland successfully tackling the job where Essex had failed, and was too valuable to incriminate. The Earl did worse: he asked to have his secretary brought to him, Henry Cuffe, an ambitious Oxford scholar of no birth, whom Essex accused of being a chief instigator 'of all these my disloyal courses into which I have fallen'. Actually Cuffe had opposed the appeal to force and took no part in the outbreak; but this settled the fate of the poor fellow. He merely registered the Earl's betrayal of his most devoted friends.

Sir Christopher Blount, Essex's stepfather, was so much 'amazed' at this orgy of confession that he divulged Essex's earlier designs when in Ireland. Essex wallowed further in the mire, like a Buchmanite, under the influence of the divines who were working on him – Prebendary Mountford of West-minster and Dr Barlow, in addition to the sainted Ashton – and now admitted that 'the Queen could never be safe as long as he lived'.

This declaration aided the old lady to make up her mind to sign his death-warrant. She havered, remembering her old affection for him – stepson of Leicester who should have behaved like a son to her – and sent Sir Edward Carey to stay the execution. Ralegh said afterwards that Essex would not have died but for the unforgivable words that he had put about, that the old woman was cankered and was as crooked in mind as in her carcase.

Essex's wife, who was Philip Sidney's widow, wrote a touching appeal to Cecil: 'Good Mr Secretary, even as you desire of God that your own son never be made orphan by the untimely or unnatural death of his dear father, vouch-safe a relenting, to the not urging – if you may not to the hindering – of that fatal warrant for execution, which, if it be once signed, I shall never wish to breathe one hour after.' (She lived to be an old lady and to marry yet a third and even a fourth husband.)

Ralegh wrote a disgraceful letter to Cecil:

I am not wise enough to give you advice [this at least was true]; but, if you take it for a good counsel to relent towards this tyrant, you will repent when it shall be too late. . . . The less you make him, the less he shall be able to harm you and yours. For after-revenges, fear them not; for your own father was esteemed to be the contriver of Norfolk's ruin, yet his son [Lord Thomas Howard] followeth your father's son, and loveth him. Somerset [i.e. the Seymours] made no revenge on the Duke of Northumberland's heirs. Northumberland that now is thinks not of Hatton's issue.

(Hatton was smeared with what had been the Earl's suicide.) And so to the odious conclusion: 'Lose not your advantage; if you do, I read your destiny.' As if clever little Cecil ever lost an advantage! It was superfluous of Ralegh to give advice in such a quarter, and unwise to put it on record.

Essex was too proud to ask for a pardon, and so the Queen eventually allowed the sentence to be carried out, within the courtyard of the Tower, as he had asked. Just before midnight he opened his casement and spoke to the guard, with his inveterate cult of popularity, apologising for having nothing to give them, 'for I have nothing left but that which I must pay to the Queen tomorrow in the morning'.

On the morrow there followed the lugubrious ritual with which we are acquainted, the Earl carefully dressed all in black, satin suit, wrought velvet gown, black felt hat. Surrounded by his divines, he was immersed in his devotions; completely at their command, he prayed long and loudly, making open confession now that he was a most wretched sinner: 'My sins are more in number than the hairs of my head; I have bestowed my youth in wantonness, lust, and uncleanness; I have been puffed up with pride, vanity, and love of this wicked world's pleasures,' etc. But, he protested, he had never been an atheist.

This was a parting shot at Ralegh, who was looking on, and whom people regarded as an atheist because he did not believe the nonsense they believed. Seated around the scaffold were several peers, knights and aldermen. Ralegh afterwards said that his purpose in being there was to answer, if Essex should object anything against him. Ralegh never curried favour with the people, unlike Essex, and so was popularly hated and misconstrued. People now thought that he had come to gloat over his enemy's end, and pressed him to leave the scene. So Ralegh withdrew to a window in the Armoury, whence he watched the execution.

Much blamed for this, when his own time came he claimed that he had shed tears at the spectacle. Such is the duplicity of human emotions, such the tangled *mêlée* in men's minds, that both are possible.

There remained Southampton, whom though condemned, everyone conspired to save. At his trial he made no defence of himself, save that he was led away by his love for Essex, and threw himself upon the Queen's mercy. He was pitied for his youth – though he was not so young as he looked; Camden says that he spoke 'with such sweet and winning expressions and such ingenuous modesty that he moved the hearts of all the standers-by to pity'. This was Shakespeare's golden youth, his patron and the young Lord of the Sonnets of a few years earlier, 1592–5. In the bitter play that Shakespeare was writing at this later time, *Troilus and Cressida* – about the disillusionments of war and love – the inset of Achilles and his Patroclus sulking in their tent describes the behaviour of Essex and Southampton before the outbreak clearly enough.

Cecil himself, now that his chief enemy was disposed of, could afford to be generous, and took credit for pleading for Southampton's life. He was just as

The portrait of the Earl of Southampton as a prisoner in the Tower.
With him is his cat which is said to have found its way to him down the chimney

IN VINCVLIS
INVICTVS.
FEBRVA·8·1600·
602·603·APRI

guilty as his friend Sir Charles Danvers, who offered ten thousand pounds to be spared. Southampton's wife wrote distractedly asking to be permitted to throw herself at the feet of her sacred Majesty to beg for mercy – considering that this was Elizabeth Vernon, who had misconducted herself as Elizabeth Throckmorton had done, it was not a good idea. His mother, whom the Queen respected, pleaded, 'God of Heaven knows I can scarce hold my hand steady to write, and less hold in my heart how to write, only for what I know, which is to pray mercy for my miserable son.'

In the event, though 'there were some looking for the Earl of Southampton this morning on Tower Hill', it turned out otherwise and he was left inside the Tower for a couple of years until the Queen's death. There he was comfortably lodged in an apartment next to the gallery of the royal apartments: the east end of it was partitioned off to make a sitting room, in addition to his bedchamber. He was closely attended by a keeper, Captain Hart, who found the confinement as bad as being a prisoner himself. The Earl had periodic bouts of fever, and the celebrated Dr Paddy gave him medical treatment. Shortly he was allowed to see his mother and the trustees of his little daughter, whose inheritance had been confiscated by his sentence – by law he was a dead man. In October he was sickly, and the Queen was graciously pleased to allow his wife regular visits.

Anticipating the Queen's death, Southampton had already written to James for a warrant for his liberty immediately upon it. Early in April 1603 he was freed, and commanded to present himself to the incoming King – a sign not only of restitution but of favour. Shortly Southampton was restored to his earldom, and given the privilege of entry to the bedchamber – but by this time he was in love with his wife: he did not become a favourite.

He had a portrait of himself in the Tower painted as a memento, of which there are several copies. There he is: the golden youth with the long hair falling on his shoulders, sadder and wiser now, fair moustache and beard incipient. In the background is a gallery window, himself leaning against the sill, upon which sits his black-and-white cat looking very much on the alert. Inset in the upper corner is a painting of the Tower, with the inscription, '*In vinculis invictus*' ('In chains unsubdued' – a somewhat boastful reflection upon his narrow escape).

It is a part of the old folklore of the Tower that his cat sought him out, and found its way to him down the chimney – if so, no less a tribute to the charm he exerted than to the loyalty of cats.

An Elizabethan plate decorated with a picture of the Tower and an inscription: 'The Rose is Red, The leaves are Green, God save Elizabeth our Queen'

We must not forget that these sensational events took place against the background of the day-to-day business of the Tower, all the coming to and fro connected with the departments housed there. These were the Armoury, the Privy Wardrobe and, much larger and more important, the Ordnance – though its main stores and business occupied the neighbouring Minories, whither we need not pursue it. The Armoury provided the armour required for the monarch and personal attendants around him, as also for the royal tournaments and tilts. Naturally the Masters were his intimate attendants: Sir Richard Guildford upon Henry VII, Sir Edward Guildford and Sir John Dudley (later Duke of Northumberland) upon Henry VIII, Sir Richard Southwell upon Queen Mary.

Elizabeth I appointed Sir Henry Lee Keeper of the Armoury, appropriately, for his prowess at the famous tilts he organised in her honour. He was less successful as an administrator. He was allowed four hundred pounds a year for upkeep from 1580, but the war with Spain strained the resources of Armoury and Ordnance alike. The armour was not only out of order, but probably passing out of date. 'That in the Tower was so bad he could not do withal. He was ashamed to see it, and pity it should be so with the armour of so great a princess. Such armour as was made over and hanged up was delivered in sundry countries [i.e. counties] and to ships, and much lost by negligence and thinned by salt water.' This was written in 1589, the year after the Armada.

So that, to the other sounds of that busy workaday place, the rumbling in and out of carts and wagons and coaches, the cries of sentinels, jangling of keys, the occasional thud upon the block, the sobs and sighs of the sorrowful, we must add the clang and hammering of armour.

Though the Queen came little to the Tower her state robes were kept there. We find payments for mending coronation and Parliament robes with 'two timber of powered ermines'; one pound of powder a month was employed on them, with an allowance of 'one load of coals to air our apparel'.

Of the Ordnance only smaller cannon were kept within the walls. Throughout most of the reign the Master was the Earl of Warwick, from 1560 to 1590, who as Ambrose Dudley had been prisoner with his brothers under Mary. There were constant complaints of inefficiency, corruption and fraud in this department, more even than in most. Nor is this surprising when we reflect on the career of the Clerk to both Armoury and Ordnance. This was William Painter, who gave up schoolmastering at Sevenoaks for the lucrative opportunities of which he made the most. From his house near the Tower and his

The Cannon Room in the White Tower. The collection includes several cannon from ships of Henry VIII's navy office within it he made a private fortune by lending from the public funds under his control. This enabled him to purchase two desirable manors in his native Kent. In 1586 he and two colleagues were ordered to refund over £7000 to the treasury; he admitted to only £1079 of the Queen's sticking to his hands. His accounts were reported to have been falsified in collusion with the Earl, his Master. Painter's son subsequently confessed to irregularities both by himself and his father.

The father was the author of the delightful *Palace of Pleasure*, dedicated earlier in expectation (fulfilled as we have seen) to Warwick. This collection of a hundred stories, out of Italian, French, Latin, Greek, formed a chief quarry for the dramatists Shakespeare, Peele, Webster, Beaumont and Fletcher.

A little peculation seems a small price to pay for so rich a reward.

PROVIDENTIA

FAMA BONA

FAMA MALA

THE HISTORY | OF THE WORLD

TESTIS TEMPORVM   EXPERIENTIA   NVNCIA VETVSTATIS   MAGISTRA VITÆ   MORS   OBLIVIO   LVX VERITATIS   VERITAS   VITA MEMORIÆ

At London Printed for WALTER BVRRE.

1614

7
Gunpowder Plot: the Wizard Earl and Ralegh

IT was not long before Ralegh took Southampton's place in the Tower, and for a much longer period, some twelve years – in fact for most of the rest of his life. We might say that, with him, incarceration in the Tower reached a twin peak with that of Sir Thomas More. Both men of genius, they were very different men: one a saint, the other very worldly, a good deal of a Machiavellian; one a man of truth, the other a congenital liar, but a man of imagination and a finer poet. In the Tower, allowed at times to walk along the walls for exercise, Ralegh became one of the sights of London; while the big book he wrote there, his *History of the World*, a classic of English literature, is certainly the greatest work to emerge from within those walls.

James I was biased against Ralegh before he came to the English throne – it seems that Ralegh was the only man whom James (a too kindly king, where young men were concerned) really hated. Ralegh, after trying in vain to win James's goodwill, became a dangerous malcontent. In the summer of James's accession, 1603, there broke a conspiracy of crazy Catholics to capture him, known as the Bye Plot, led by a possibly lunatic priest, Father Watson. These people got in touch with the foolish Lord Cobham, a close friend of Ralegh, and they proceeded to egg each other on. Cobham was treating with a Spanish envoy for peace, lured on by the offer of an enormous sum; Cobham's still baser brother, Brooke, was in touch with the Catholic desperados of the Bye Plot. Brooke made a confession which inculpated his brother; Ralegh, when questioned, gave a disingenuous account of these contacts, and henceforth could never clear himself. A dreadful phrase passed from mouth to mouth about killing 'the fox and his cubs'. The government was convinced that, behind the Bye Plot, was a Main Plot involving Ralegh.

What indeed was he up to?

No one has known for certain from that day to this; but to my mind the explanation is clear. Ralegh was hoping to recover his position by a dramatic *coup*: he tried to lure Cobham to his island of Jersey, where he was governor,

The title-page of Ralegh's *History of the World* which was written during his twelve-year imprisonment in the Tower could pounce on Cobham, reveal the whole business to James and put him under an obligation to treat him henceforth with some favour. Of course Ralegh could never plead this in his own defence, at the expense of reputation and character for ever. On the other hand, he never varied from his story that he never had the least intention of ill towards the King and his children. The trouble was that nobody believed him – except Cecil, who would have known what the truth was; but Ralegh had offended him and Cecil wanted him out of the way. So Ralegh went to the Tower.

Arrived once more within those walls, he behaved so badly as to confirm people's view of him as guilty. The Lieutenant 'never saw so strange a dejected mind. I am exceedingly cumbered with him. Five or six times in a day he sendeth for me in such passions as I see his fortitude is not competent to support his grief.' (Might the Lieutenant succeed to Ralegh's delectable island for the trouble he was taking? He might, and did.) Ralegh now made matters worse by entering into collusion with Cobham as to what they should confess. Confronted with this, Cobham went back on his confession; then Ralegh retracted his. Nobody knew what to think, except that they were all liars, and all guilty. And Ralegh could never plead what was the truth, and his real defence.

When he was brought out of the Tower and taken through the City on his way to Winchester for trial, he was so hated that it was 'hob or nob whether he should have been brought alive through such multitudes of unruly people as did exclaim against him'. If a single hare-brained fellow had got through to him he would have been lynched. At Winchester it was a foregone conclusion: he was condemned to death. But James wanted to begin his reign with a notable example of clemency; so Ralegh was left with the sentence suspended over his head, like Southampton, and back he went to the Tower.

There he never gave up the struggle. With his excess of energy, both physical and mental, he made a most uncomfortable, clamorous, exhibitionist prisoner. He constantly protested his innocence, indeed he constantly protested about everything, both he and Lady Ralegh made confounded nuisances of themselves to the overworked, if all-powerful, Cecil, and to the hostile Council. Ralegh never ceased to draw attention to himself – he had a genius for that, too, among other things. He wrote tracts, giving his political advice, when no one asked for it. He was all in favour of continuing the war with Spain – so like him – when James and Cecil, not to mention the country, wanted an end to the long war. He improved on any and every occasion to make himself heard. A new Lieutenant, Sir William Wade, complained that when Ralegh returned from being examined anew by the Council, he showed himself 'upon the wall in his garden to the view of the people, who gaze upon him and he stares at them, which he does in his cunning humour that it might be thought that his being before the Lords was rather to clear than to charge him'. He was indeed becoming one of the sights of London, and public opinion, typically, was beginning to turn in his favour.

For his first two years Ralegh entertained the hope that he might be released. Then came the tragic idiocy of Gunpowder Plot, which changed the whole atmosphere – the honeymoon period of the new reign. Apart from the suffering this piece of lunacy entailed for the young Catholic conspirators responsible, and for those who were not, one by-consequence was that it put paid to Ralegh's hopes of release.

This fantastic plot, which made such a sensation at the time and has gone on reverberating ever since – we still celebrate Guy Fawkes Day on 5 November – was thought up by Robert Catesby, of that old family involved in Richard III's misdeeds. Catesby had already been involved in Essex's rebellion and had been let off with a heavy fine. The original knot of five conspirators were gentlemen of good Catholic families, so that they could trust each other. But they were desperados, willing to embark on anything to advance 'the Cause'; in the event they practically ruined it.

Today we have difficulty in understanding the motives and temper of such people: we value our lives, they did not. Thomas Winter, the only one of the original five to fall into the hands of the government, replied when approached to take part in the plot: 'I had often hazarded my life upon far lighter terms, and now would not refuse any good occasion wherein I might do service to the Catholic cause.' Sir Everard Digby, who had been brought in later by Catesby, who lied to him about their prospects of foreign support, nevertheless said in the Tower, 'Oh! how full of joy I should die, if I could do anything for the Cause which I love more than my life.' And Digby wrote to his wife that he had asked the Jesuit Superior Garnet to interpret the Pope's ruling on action in general, before he knew the full secret of the plot. Garnet had replied that, though priests were not to procure stirs, 'yet they would not hinder any, neither was it the Pope's mind they should, that should be undertaken for the Catholic good. I did never utter thus much, nor would not but to you; and this answer, with Mr Catesby's proceedings with him [Father Garnet] and me

Robert Winter   Wright   Iohn Wright   Thomas Percy   Guido Fawkes   Robert Catesby

8   DEO trin-vni Britanniæ bis ultori In memoriam Classis invincibilis subverſæ submerſæ | Proditionis nefandæ detectæ dilectæ.
To God, In memorye of his double deliveraunce from ye invincible Navie and ye unmatcheable powder Treason

דָכַרְתּ

Diſflo   Diſſipo
I blow and ſcatter
Ick blaes en verſtroy

VIDEO RIDEO
I ſee and ſmile

Opus tenebrar
A deed of darke

88

Tylbury Campe

In perpetuam Papiſtarum infamiam

Ventorum Ludibrium

In foveam quam foderit

Faux

Quantillum abſt
Hoc nae
How nye

CTOGESIMUS OCTAVUS, mirabilis Annus
Clade Papiſtarum, fauſtus vbique agis

Perditione prius nunc proditione petebant
Perdita perditio eſt prodita proditio

Fauſta et feſta dies lux aurea QVINTA
Anglis ſulphureum vedidit illa nefás

give me absolute belief that the matter in general was approved, though every particular was not known.'

Not that the fanatical Catesby would take any heed anyway. When Garnet heard indirectly of the Plot from Father Greenway who heard all about it in confession from Catesby – and gave both him and Winter absolution – the Jesuit Superior gave him warning of possible Papal disapproval, 'he told me he was not bound to take knowledge by me of the Pope's will'. Catesby went ahead, a singularly handsome man with very winning and persuasive manners, all the more effective – and all the more's the pity. When, after the discovery and the hue and cry were up, the house at Holbeach surrounded and Catesby and Tom Percy shot down together, Catesby dragged himself over to a picture of the Virgin, which he kissed before he died. Of the hundreds that they would have blown up with all the gunpowder stacked in the cellar beneath Parliament for its opening by the King, Digby stated, 'I do not think there were three worth saving that should have been lost'! This lets us into the spirit of these desperate young men's undertaking.

Actually it was through someone taking care for those three or four that the guns were spiked at the last moment. A larger circle outside the conspirators knew that something was afoot, if they did not know actually what or when. Lord Monteagle hardly needed the notorious letter from his brother-in-law, Francis Tresham, to head him off from attending Parliament that day: he was already a malcontent himself and thought that the moment was a good one to take arms, 'the King is so odious to all sorts'. The Jesuit Superior had a general knowledge that something was afoot, and specific information of the plot by way of confession – ordinary Englishmen were unable to distinguish between the two: for them, all that mattered was that he *knew*.

The great historian S.R. Gardiner summed up the situation, when Father Garnet first heard of the matter in the summer of 1605 and expressed his doubts, 'it was certainly rather mild condemnation of a design which, as Garnet understood, would involve considerable loss of life'. And subsequently, 'he could surely have found Catesby out between July and November, and this omission is perhaps the most fatal condemnation of Garnet's course'. From the private exchange of letters between the King and Cecil (now Lord Salisbury) we can see that the King did not wish people to be condemned on account of their religion, as in Catholic countries. Nor did Cecil: 'I confess I shrink to see them die by dozens'; but he regarded the Jesuits as 'absolute seducers of the people from temporal obedience, and consequent persuaders to rebellion'.

Opposite above: A contemporary Dutch print showing the Gunpowder Plotters.
Below: A Dutch satire on the failure of the Plot

Father Parsons had been at it for over twenty years, and nobody had caught him; now Father Garnet, who had lived quietly in England for twenty years and been the Jesuit Superior for fourteen, was to pay the price for Parsons' activities.

The government's aim was to fix the responsibility on Jesuit meddling in matters of state; the contrivers of the Plot were Catholic laymen, the poor priests the victims of their criminal folly. Father Garnet took refuge in the Habingtons' big house at Hinlip, near Worcester, which was honeycombed with hiding places. But his presence there was betrayed by a fellow-Catholic, Humphrey Lyttelton, anxious for his own safety; after a week's search the two Jesuits, Garnet and Oldcorne, were hoiked out of hiding and taken to the Tower. Garnet himself reported that the Lieutenant, Sir William Wade, 'is very kindly in his usage and familiarity, but most violent in speeches when he entereth matters of religion' – so much for what Parsons' incessant propaganda had achieved. The Lieutenant, like everybody else, believed that the Jesuits were all 'plotters of treasons': their case was pre-judged. Actually Garnet 'cared not for my life: death was welcome', but he stood to his defence, denying specific knowledge of the Plot.

The weakness of his case was that he *had* known about it through confession, and English law did not recognise such an excuse. Nor did ordinary English people understand the Jesuit doctrine of equivocation when Garnet fell back on it for defence: to them it merely compounded the offence, they regarded it as plain lying. The ordinary man's point of view is reflected in the play that Shakespeare was writing at the time, *Macbeth*, with its references to 'equivocation' and 'equivocators': one sees the unfavourable impression that such casuistry made upon the public:

> To doubt the equivocation of the fiend
> That lies like truth . . .

Again: 'Much drink may be said to be an equivocator with lechery: it makes him, and it mars him; it sets him on, and it takes him off' – this last phrase has a sinister double meaning, a reference to hanging.

The government's difficulty was to get direct evidence of so oblique a matter. For this purpose a trap was laid to catch the two Jesuits in the Tower. Garnet's keeper was to feign sympathy for his plight and discover to him a hole in the wall through which Garnet and Oldcorne could communicate; their admissions and mutual confessions were of course overheard. Garnet admitted

The Council Chamber in the Queen's House, where Guy Fawkes was interrogated

that Catesby had misled him and done him much wrong; and Father Tesimond, alias Greenway, revealed Catesby's unyielding resolution: he 'had a design to save all noblemen whom he did respect, yet he was of mind, rather than in any sort the secret should be discovered not to spare his own son if he were there'. All that the Jesuit Superior had done throughout that summer to stop him was that he had 'ceased not to commend the matter daily to God'. No doubt . . . and if the attempt had succeeded?

In the end, Garnet confessed that, though he had never approved of the Plot, 'it was not my part (as I thought) to disclose it'. This was enough even for the Catholic Councillor, Northampton – who, as Lord Henry Howard, had been in the Tower on behalf of Mary Queen of Scots years earlier. He was one of two Catholic peers on the commission investigating the Plot, and he reproached Garnet for not prohibiting it: 'Why did you not make it known to those that could and would have hindered it?'

This is the whole point of the government's proceedings. It is often overlooked amid much modern propaganda – and some downright lying – how successful they were. They did not stop Catholic religious activity, nor Catholic proselytising; but they put paid to Jesuit meddling in English politics. After the Plot we hear little of Parsons: even abroad, he was effectively shut up.

Poor Garnet went to his death in St Paul's churchyard, really a victim of the Papal Bull of Excommunication and Deposition posted up there thirty years before. As he left his cell, Garnet said to one of the Tower cooks, 'Farewell, good friend Tom: this day I will save thee a labour to provide my dinner.' It was in the spirit of Sir Thomas More. So, alas, was his rebuff to the Dean of St Paul's, who wished to pray with him: 'Mr Garnet, we are all Catholics.' The Jesuit denied this: the Dean was a heretic, only Catholics could be saved.

Thus do men's beliefs make fools of them.

The treason of Catesby's friend Percy – 'Stand by me, Tom, and we will die together' – brought into the Tower one of the grandest peers in the realm, the 'Wizard Earl' of Northumberland. He was the son of that Earl who had committed suicide there in order that his great estates might not be confiscated by attainder – and so they came to his son. Brought up as a Protestant, he was not much of a believer and neglected his boring duties as a Border grandee. He was a difficult, haughty man, of saturnine countenance and intellectual interests; he took it as a personal slight that James was unable to fulfil expectations of toleration, and retired from Court to sulk at Petworth.

But he was gravely compromised by his cousin Tom. As Captain of the Gentlemen Pensioners attending on the King, the Earl had admitted him as one without taking the oath of Supremacy (for he was a Catholic). As the Earl's steward, Percy had been able to bring to London a large sum out of the Earl's rents. It was he who, when joining the knot, had given the word, 'Shall we always, gentlemen, talk and never do anything?' It was he who had used his position at Court to hire the premises next to the House of Lords for the gunpowder and, when those would not do, hired the cellar under it. On Gunpowder eve he had dined with the Earl at Syon.

The case against Northumberland indeed looked black. He was condemned in Star Chamber for misprision of treason, to pay an enormous fine of £30,000 and to be imprisoned in the Tower for life. In the event he managed to pay some £11,000 (multiply by perhaps a hundred now!) and remained there for some sixteen years – longer than Ralegh. These two lofty spirits were friends, and they made good companions for each other in the Tower. Both interested in mathematics and navigation, chemistry and astronomy, they drew around them a distinguished circle of scientists and scholars. Both Ralegh and Northumberland had considerable libraries with them, and Ralegh turned a henhouse in the garden into a chemical laboratory, where he conducted his experiments and distilled his celebrated 'Cordial'. Never did the Tower hold such a distinguished lot of brains as in James's reign; for a decade and a half it was something of a university, or at least a college.

Northumberland was rich enough to keep open table and to pension Thomas Hariot, the brilliant mathematician, along with Walter Warner and Thomas Hughes: his 'Three Magi'. Nicholas Hill aided him with his astrological and alchemical studies. His library had many Italian works on the art of war and fortification, navigation and American voyages, on astrology and medicine; it also contained Tasso and Machiavelli, by whom both he and Ralegh were much influenced. One sees the Wizard Earl in his portrait at Alnwick, discontented and dark and brooding – he had plenty to brood over and plenty of time to do it in. A few random notes and accounts take us behind the scenes and into their intimate life within the Tower: payments to the Lieutenant for the Earl's privilege of having his own cook, diet and supplies, for mending the chimney in the kitchen, for his still-house, for paving his walk upon the walls. The Countess buys rubies for the Lieutenant's daughter, to keep him sweet – it was a very profitable post, not without its hazards. The young heir, Lord Percy, occasionally resided there. Then there were all the messengers to Syon, the Court and law-courts about estate affairs; repairs at Syon, rent for the Countess's house on Tower Hill, immense quantities of groceries and stores, considerable sums for books; a small sum for the preacher in the chapel; much larger ones for tobacco, of which Northumberland, like Ralegh was an addict – and that would not endear either of them to King James, who hated the noxious weed.

The Earl and his Countess, Essex's temperamental sister, did not get on well, and often his daughter Lucy was his companion. Then she fell in love with James Hay, an earlier favourite of the King; this was gall and wormwood to the Border magnate, who besides hated all Scots. But Hay was of a popular nature; he had extracted over £100,000 from the Scotch King's favour – James was a perfect sugar-daddy where boy-friends were concerned – and won popularity by spending it all. The marriage took place against the Earl's wishes, in 1617, and Hay made every effort to obtain his release, to overcome his father-in-law's bias against him. It was not for four years that James was induced to yield, and then it was with difficulty that Northumberland was induced to quit. He was persuaded to visit Bath for his health, to which the new favourite, Buckingham, had driven in a coach-and-six; so the Earl proceeded to the West Country more grandly in a coach-and-eight. As Countess of Carlisle later, his daughter was the person who reported every secret and every move of Charles I at Court to Pym and the Parliamentary leaders at Westminster – a kind of revenge upon the Stuarts.

We have a memorial of these years in Northumberland's well-known *Advice to his Son*, the major portion of which was written in 1609. He had been a spendthrift in his youth and wasted scores of thousands from his great estate. He put it down partly to 'an ignorance fostered in me by my father's concealing of that was fit for me to have been made acquainted withal, either to cause obedience in keeping me under, or to hinder some prodigal expense in some small trifles'. The purpose of the book was to lay down rules of guidance for his heir to safeguard the estates; it must have taken a good deal of time in the Tower supervising his stewards and agents. The burden of the book is that there is no alternative but to acquaint oneself thoroughly with one's own affairs, however complicated and burdensome. He had taken time to reduce them to order, so that his son could now follow them clearly, with ease and profit. The book is very characteristic of its author, with its disapprobation of women's government: 'In this state of England wives commonly have a greater sway in all our affairs than in other nations.' There is a certain pathos in

The 'Wizard' Earl of Northumberland who was imprisoned at
the same time as Ralegh and undertook scientific and other
studies while in the Tower for sixteen years

the last sentence: 'Be but the giver yourself of your gifts, and all these lime twigs can take no hold, nor you remain other than a free man, and at liberty.'

It was still twelve years before he would regain his liberty.

Meanwhile, how was his friend, Sir Walter, getting on in the Tower?

Ralegh was not a rich Earl, and his affairs were much burdened; but he carried on, courageously and arrogantly, in some style. He had leave for two personal servants, one to go abroad about his master's business; but he had soon drawn about him 'a preacher and three boys in ordinary'. He had faithful John Talbot as tutor for his son, Walter, and to act as his amanuensis: Talbot spent all these years in attendance, wrote out the fair copy of the great *History of the World*, and died on the last, fatal voyage to Guiana. Ralegh was allowed to walk in the Lieutenant's garden, where sometimes courtiers walked in and 'complimentarily' talked with him. Visitors were allowed him, and at times the Council had to restrict the coaches rolling in and out to call upon the Tower's famous inhabitant.

Lady Ralegh had her coach, and her house on Tower Hill; but this meant two establishments and two tables, so at times she joined her husband in the Tower. A second son was born to them, Carew Ralegh, baptised in St Peter-ad-vincula on 15 February 1605. But, perpetually badgering Cecil, she was sometimes ordered out to her own house. Cecil had extended a measure of protection to Ralegh, to prevent him from ruin at the hand of the Howards, who were both persecuting him and dunning him for arrears on his lost monopoly of granting licences to sell wine. He did what he could to keep in touch with colonial enterprise and to support a voyage across the Atlantic. But to raise cash he had to sell jewels, and this annoyed Lady Ralegh, of whom he came to stand in some awe – serve him right for marrying her. On one occasion, when he had had to part with a magnificent jewel Queen Elizabeth had given him, Lady Ralegh was so angry that she refused to come to dinner with him.

Before his troubles Ralegh thought that he had made his tenure of Sherborne safe by a conveyance; but now in 1609 a flaw was found in the deed, and James wanted the estate for Robert Carr, the reigning favourite, whose long legs had been too much for the susceptible Stuart. The shambling son of Mary Stuart and Darnley was totally without dignity: 'I maun hae the land; I maun hae it for Carr,' he kept repeating – and Carr had it, a suitable equipment for his later earldom of Somerset. Ralegh was distracted by the blow; though he was given a cash compensation, this destroyed the hopes of founding a landed family

The portrait of Sir Walter Ralegh painted in 1588
and attributed to the monogrammist 'H'

De Toubr van London aen de Refierre Legende 1615

for which he had taken such a risk in marrying Bess. The Raleghs kept up their clamour for the return of Sherborne, after Carr's downfall and the accession of the Digbys, and into the next generation; but they never got it back.

Ralegh lashed out with fiercer protests and seems to have made them public. He was no silent prisoner: he was writing forward-looking tracts on sea-power and ship-building, circulating his manuscripts, if he could not publish them. The Council pounced down on him: he was put under close restraint, Bess, her children and womenfolk ordered out of the Tower. Ralegh took nothing lying down; at once came the request that 'my wife might again be made a prisoner with me, as she hath been for six years last past'. This was a typical exaggeration. The Councillors bore down upon him in the Tower, headed by his inveterate enemy, Northampton, who reported to Carr for the King's ear:

We had a bout with Sir Walter Ralegh, in whom we find no change – but the same boldness, pride and passion that heretofore hath wrought more violently, but never expended itself in a stronger passion. Hereof his Majesty shall hear when the Lords come to him. The lawless liberty of the Tower, so long cockered and fostered with hopes exorbitant, hath bred suitable desires and affections. And yet you may assure his Majesty that by this publication he won little ground.

Ralegh had now won two exalted friends in James's Queen and her elder son, Prince Henry, who became an enthusiastic admirer: 'Who but my father would shut up such a bird?' Next year Ralegh was protesting to Queen Anne that he was still, after eight years, 'so straitly locked up as I was the first day', and that he could not obtain 'so much grace to walk with my keeper up the hill within the Tower'. As long before, with another greater Queen, his self-pity inspired him to poetry:

> My days' delight, my springtime joys foredone,
> Which in the dawn and rising sun of youth
> Had their creation and were first begun,
>
> Do, in the evening and the winter sad,
> Present my mind, which takes my time's account,
> The grief remaining of the joy it had . . .
>
> Moss to unburied bones, ivy to walls,
> Whom life and people have abandoned,
> Till th'one be rotten stays, till th'other falls.

Queen Anne, a kindly woman, begged again for his release, but no one took any notice of her.

A view of the Tower in 1615 depicted by a Dutch traveller

In 1612 he had the satisfaction of writing a bitter epitaph on his former friend, Cecil, whom he had come to regard as his chief enemy – for, of course, Cecil could have got him out, if he had wanted to.

> Here lies Hobbinol, our pastor whil'ere,
> That once in a quarter our fleeces did shear . . .

This referred to his office as Lord Treasurer:

> For oblation to Pan his custom was thus,
> He first gave a trifle, then offered up us.
> And through his false worship such power he did gain
> As kept him o' the mountain and us on the plain.

There was the rub: Cecil had always kept Ralegh *under*. So, after his death, he got what was coming to him: the little hunchback who monopolised the two great offices, both Secretary of State and Lord Treasurer, and ran the country, was a dab with women:

> Till Atropos clapped him, a pox on the drab,
> For – spite of his tarbox – he died of the scab.

After that (as with Swift later) it was unlikely that ordinary conventional people would let up on Ralegh: for a man with political ambitions, it is a mistake to be too expressive; a born writer is at a disadvantage.

He was slandered also for his chemical and medical activities – naturally, a man of genius, he never fitted into the categories of fools. Queen Anne, a rather hypochondriacal woman, thought that she had profited from the strong waters of Ralegh's Cordial (she drank). But when another client, the Countess of Rutland, died people said that it was his pills that 'despatched her'. The Rutland family were addicted not only to his medicines but to his tobacco, and he supplied the horrid stuff, along with the pipes to smoke it in, to Belvoir. Neither could this activity be expected to recommend him to the royal author of *The Counterblast to Tobacco*.

Now, too, in these years when Ralegh was writing, with his usual furious energy, his greatest work, Prince Henry called him into public activity by asking him to give his advice on the marriage of the Princess Elizabeth. Hardly ever can a prisoner in the Tower have been so publicised a participant in affairs – and this gave further annoyance in the right quarters. James would have preferred, for his own reasons, partly snobbish, a French or a Spanish marriage for her. Not so Prince Henry or Ralegh: they wanted a Protestant marriage.

The Bloody Tower where Ralegh spent his long imprisonment

Ralegh argued the case in two tracts, impressive for their knowledge of European and English history. He argued for a marriage with the Protestant Prince Frederick of the Palatinate: this recommended itself to Parliament, and this is what came about.

Notice that opinion was changing about Ralegh: he was becoming something of a mentor to Parliament, and of increasing favour with the public that had once hated him. Observe also what is so symptomatic of him: the Palatine marriage, which was in the short run disastrous, in the long run produced the lucky Hanoverian line still with us. He was a poor politician, but something of a prophet.

He wanted to write the history of Elizabeth's reign; it would have been wonderful if we could have had it, for he knew many of its secrets, but Cecil would not allow him to see the state papers. However, he wrote down his criticisms of the late war: he belonged to the maritime school, placing reliance on the Navy as the first line of defence, emphasising commerce and colonial expansion – here, too, prophetic of the way the future was to go. At home he looked forward to something like parliamentary government – at any rate, a larger share of Parliament in government. It seems that he had long played with

the idea of writing a history of the world, but during earlier years in the Tower kept hoping for release. It was during the winter of 1608–9 that he began at last to concentrate on the work.

He was encouraged by Prince Henry: 'It pleased him to peruse some part thereof', and he must have been much interested, for he got Ralegh to enlarge the plan, and this meant more work, more reading. Over five hundred authors are cited in the course of it; he cannot have had all those books with him in the Tower at one time – Elizabethans were apt to keep their books in chests rather than on shelves. He could always borrow and, a superior spirit, could command aid: he was helped with his Hebrew, and Ben Jonson claimed that he had contributed a piece about the Punic war, when the book became so famous. It was announced for publication in 1611, but the immense increase in scope – it was now planned to take three volumes – postponed publication of the first till 1614. By then the Prince was dead. The very stars fought against Ralegh – perhaps because he minded so much, was so anxious to achieve, before the light went out.

The Prince had got James to promise Ralegh's release that Christmas, and he had bought Sherborne from Carr, whose favour was expiring with his looks and his marriage – it was said, with the idea of restoring it to Ralegh. It would have been a proper reward for the *History of the World*. When the book came out, printed by Jaggard – who was shortly to bring out a still greater work, the complete Plays of Shakespeare – James made a personal intervention to suppress it. He recognised his own portrait well enough in that of Ninias, successor of a famous Queen, a man 'esteemed no man of war at all, but altogether feminine, and subjected to ease and delicacy'; and Ralegh never failed to express his contempt for sodomites in history.

Aubrey, in his *Brief Lives*, tells us that 'when Serjeant Hoskins was a prisoner in the Tower he was Sir Walter's Aristarchus', i.e. that it was his function 'to review and polish Sir Walter's style'. This celebrated lawyer and wit had been sent there for speaking too freely about James 1's Scotch favourites, and their gold-digging propensities. Hoskins was kept close prisoner, i.e. with his windows boarded up. 'Through a small chink he saw once a crow, and another time a kite; the sight whereof, he said, was a great pleasure to him. He, with much ado, obtained at length the favour to have his little son Bennet to be with him; and he then made this distich:

> Parvule dum puer es, nec scis incommoda linguae,
> Vincula da linguae, vel tibi vincla dabit.

Thus Englished by him:

> My little Ben, whilst thou art young,
> And knowst not how to rule thy tongue,
> Make it thy slave whilst thou art free,
> Lest it, as mine, imprison thee.

There was no suppressing Ralegh: the attempt to do so only increased the demand for the book; it became the best-seller of the century, far more so than the Plays of Shakespeare. Its influence upon its time was even more important, for it became favourite reading with Sir John Eliot and John Hampden, Milton and Oliver Cromwell. Contradiction, inner tension, paradox are of the essence of genius: here is another paradox – that the book of this man who detested Puritans became a guide and an inspiration to them. All over the country people responded, consciously or unconsciously, to its motivation and its implications, its tone and temper.

Angry at the attempt at suppression, furious with fate, Ralegh burned the apparatus he had collected for the second part, with 'If I am not worthy of the world, the world is not worthy of my works.' Nothing could be more characteristic of him. That same spring of 1614 he made himself ill from one of his chemical experiments, and seems to have suffered a slight stroke that left him a little lame. But he was undaunted, for a new prospect was opening before him. All these years he had kept some touch with the visionary projects that he had initiated in regard to 'the Large, Rich, and Bewtiful Empyre of Guiana'. Ever since his voyage of 1595 it had possessed his mind; there was gold there, and a new turn in the political kaleidoscope, allied to James's ever-pressing need for money, combined at last to let Ralegh out for his last and fatal venture.

In March 1616 he was released, to go about the City, still attended by his keeper, to prepare the Voyage, supervise the building of his fine new ship, the *Destiny*. Stick in hand, filled with new zest, he went about sight-seeing, viewing the changes in all the years of his imprisonment. But he was himself one of the sights, as an observer noted, the only man left of those who had beaten the Spaniards in '88: an heroic figure left over from the heroic age.

Some characteristic figures of the new reign were already falling from the skies. In September 1613 Sir Thomas Overbury had died in the Tower, poisoned by the wife of the ex-favourite Carr, who had been made Earl of Somerset to qualify him for her hand as ex-Countess of Essex. Ralegh's apartments in the Tower were now available for the deplorable couple: they took his place there.

8
Arbella Stuart: the Murder of Sir Thomas Overbury

NEVER did the Tower house a more exalted or more interesting number of occupants together at one time than in James I's reign. There now came to join Ralegh, Northumberland and the rest, as a permanent resident, no less a person than James's first cousin and next heir to the throne after his family, Lady Arbella Stuart. She, too, was a malcontent, and the ever-dangerous proximity to the succession proved her undoing.

She was the child of Darnley's brother, Charles, Lord Lennox and a daughter of Bess of Hardwick. More to the point, she was the grand-daughter of two ambitious, designing women who had plotted the marriage: Bess herself, now the rich and grand Countess of Shrewsbury, with her eye towards the throne – not bad going for a small Derbyshire squire's daughter; and Margaret, Countess of Lennox, grand-daughter of Henry VII. For this offence Queen Elizabeth had sent both to the Tower, comfortably enough in the Lieutenant's Lodgings, where Margaret had been before for her intrigue to marry her other son, Darnley, to Mary Stuart. An inscription above a fireplace recalls her earlier sojourn in 1566 and the terrible upshot of Darnley's marriage.

Now, with both grandmothers and her parents dead, Arbella was left in lonely isolation at James's Court, going through the weary round year after year, with no marriage in prospect. Though her status was that of a princess of the blood royal James had no interest in finding a marriage for her; and at last, at the very mature age of thirty-five, when she fell in love, she took the matter into her own hands. Unfortunately, the man she favoured was the Earl of Hertford's son, William Seymour, over twelve years younger than she; at this James woke up and prohibited the match, for Seymour was also of royal blood, the son of Hertford's union with Lady Catherine Grey, which Elizabeth had prohibited. James specifically ruled out this 'combination of titles' – she might marry anyone else, except the man she loved.

Arbella – with a combination of Stuart fecklessness and Bess's hardihood –

A painting of Lady Arbella Stuart by Carl van Mander

pressed the young man into a secret marriage in her private apartments at Greenwich. They had no more than a fortnight's bliss (we hope) before Seymour was sent to the Tower and Arbella rusticated – it was intended, to remote Durham, which she evidently regarded as the North Pole.

The couple planned to escape – or, rather, it was planned for them by Arbella's designing aunt, wife of Gilbert, Earl of Shrewsbury: another daughter of Bess, and evidently a chip of the old block. The Countess had become a Catholic and, with all the enthusiasm of a convert, her plan was to spirit Arbella abroad to become a Catholic pretender to James's throne. Rich, she raised a large sum of money to back the attempt – only five years after Gunpowder Plot! One would say that these people were incorrigible, to put it mildly.

Disguised as a man, though impeded by attendants and a suspicious amount of luggage, Arbella made for the Thames where a boat took her down the estuary for her assignation with Seymour. Missing him, she got a ship to take her across Channel, where she awaited him off Calais. Seymour was confined in the Tower over Traitors' Gate, not far from the western entrance. In disguise as a carter's boy, he followed a cart which had brought faggots for his lodging, unchallenged by the guards. But he missed his rendezvous with Arbella. Meanwhile, the hue-and-cry was up: the Countess of Shrewsbury was sent to the Lieutenant's Lodgings, while Arbella was tracked to Calais, where she was idiotically waiting outside the harbour for Seymour and was caught. He came ashore safely at Ostend, and within the year was received into the Catholic Church.

All this blackened the case for Arbella, who spent the rest of her short life in the Tower. She received a large allowance and was treated with becoming state. Her fantasies turned into delusions: she ordered dresses to the tune of £1500 for the marriage of Princess Elizabeth she would not be attending. After the collapse of a scheme to rescue her, she gave up hope and took to her bed, rejecting physic and attention. Sunk in despondency, she described herself as 'the pattern of misfortune', 'a spectacle of his Majesty's displeasure'. Refusing to be a spectacle any longer she died in 1615, aged forty.

The Countess, closer to Bess, without any Stuart admixture, was made of sterner stuff. Tried before Star Chamber, she was quite unrepentant and remained, stiff-necked and proud, in the Tower. She was allowed out for a month or two to attend her dying husband, but had to come back and was released only in 1618 on the payment of a fine of £20,000. She was enormously rich, however, and made a much better investment by becoming virtually a second foundress of St John's College, Cambridge.

Already she had worked her revenge upon the Howards, set in train the explosion over Sir Thomas Overbury's death which brought them down and rocked the state to its foundations.

John Aubrey says of Ralegh that 'he was a tall, handsome, and bold man: but his naeve was that he was damnable proud', and that at the time ''twas a great question who was the proudest, Sir Walter, or Sir Thomas Overbury, but the difference that was, was judged on Sir Thomas' side'. Overbury belonged to the younger generation, born in 1581: his importance was, not so much that he was the boy-friend of the favourite Carr – with whom James was in love – but that he was his mentor, immensely his superior intellectually, indispensable to him if he was to play any part in the King's counsels. Overbury was well-educated and well-informed about foreign affairs; but he was arrogant, insensitive and tactless, and was unaware that James disliked him and was – perhaps naturally – jealous of a more youthful rival.

With Cecil's death in 1612 things fell into a pretty mess: James thought that he could manage the Secretary's business himself with the aid of Carr, but Carr could not function without Overbury. This situation went to Overbury's head: immensely ambitious, he aimed at the Secretaryship himself and had the folly to challenge the Howards, Northampton and Suffolk, who were now poised to acquire Cecil's power in the state. To make sure of their direct line to James, they had a candidate for Carr's unmarried hand in Suffolk's beautiful daughter, Frances Howard. Unfortunately she was married to Essex's son, whom she detested and whom – herself only nineteen – she had already tried to

Robert Carr,
Earl of Somerset,
favourite of
King James I

poison. She wanted the handsome favourite physically, quite as much as her family wanted him politically. She was an addict of the black arts, and a client of Dr Forman's, to whom she resorted for philtres, love-potions, phallic and other figurines, to compel his love. At last, beautiful as she was, with an expression of angelic innocence, she won it: the fool became infatuated.

This went clean counter to Overbury's plans for Carr and himself. Actually his idea for Carr was the right one – that, as the King's favourite, he should not fall into the hands of either of the factions at Court, but maintain independence of both. Carr was now in the clutches of the Howards, the clever and reptilian old Northampton – whom we have met as Lord Henry Howard; who proposed to free his great-niece by nullity proceedings, and this meant keeping Overbury out of the way until they succeeded. The lady, however, meant to go further: she proposed to murder him.

Overbury knew far too much: in the early stages of the affair, the clever man had written Carr's letters for him to the great lady, never thinking – so like an intellectual – that a normal fool would fall for the bitch, 'that woman' as he called her, as well as 'whore' and 'bawd', which she was. He had evidence against her that would nullify all nullity proceedings. It was necessary to get rid of him. Clever old Northampton thought up the plan. He got James – who had his own reasons for wanting to see Overbury off the premises – to offer him the choice of two embassies. He turned down both, which, in those days, was regarded as an insult to the King. On 26 April 1613 Overbury found himself, to his surprise, close prisoner in the Tower. Wise Sir Henry Wotton prophesied that he 'shall return no more to this stage'. But his ghost did.

The Lieutenant of the Tower, Sir William Wade, was a man of integrity. A follower of old Burghley, he had been sent on many confidential missions in his time, to Philip II and Mary Stuart, whose coffers he had had to ransack once, while she was out hunting. Another time he had sent fifty rare seeds from Italy to Burghley, who had a passion for gardening and for improving his country. He had been clerk to the Privy Council, was one of the Council of the Virginia Company, had taken part in examining the Gunpowder Plot conspirators, as we have seen. In sum, he was a thoroughly experienced man, who interpreted his instructions strictly and refused to allow messengers to get through to Overbury. This attitude defeated the Howards and Carr – now elevated to the peerage as Viscount Rochester, in prospect of his grand marriage; Overbury might turn nasty and delate them from the Tower: he must be softened up.

Sir Thomas Monson, Keeper of the Armoury, was already a Catholic dependant of the sage Northampton, who now arranged a frame-up against Wade, on the grounds of carelessness in guarding Arbella Stuart. Northampton got him superseded by a creature of his own, a fellow Catholic, Sir Gervase Elwes, who would be more pliable. For this profitable post Elwes paid £1200, the cash collected by the Catholic poet and doctor Thomas Campion. The post was, in the end, to cost Elwes his head.

In the meantime, as the first reward of this change of posts, Overbury's incorruptible attendant, Carey, was dismissed and his place taken by Weston, a creature of the Countess, prepared to do her bidding, introduced into the Tower by the virtuous Monson. Overbury now, unaware to himself, lay wide open to his enemies.

The first attempt to poison him was with arsenic in his soup. Weston had the poison in a glass phial, a bowl of soup in the other, when he was intercepted by Elwes, who asked what was in the glass. 'Sir, know you not what is to be done?', said Weston, surprised in his turn. 'They will have me give it him, first or last.' Elwes: 'Let it be done so I know not of it.'

Elwes realised that he was now in a trap, no less than Overbury: he kept watch and tried to deflect poison going directly in to Overbury, but he was not the man to risk delating such all-powerful patrons. Overbury was deluded into thinking that his friend Carr was working on the King to deliver him, and to this end he was to feign sickness to strengthen Carr's appeal to the King's sentimentality – they had both been used to playing up James in this way, much as the former Essex used to play on Elizabeth's heart by absenting himself for sickness, real or feigned. So Overbury dosed himself with harmless vomits concocted by the amateur Sir Robert Killigrew.

The real thing, however, went in with the constant supplies of venison pasties, tarts, jellies, drinks sent indirectly through the Lieutenant's kitchen. Taking warning and not touching the stuff, he noticed it became black and furred in a day or two. All this was supplied by the handsome Mrs Turner, a fellow-client of Dr Forman's with the Countess, mistress of Sir Arthur Mainwaring, mother of his children, and a practising Catholic. (The poison did not come from Forman, but from an apothecary, Franklin.) Meanwhile, the nullity proceedings at Lambeth were dragging on: the good Archbishop Abbot was proving difficult, Higher Church bishops, like the sainted Lancelot Andrewes, more accommodating. A jury of matrons was called upon to examine the unbroken virginity of the Countess, under a cloud of veils to protect her modesty – though it was said that the veils served to cover up the identity of Monson's daughter in her place, an undoubted virgin.

Meanwhile, Overbury was still alive, recovering from sickness, and in a position to abort the proceedings, should he realise that he was being duped and that in fact his friend was holding him there until there was a happy issue out of his afflictions. When Weston came to Mrs Turner for his money – she was doing the dirty work for the great lady – she said, 'the man is not yet dead: perfect your work and you shall have your hire'. The Howard code-word for Overbury was 'the scab'; by this time, what with the vomits he was taking, and the poisons getting through to him, he was scabby indeed. But he did not die – perhaps the vomits counteracted the poisons – he lingered; so did the nullity suit, with which his life was inextricably entangled. At last he began to suspect, 'does Rochester juggle with me, or no?' We have his last despairing letters to his friend, turned traitor, adjuring him to get him out; at last he made his submission to the Howards – in vain: too late. The divorce commission had another fortnight to run. In despair he turned to threats: he knew enough to blackmail not only the Countess, but even Carr and the King. This sealed his fate.

Everybody by this time had given him over and wanted to see an end. Elwes preferred him dead and was sucking up to Northampton with reports of everything the 'scab' said or wrote. Early in September the Lieutenant moved him into closer quarters, dark and damp. All was ready for the kill. Elwes was not responsible for the final move: the Countess and Mrs Turner bribed the doctor's boy to put mercury sublimate into Overbury's next enema. After a night of agony, with Weston in attendance, he died about dawn on 15 September 1613.

Immediately Northampton dispatched a number of hurried and guilty notes to Elwes:

Noble Lieutenant, If the knave's body be foul, bury it presently [i.e. immediately]: I'll stand between you and harm. But, if it will abide the view, send for Lidcote [Overbury's friend] and let him see it to satisfy the damned crew. When you come to me, bring this letter again yourself with you, or else burn it.

And again:

See him interred in the body of the Chapel within the Tower instantly. . . . Let no man's instance move you to make stay in any case, and bring me these letters when I next see you. Fail not a jot herein as you love your friends; nor stay one minute, but let the Priest be ready; and if Lidcote be not there, send for him speedily, pretending that the body will not tarry. Yours ever, N.

Sir Thomas Overbury, whose poisoning in the Tower brought down the Earl of Somerset

To Rochester, the devout Earl was able to report:

He stank intolerably, in so much as he was cast into a coffin with a loose sheet over him. God is good in cutting off ill instruments from off the factious crew. If he had come forth, they would have made use of him. Thus, sweet Lord, wishing you all increase of happiness and honour, I end. Your Lordship's, more than any man, Henry Northampton.

Overbury's body was buried the same afternoon that he died; the Lieutenant reported to the Earl, 'I kept it overlong, as we all felt.' The Howards put it about that he had died of the pox; but the stench remained.

The Divorce Commission ended its labours with a report in favour of the unsullied virginity of the Countess. The pliable bishops were rewarded; even the Archbishop bent before James's plea of 'some skill I have in divinity', and 'no honest man doubts of the uprightness of my conscience' – with a half-promise of the see of Lincoln for the Archbishop's brother.

The marriage that followed was one of the most splendid in the annals of the English Court. It took place in the Chapel Royal, James paying for it all and – though the Crown was three-quarters of a million in debt – giving the bride £10,000 worth of jewels (multiply by a hundred for contemporary value). Everybody had to follow suit and heap presents upon the loving, and lovely, couple – Rochester was as handsome-bodied as his bride was beautiful. He had received his 'increase of honour' and been made Earl of Somerset to make him worthy of her, and that she might not be lowered in status by marrying him. The happiness promised by old Northampton – himself unmarried, of course – was now in hand.

The whole thing was a spectacular Howard triumph; when the bride entered the Chapel on the arm of her great-uncle, her hair falling to her shoulders in token of her virgin status, all noticed her bewitching expression of child-like innocence. The bridal masques were written by Ben Jonson and Campion; Donne wrote the Epithalamium:

> Then from wombs of stars, the bride's bright eyes
> At every glance a constellation flies,
> And sows the Court with stars . . .

In June 1614 Northampton died, declaring himself a member of the 'Catholic and Apostolic Church' and leaving the immense fortune he had scrounged from the state to his nephew Suffolk and his great-nephew, Arundel. He had been the brain behind the cornering of poor Overbury, though the murder was the idea of the lady – a bungled feminine affair which far too many people had been involved in to keep secret. Rumours began to circulate. The Countess of Shrewsbury searched out the gossip within the Tower, and saw that it was passed on to Sir Ralph Winwood, an upright Secretary of State and an enemy of the Howards. James was no longer under the spell of the Somersets: a combination of the respectables at Court, headed by the Archbishop of Canterbury, had promoted young Villiers to his attention – and he was far more handsome than the late Carr, his progress upwards correspondingly more rapid. The Somersets were now dangerously exposed.

At length Winwood went to the horrified King, who realised how he had been taken advantage of and in what an unfavourable light he appeared: he *looked* even guilty. He ordered a thorough investigation, which the aggressively Protestant Attorney General Coke was delighted to conduct. Gradually the whole unsavoury story was uncovered, and the investigation reached higher and higher, the lesser criminals suffering first. Wade was able to get his own back on Elwes by gathering information from Tower warders. Then Elwes made a complete confession and an edifying end on Tower Hill: he had been a great gambler and, after one session in which he lost heavily, had cried out, 'Oh, God, if I ever play again, let me be hanged.' Now he was.

Coke was flying for higher game. He attempted to bring Sir Thomas Monson into danger and bullied him for his Catholicism; but Monson was guiltless of the murder and was remanded on bail, where he lived, comfortably enough, in the lodgings of the new Lieutenant, Sir George More. It did not, however, make a good impression that, at Monson's former musical parties, the experienced Mrs Turner had supervised the catering. The celebrated bibliophile and scholar Sir Robert Cotton was imprisoned for months, for destroying what he could of Northampton's correspondence to save Somerset. Then the deplorable Countess made a full confession in the hope of pardon – she was now pregnant, and pregnant women were not executed. After the birth of her child she was taken to the Tower and had hysterics when she found that she was to be put into Overbury's chamber there. The Lieutenant hurriedly got ready for her the apartment just vacated by Sir Walter Ralegh.

Somerset remained obdurate, pleading his innocence. There is no reason to suppose, or at least no evidence, that he had anything to do with the poisoning. But James was clearly alarmed at what he might reveal under a prolonged trial, and prevailed on him, with difficulty, to plead guilty along with his wife. This helped: a long trial was avoided; both were sentenced to death, and a crowd gathered on Tower Hill, hoping to see them suffer. But James could hardly afford to take the risk of executing them – he may have promised Somerset his life, in return for silence. But the affair gave rise to a damaging spate of publications, including John Ford the dramatist's *Sir Thomas Overbury's Ghost.*

The Somersets lived in the Tower in considerable state: the Countess moved in her bedroom furniture of crimson velvet trimmed with gold fringe, satin-covered chairs and hangings, three maids to wait on her. Within a week she was being visited by her grand family friends and seeing her baby daughter. The Earl had a plentiful supply of plate, continued to wear his George and Garter about the place, and was shortly visiting Northumberland. The precious couple occupied Ralegh's old apartments, with a communicating door. It was not long before they were quarrelling.

Soon the beautiful Countess, who had such an acute interest in marrying and giving in marriage, was up to her neck in the intrigue to marry Lucy Percy to James's earlier favourite, James Hay, in the teeth of her father's opposition. Meanwhile, Suffolk's avaricious wife had provoked the hostility of the new favourite, now promoted Buckingham, by trying to oust him in James's favour by presenting to him Monson's son, posseted and curded, curled and scented. This was an insensitive mistake, for this was not James's type. It provoked Buckingham to make his first political intervention on the side of virtue, and to have Lord Treasurer Suffolk brought to book for his vast peculations from the Treasury he presided over, and out of which he built Audley End. No wonder easy-going James observed that the house was too big for a king, though not so for his Treasurer.

So the Suffolks fetched up in the Tower for a short spell in 1619. What with their son and Secretary Lake, a Court wag observed that an alternative government could be provided within the Tower, 'with a Lord Treasurer, a Lord Chamberlain, a Captain of the Pensioners, and a Secretary'.

In 1622 the Somersets were released, and rusticated to Rotherfield Greys in Oxfordshire, where tradition says, they lived at opposite ends of the house, having ceased to speak to each other. The Countess died still young, in agony, of cancer; Somerset lived on right up and into the Civil War these events helped to bring on; but she had ruined his life. It is said that Somerset had one last meeting with James before he died, secretly in the garden at Royston – when Buckingham was away – and that they fell on each other's necks and wept. They had much to remember, and much to be sorrowful for.

Frances Howard, Countess of Somerset, who arranged
the poisoning of Sir Thomas Overbury

SIR IOHN ELIOT.
Painted a few days before
his Death in the Tower
A.D. 1632.

9
Victims, Royal and Parliamentary

RALEGH's real successor in the Tower was his fellow West Countryman, Sir John Eliot. We have seen that Ralegh's posthumous influence was far greater than any he enjoyed in life, particularly in the formation of the Parliamentary tradition, and that Eliot possessed a manuscript of *The Prerogative of Parliaments*. Eliot, like Ralegh, had more than a due share of Celtic temperament: a Cornishman, he was both sensitive and combative; a personality of some charm with a gift for friendship, he was highly intelligent but impulsive. All this went into the making of a first-rate Parliamentary orator: he became the leader and inspiration of the Opposition to Charles I and Buckingham. But his oratory led him away. When he made his famous 'Sejanus' speech, specifically naming the minister and minion of Tiberius, there was no doubt about the implication. For this Eliot spent a few days in the Tower in 1626.

In the Parliament of 1629 he led the attack on the King's policy with regard to the Church and the new High Church leadership inspired by Laud. For the attempt to impeach Buckingham, Eliot and eight other MPs were sent to the Tower. When his case came to trial Eliot refused to acknowledge the jurisdiction of the court: he would never surrender on the principle of Parliamentary privilege. And so he stayed in the Tower the rest of his short life. Perhaps the consumption of which he died had something to do with his feverishness.

During these years, 1629–32, he wrote a great deal, feverishly too: two long and boring works of political theory, *The Monarchy of Man* and *De Jure Maiestatis*; a philosophical tract in his own defence, *An Apology for Socrates*; and the first part of a more interesting work, since it was historical and dealt with real events, those of Charles's first Parliament, *Negotium Posterorum*. In addition there was a voluminous correspondence of which only part survives, though over forty people appear in it, some of them of the first importance.

Of these the foremost was John Hampden, to whom Eliot was related and to whom he confided the oversight of his sons as well as the criticism of his

Sir John Eliot, Parliamentarian leader of the
opposition to Charles I and the Duke of Buckingham

works. Hampden was constructively critical: he thought that the super-abundance of examples and precedents might be cut down with good effect. No doubt: for Eliot was steeped in the literature of republican Greece and Rome, which – Thomas Hobbes considered – had so deleteriously stuffed contemporary heads with republican ideas and so helped on the Civil War. Eliot's actual life in the Tower is more interesting.

In the high summer of 1630 he reports, in agreeable humour, to Hampden: 'I have no news to give you but the happiness of this place, which is so like a paradise that there is none to trouble us but ourselves. All company is gone but the books and the records.' Political society would have gone into the country, but never a word of regret for the woods and waters of Port Eliot, the healthful vistas down the St Germans river to the Hamoaze and the open sea. 'Amongst the other rarities of this sphere there is newly here exposed some part of the Jewels to be seen, the font the Prince [the future Charles II] was christened in and such others. To that spectacle like a white house the doves repair, and every day has variety of admirers.'

A new Lieutenant had been appointed, on the death of Sir Allen Apsley, whose daughter, Lucy Hutchinson, has given a perhaps too favourable portrait of him in her celebrated *Memoirs*, as 'a father to all his prisoners'. He was not so to Eliot, of whom he probably disapproved: though he himself had been an Essex man earlier, following him to Cadiz and to Ireland, while Lady Apsley had taken a hand in Ralegh's chemical experiments. More recently, Apsley had been with Buckingham on the unhealthy Ile de Rhé expedition, contracted fever and died of it. So perhaps there was consumption in the air.

Among other correspondents was gallant Sir Bevil Grenville, from Stowe upon the wild cliffs of North Cornwall, writing that he 'cannot be quiet without saying something: farewell, and love him that will live and die your faithfullest friend'. In the event Grenville was to die at Lansdown, fighting for the King, in the superfluous Civil War. Eliot was not without gallantry himself: he pleaded that it was only the perversity of fortune that prevented him from kissing Lady Grace's hands at Stowe. To 'Sweet Mistress Corbet', for whom he had much tenderness, he wrote: 'I have no apprehension of restraint but in the want of so much liberty as might carry me to your presence.' He has no power to visit his friends; otherwise he has the same days and nights, the same air and elements, sun, moon and stars, the same seasons.

Such charm is worth tons of political theorising.

To his men-friends he occasionally expressed his anxieties. He was much worried by the misbehaviour of his second son, Richard, at Oxford. He arranged to take both boys away and send them to the Continent for their education. With both a large estate and a large family there was considerable business to transact from the Tower. Sometimes he could help his friends in return, as when he arranged for a large supply of copper coins needed by Sir Oliver Luke. To him he wrote, 'the deadness of this place prevents all occasions of intelligence, and we are so unactive of ourselves as we are hardly capable of the knowledge of what is done by others'. But to John Hampden he wrote that he had with him 'the continual presence of your love', and this must have been a continuing inspiration in the struggle before Hampden, when his time came on Chalgrove Field.

Among other correspondents was the most brilliant and philosophic brain of them all, John Selden, who came to see the silliness of both sides. Eliot, Hampden, Charles I himself in the end: they all sacrificed their lives – for what?

Early in 1632 Eliot wrote that his lodging in the Tower had been changed ten times without making any alteration in his mind. Just before Christmas he had been put under close surveillance and removed 'where candle light may be suffered but scarce fire. None but my servants, hardly my son, may have admittance to me. My friends I must desire for their own sakes to forbear coming to the Tower.' Shortly he was racked with a dangerous cough. He petitioned for so much liberty as to take the fresh air – how he must have longed in that fetid place for the fresh air of Cornwall. Charles I replied that the petition 'was not humble enough'.

By the autumn he was dying. We have a portrait of him which his friends had painted, to remember him by: the long laced nightgown, peaked beard and dark hair, the haunted look in the eyes, prayer-book in hand. In the early hours of the morning of 28 November 1632 he died. When the family begged for his body, to be carried home to Cornwall, the King gave the reply for which he was never forgiven: 'Let Sir John Eliot's body be buried in the church of that parish where he died.'

The respectable Eliot was shocked when, in 1631, the naughty Irish peer the Earl of Castlehaven was brought into the Tower, for a sexual scandal which made an even greater sensation than that of a later Irish exhibitionist, Oscar Wilde. We cannot go into the disagreeable details of Castlehaven's naughtiness here and the goings-on in his household which have given surreptitious delight to generations of readers of the State Trials.

The long and short of it was that this doddery peer was convicted of rape upon his wife and sodomy with a man-servant. Sodomy had become a felony only since the Statute of the moralistic and prudish Henry VIII; rape may be regarded as more important as liable to have consequences. In fact there was an element of frame-up in the indictment of this elderly peer, for it was known that his wife was a loose woman who had no objection to the sexual entertainments that enlivened the boredom of life at Fonthill Gifford in Wiltshire. The action may have been a collusive one with her son, for her virtue would have lain open to grave imputation if she had not protested her resistance, while her son was anxious to inherit. It is a well-known fact of anthropology that in less sophisticated societies sexual activities are mixed up with religion, and deviations apt to be regarded as blasphemous. Though we might not approve of the goings-on at Fonthill on aesthetic, or possibly disciplinary, grounds, today they would hardly be taken so seriously as to merit an execution on Tower Hill, pandering to the worse excitement of a mob of spectators with curiosity unslaked.

The poor Earl made a sufficiently edifying end, 'his coffin carried into the Tower about a week before, that he might the better prepare himself for death'. The Dean of St Paul's was appointed to soften him up, visiting him daily 'to see how he stood and to settle him in his religion'. To such good effect that the Earl surprised the mob on the Hill, 'showing to them all a very noble, manly, and cheerful countenance, such as seemed no wise daunted by the fear of death'.

This happy Caroline decade of peace and prosperity, directed by such civilised spirits as Charles I, Archbishop Laud and Strafford, witnessed a suspension of persecutions for witchcraft to which Puritans were so addicted. Both Charles and Laud were cultivated men who wished to repair some of the ravages of the Reformation in the churches, to rail in the altar from the familiarities of dogs, place it once more at the east end, and work towards seemly order, with a proper element of ritual, in the services. Laud's insistence on uniformity, like Elizabeth's, was a matter of external order; an excellent scholar, he was intellectually and theologically more tolerant and less narrow-minded than the maniacs for predestination.

This was anathema to Puritans like the prolific Prynne, who wrote book after book urging Parliament to suppress anything contrary to Calvinist doctrine and to force the English clergy to subscribe to the Predestination and Eternal Damnation doctrines of the Synod of Dort. In 1632 he published

The Tower in Stuart times, from an etching by Hollar

Victims, Royal and Parliamentary

Histriomastix, a whole-hogging Philistine attack on plays and masques, and describing women acting in them as no better than whores – under which heading, in his Index, he brought Charles's Queen, Henrietta Maria. (She was a silly woman, but she was not that.) For this gentlemanly stricture he spent a year in the Tower, and at his trial was condemned to pay a large fine and have his ears – rather than his tongue – nipped. Nothing would stop a Puritan: he continued his intolerable campaigns of seditious libel until a court condemned him to be branded with S.L., for the seditious libeller he was. After this, holding Laud responsible, he became his implacable enemy and pursued the Archbishop to the death.

Charles and Laud were poor politicians, though the latter was an industrious administrator; to his only truly great minister, Strafford, Charles did not give his confidence, until too late, but kept him away from the centre of power, in the North or in Ireland, while Henrietta Maria did her best to undermine him. (In later life she repented of this with tears.) The Puritans and Parliamentarian upper classes – nobility and gentry – were mad at the suspension of Parliament and their exclusion from power. Charles and Laud, not knowing what they were up against, provoked the religious fanaticism of the Scots, with a new prayer-book, and a quasi-national resistance which defeated and humiliated royal government. In collusion with the Parliamentary leaders – for Charles was forced by defeat to call a Parliament – revolution was unleashed. The rock that unloosed the avalanche was the prosecution of Strafford

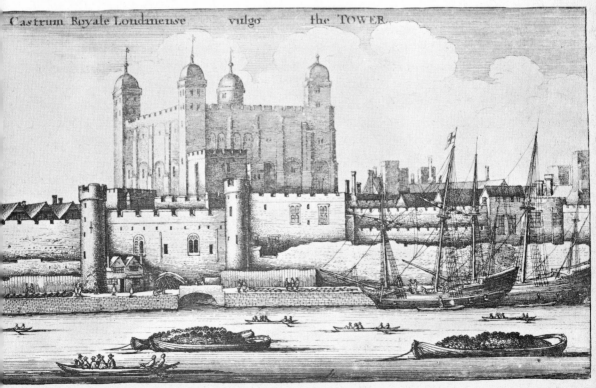

Castrum Royale Londinense   vulgo   the TOWER

to death; as a Puritan MP shouted on his condemnation, 'Now we have done our work; if we could not have effected this, we could have done nothing.'

In November 1640 the Long Parliament met, which carried through the revolution and, with more success, the Civil War. John Pym, an abler political brain than Eliot, led Parliament in an onslaught on Strafford. It was a duel to the death, from which only one would emerge alive: as Pym said, 'Stone-dead hath no fellow.' In these revolutionary circumstances the Tower was not only a key-point, it had a part to play. Strafford proposed to parry Pym's attack by a characteristically bold move: to charge the Parliamentary leaders who had invited the Scottish army into England with high treason. On 11 November the King was to hold a review at the Tower: if he carried those named with him thither, there would be an armed force within to receive them. The plan was betrayed, as every move Charles made was leaked from Court, notably by Lady Carlisle and Sir Henry Vane. Pym got his blow in first and carried the Commons' impeachment of Strafford to the Lords: it was Strafford who was committed to the Tower. He was conveyed there on 25 November in a closed coach through shouting, insulting crowds.

Parliament was bent on bringing the great man down: they could not win their victory over the royal government while Strafford remained alive. The situation was a strange one, if not unique: 'Like no other minister, while in the Tower awaiting his trial for high treason, he was still the greatest power behind the Crown.' In the struggle that ensued Charles made every possible mistake; his ineptitude played into Pym's hands; in the end, when Strafford's life hung on Charles's word, the King betrayed him.

While Pym raked together all the evidence he could get against every aspect of Strafford's rule in the North and in Ireland, Strafford felt confidence in his innocence. He wrote to his wife: 'Sweetheart, the charge is now come in, and I am now able, I praise God, to tell you that I conceive there is nothing capital. And for the rest, I know at the worst, his Majesty will pardon all, without hurting my fortune, and then we shall be happy, by God's grace.' Strafford was a man of integrity; unfortunately, integrity is not enough in politics. On 1 March 1641 another man of absolute integrity joined him in the Tower: Archbishop Laud, brought there too in a coach through the hooting mob.

Strafford's impeachment before the Lords turned into a triumph; his defence was so masterly that not even Vane's evidence that Strafford proposed to use his Irish army against the Opposition in England carried conviction. At

Opposite: A portrait of the Earl of Strafford by Van Dyck
Overleaf: The Tower at the time of the Revolution of 1688

the end of the proceedings Strafford and his master exchanged a significant smile; but this was not the end. Returned to the Tower, Strafford felt that 'he had saved himself; he walked up and down in the Tower in high spirits, even singing songs of thanksgiving'. Moreover, he had the word of a king behind him: 'I cannot satisfy myself in honour or conscience without assuring you now, in the midst of your troubles, that, upon the word of a king, you shall not suffer in life, honour, or fortune.'

But the House of Commons could not allow Strafford, whose very personality daunted them and aroused their hatred, to escape; with the impeachment hanging fire, they resolved to proceed by attainder, i.e. kill him by act of Parliament, justice or no justice. It was at this point that the Tower became decisive in Strafford's fate.

Charles and Henrietta Maria, incompetent politicians, incapable of saving their minister by political means, committed themselves to an Army plot to seize the Tower and enable Strafford to escape. Sir William Balfour had been appointed Lieutenant, in succession to Apsley; Charles was always partial to Scots, and Balfour had been favoured with a lucrative patent for minting gold and silver there. Nevertheless, according to Clarendon, he 'forgot all his obligations to the King and made himself very gracious to those people whose glory it was to be thought enemies to the Court'. When Captain Billingsley appeared at the Tower gate, requesting in the King's name the admission of a hundred men, Balfour refused the request. At the end of the year Charles got him to resign his post: he went on to become a lieutenant-general of Parliamentary horse in the Civil War.

At this juncture the King, in the hope of conciliating his opponents, made one of those concessions which only encouraged them. He made the Earl of Newport, an enemy of Strafford, Constable of the Tower. This man, Mountjoy Blount, was one of the illegitimate family that Elizabeth's talented Mountjoy – suitably named – fathered upon the beautiful Penelope Rich (Sidney's Stella) while she was the wife of Lord Rich. Left already rich by his father, as Master of the Ordnance he made large sums out of the public for his private purse, in the manner of the English aristocracy. With Strafford's attainder through Parliament and the King hesitating to sign it, the new Constable announced that he would execute Strafford without warrant, if the King did not give it. This provides some idea of the hatred that the superior spirit of Black Tom Tyrant aroused in opponents.

Every kind of pressure was brought on the King to make him give way;

The Chapel of St John the Evangelist on the first floor of the White Tower thousands of the London mob came down to Whitehall to howl at the palace windows for Strafford's blood. In this fearful dilemma Strafford made the noble offer of his life to purchase peace for his master. 'May it please your Sacred Majesty, I understand the minds of men are more and more incensed against me, notwithstanding your Majesty hath declared that, in your princely opinion I am not guilty of treason, and that you are not satisfied in your conscience to pass the bill.' He asked the King to pass the bill and 'by this means to remove, I cannot say this accursed, but I confess this unfortunate, thing, forth of the way towards that blessed agreement which God, I trust, shall ever establish between you and your subjects.' Having made this magnanimous offer, Strafford began to hope again for life, and offered Balfour £20,000 to allow him to escape – but to do so was more than the Lieutenant's life was worth.

Down at Whitehall Charles was in an agony of indecision, and sent for his bishops: Ussher and Juxon (who was to attend the King on the scaffold) urged him to stick by his conscience, the politic Williams to give way. With useless tears he signed the Bill: 'My Lord of Strafford's condition is happier than mine.' For the rest of his life he repented this action. There are two stories of how Strafford received the decision. Archbishop Laud was assured that he took it with resigned acceptance; another said that he repeated the words of the Psalmist, 'Put not your trust in princes, nor in the sons of men: for in them there is no salvation.' There is no reason why both should not be true; both had failed him. In the days of his power he had particularly protected the interests of the small men, who now howled for his blood, against the great, who made more effective friends – and enemies.

Strafford spent his last days mostly with Ussher, preparing for death. Before going to the Tower the Archbishop bitterly reproached Charles for breaking his word as King – who could ever trust him after that? As Clarendon said, 'he knew neither how to be, nor to be made, great': he was a small man in every way. On 12 May 1641, a sea of faces crowded Tower Hill to watch the great man die – there was even a fear that he might be lynched. A still greater man, Oliver Cromwell, knew what to think of average humans: he said to Lambert one day of the crowds that were cheering them when they set out against the Scots, 'Do not trust to that: these very persons would shout as much if you and I were going to be hanged.'

The Lieutenant was afraid for Strafford to walk up Tower Hill, and wanted to send for his coach. 'No,' he said, 'I dare look death in the face, and I hope the

An etching by Hollar of the execution of Strafford

people too. I care not how I die, whether by the hand of the executioner or by the madness and fury of the people: if that may give them better content, it is all one to me.' But he did care for the blessing of that other worthy servant of an unworthy master, Archbishop Laud. As he passed under the old man's window he asked for his prayers and blessing. Laud held out his hands over the bowed head, and then fell senseless at the horror of the scene, not with fear for himself but grief for his friend. So Strafford prayed for him: 'God protect your innocency.'

The strange dark figure, with the saturnine countenance and magnetic eyes, walked on erect, imposing silence on the vast crowd: 'He walked,' they said afterwards, 'like a general marching to victory, his face grave and steadfast in the spring sunshine.'

Of course Strafford's death purchased no respite for the King: it only exposed the utter weakness of the monarchy and opened the way to revolution. Not until this became evident did a party rally round King and Church. Meanwhile, control of the Tower was disputed by Parliament – a pointer to the way things were going. In August 1641 Parliament ordered the Constable himself, Newport, to take up his residence within the Tower and see it safely guarded. In December the King managed to appoint a supporter of his own, Lunsford, as

A Doctor Vfher Lord Prim[...]
le of Ireland.
B the Sherifes of London
C the Earle of Strafford
D his kindred and Friends

Lieutenant. Upon this, Parliament commanded the Constable to take personal charge – something new – whereupon the King dismissed him. Yet, in the Civil War into which the two sides gravitated in 1642, Newport followed the King and took up arms for him in the North, all his equipment left behind in the Tower. Parliament took possession of them, and of him when he returned. It is a nice epitome of the changes and chances of the time, when order had broken down in the country. At the centre Parliament moved into the vacuum.

Amid all these excitements Archbishop Laud lived on in the Tower, attended by two servants. For a brief spell at New Year 1642 he was joined by a dozen bishops, for protesting that a Parliament which excluded them against their ancient and lawful right was no free Parliament – nor, of course, was it. They were headed by Archbishop Williams of York: he and Laud should have worked together for the good of the Church, instead of which they hated each other so much that their personal feud had helped to wreck it.

Laud kept himself busy in the Tower – he had always been a busy-body – arranging his papers over the whole range of his administration, keeping a regular routine of prayer and business. Heart-breaking news came through to him, all that he had worked so hard for now overthrown. The stained-glass windows he had put up in the chapel at Lambeth, the religious pictures in the gallery smashed; at St Paul's and the Abbey, historic monuments defaced; in the churches the altars once more overthrown – the House of Commons would not take communion at St Margaret's until the communion-rails were broken down and a supper-table placed in the middle of the church.

He was harassed by Parliament to present their nominees to benefices still legally in his gift, sometimes of persons of whom he could not approve. One upright Puritan peer offered a large bribe to Laud's servant to get the rich living of Chartham for a dependant. Sometimes, when the Archbishop attended chapel, the preacher from the party now in the ascendant reviled him to his face, while the women and boys stood up to see how he was taking it. He was now lame and had to be helped to chapel by his man; on another occasion when he was railed on he wrote, 'But I am better acquainted with patience than they think I am.' A minister who had been suspended and gone to New England, now returned with Hugh Peters and others of the Saints, came to the Tower to taunt him. Let in by a new Lieutenant's son, Pennington, the New Englander asked the old man whether he repented or not; Laud patiently answered that, if the preacher had been suspended, it had been according to the law.

But the odious Prynne was not forgetting his old enemy; when it was necessary, in 1643, for Parliament to purchase the support of the Scotch Presbyterian Army, Laud's trial was implicitly part of the purchase price. Prynne exerted himself with all his indefatigable industry to supply the evidence. He arrived at the Tower with a posse of soldiers to search the Archbishop's apartment, rifled his pockets, went through everything. He took away twenty-one bundles of papers the methodical Laud had prepared for his defence, of which only three were ever returned, and even his Diary and book of private devotions.

The trial was months in preparing, for not all Prynne's industry and in-genuity, his tampering with the evidence and suppressing whatever was in Laud's favour, could substantiate the case against him. He was charged with high treason for subverting the laws of the realm and attempting to reconcile it to the Church of Rome. Laud was able to show that all that he had done was in keeping with the laws, and that in fact he had personally converted a number of Catholics to the Church of England. True, he had been offered a cardinalate to bring about a union with Rome, but he had never accepted the offer. To Calvinists, of course, the unity of Christendom, the re-union of Christ's Church, was not only a sin, but a crime. We cannot think that a more enlight-ened man like Laud saw it in that light – any more than sensible people would in our time: he died for being, among other things, ahead of his own.

His trial lasted many days, with an incredible amount of detail raked up before the Lords. But Laud was more than a match for Prynne: anyone who reads the lengthy proceedings must be struck by the old man's retentive memory, without his papers – he had always been one for meticulous detail, part of his failings. One day in January 1643 'the Thames was so full of ice that I could not go by water [to Westminster]. It was frost and snow, a most bitter day. I went therefore with the Lieutenant in his coach, and twelve warders with halberds went all along the streets . . . which was as good as to call the people about me.' So he was hooted at and reviled all the way to Westminster: 'God of his mercy forgive the misguided people.' Another day at Westminster, the Archbishop was railed upon by a minister from New England whom he did not know: this was the celebrated Hugh Peters, I regret to say – for he was a Cornishman.

Among the numerous small charges against the Archbishop was that he had interfered with marriages in the Tower and prohibited them. This was true, and Laud was able to show that it was for the people's own sake, 'for many of their sons and daughters were there undone', with neither banns nor licence. He was answered that it was the King's free chapel, not his to interfere – any argument to suit their book. But it was found impossible to prove the charge of high treason and, when the Archbishop was brought before the House of Commons, he made such an admirable defence of his proceedings that even Prynne grudgingly admitted that it was as able as the merely human wit could devise. So, as with Strafford, they resolved to proceed by attainder, i.e. kill him by act of Parliament. Even the rump of the House of Lords that remained – for all revolutions are conducted by determined minorities – stuck at this, and the judicious Commons waited till there was a day when there were hardly any lords present, and got their bill through.

It may be said that William Laud welcomed death: everything that he had worked for lay in ruins about him. As he wrote in the will he made in the Tower, 'I most willingly leave the world, being weary at the very heart of the vanities of it.' The night before his execution he slept soundly, and from the scaffold he preached a good sermon, after his old-fashioned manner: 'I am going apace, as you see, towards the Red Sea, and my feet are now upon the very brink of it: an argument, I hope, that God is bringing me into the Land of Promise.' Coming to the block he noticed through the chinks of the boards that some of the idiot people had stationed themselves right under it where the blood would drip through. So he called on the officer to lay some sawdust or else remove them, saying – without irony – that 'it was no part of his desire that his blood should fall upon the heads of the people'.

In truth, his life's work had not been in vain. Today the altars and stained-glass windows, even the images, are back in the churches and everyone pays tribute to the ecumenical spirit: even Christians are ceasing to hate one another.

And where is Prynne?

After Laud's death Prynne was charged by the triumphing House of Commons with the task of justifying it. But though he produced next year a ponderous folio, *Canterbury's Doom*, it was only a first part and he never finished it – perhaps even he felt less convinced of his case as he went further into it. And now there were other enemies to attack: he hated the Independents as much as he had hated the bishops. From the Independents he got as good as he gave, and even Milton, whom he attacked with his usual injustice of mind, has a scornful reference in a bitter sonnet to 'Marginal Prynne's ears'. Cromwell's government very properly put him in prison at remote Pendennis Castle –

though the Scilly Isles would have been still more appropriate. Before long he was eagerly agitating for the Restoration of the King.

As a mere scholar, Prynne survived the deluge; abjuring politics, he gave himself up to research, the better side of him. At the Restoration he was made Keeper of the Records in the Tower at a good fat salary, and as such he did his best work. As early as 1662 he was ready with his *Brevia Parliamentaria*, which he dedicated to the King, whose mother he had once insulted. Year after year the works poured out from the press, concluding with his *Exact Abridgment of the Records in the Tower of London*, published in the year of the Revolution, 1688–9.

Like other researchers, he was always asking for more accommodation for his work in arranging and transcribing the records there; unlike some, he produced the goods. And he was always helpful and encouraging to young researchers. Anthony Wood tells us that 'Mr Prynne received him with old-fashioned compliments, such as were used in the reign of King James I, and seemed to be glad that such a young man as he was should have inclinations towards venerable antiquity.' John Aubrey describes him for us, in his later manifestation:

He wore a long quilt cap, which came two or three inches over his eyes, which served him as an umbrella to defend his eyes from the light. About every three hours his man was to bring him a roll and a pot of ale to refocillate his wasted spirits. So he studied and drank, and munched some bread; this maintained him till night, and then he made a good supper.

As Chancellor Adenauer once said to the present writer: 'Es ist besser als die Politik.'

Archbisop Laud (*left*) and William Prynne (*above*), the man who brought about his trial

10
The Tower in Civil War and Revolution

ATURALLY in time of Civil War and Revolution the Tower was
busier than it had ever been, more crowded with prisoners and of
more kinds. We cannot hope to deal with such an overflowing
volume of material in a chapter: it would need a whole book. But
we can watch, with horrid fascination if selectively, what happens when the
lid is taken off the top of society and the contents boil over. The social break-
down gives their head to all sorts of unquiet spirits, agitators, dissenters, radicals,
levellers, fanatics, lunatics; one sees the revolutionaries eating each other up,
as we have witnessed in contemporary Russia. Until the saner elements in
society, the country at large, have had enough and decide to put an end to it.

The Tower provides more clearly than ever a barometer registering the
political climate, the ups and downs of power. The gathering crisis is observable
in 1641: the country stands on the verge of civil war. One M.P. is sent to the
Tower just for daring to urge moderation in the treatment of Strafford;
another for opposing an armed guard for Parliament; Sir Ralph Hopton for
opposing the Grand Remonstrance; the Earl of Bristol and Judge Mallet
simply for having had information of the Kentish Petition. Lord Montagu of
Boughton was imprisoned at eighty for expressing disapproval of disobedient
behaviour to the King – the current cant of Parliament was that all they were
doing was in the service of the King – and there the old man remained till his
death. Meanwhile the Lord Mayor of London, Sir Richard Gurney, was so
misguided as to be on the King's side: he was deposed and kept in the Tower
practically till his death. A new Lord Mayor was intruded, one Pennington,
who was so sage a Puritan that he decreed that on the Sabbath no milk should
be sold in the City after 8 a.m. To add insult to injury, he became Gurney's
keeper as Lieutenant of the Tower and, as such, had the pleasure of conducting
Archbishop Laud to the scaffold. At the Restoration he was convicted as a
regicide, returned to the Tower as a prisoner and died there.

'Thus the whirligig of time brings in his revenges.'

General George Monk who engineered Charles II's Restoration

Not only the Tower but, as Clarendon tells us, 'all the prisons of London were filled with persons of honour and reputation, by the Parliament. New prisons were built for their reception, and many of quality, both of the clergy and laity, were even placed on board ships in the river, where many lost their lives.' In such circumstances it is pleasant to record that there were more escapes than usual. Daniel O'Neill had a fascinating career as a soldier of fortune, and was involved in the Army Plot. Sent to the Tower in January 1642, in May he escaped, dressed as a woman, and survived happily to the Restoration. Two more Irishmen made a getaway: Hugh MacMahon and Lord Maguire, who had plotted the rebellion in Ireland which so much exacerbated feeling in England. Held in the Tower from 1642 to 1644, with the help of two priests they made their escape by swimming the ditch. A few weeks later a servant betrayed them in a house in Drury Lane; Prynne as prosecutor pressed home the case and they suffered the usual penalties.

Later on, the forces that had made the revolution split in two: Presbyterian against Independent, Parliament against Army, almost everybody against Cromwell, the greatest man of them all – both the ablest soldier and the ablest politician. Massey and Middleton were Parliamentarian and Presbyterian officers who were opposed to Cromwell, and went over to Charles II, served him in Scotland, and were captured at the battle of Worcester in 1651 – there was no defeating Cromwell. Taken to the Tower in November 1651, Massey – of middle stature, brown hair and sanguine complexion – escaped in August 1652, to become a leader of the Presbyterians, disillusioned at the way things had turned out, who were working for the restoration of the King. John Middleton was another, who followed the same course and was wounded at Worcester. Brought to the Tower, he escaped in his wife's clothes, to join the King in Paris and become an earl at the Restoration.

Meanwhile, a survivor of the old régime lived on in the Tower throughout the whole *épopée*: Bishop Wren, Sir Christopher Wren's uncle. As Bishop of Norwich and then of Ely, he had roused the fury of the Puritans by his activity in restoring order and decency in the churches and curbing obstreperous preachers. Impeached by the Commons, they could find nothing for which to kill him, so he spent years in the Tower. Like Laud he was busy enough: he conscientiously dealt with institutions in his diocese and kept his register going himself. He was consulted by Hyde and others on Church affairs, and Cromwell more than once offered him his liberty. An upright Anglican, devoted to Church and King, Wren would never accept this favour at the usurper's hand

Bishop Matthew Wren who was imprisoned in the Tower throughout the Protectorate of Oliver Cromwell

or acknowledge his authority. Scholars like Laud and Wren had an advantage during imprisonment in that there was always something to occupy their minds: Wren wrote his *Critical Meditations*, afterwards published by his son. Restored with the King, Wren continued the regular Anglican line of Laud as before. When easy-going Charles, who had not much in the way of belief, urged compromise on Wren, he replied, 'Sir, I know the way to the Tower.'

We cannot go in detail into the ordinary exchanges of civil war – the hangings and beheadings for treason, i.e. against whichever party was in power, for popping over from one side to the other, for having second thoughts. The most interesting cases are those that come under the last two headings. There were a large number of sensible people in the middle who deplored the crazy conflict and sought an accommodation. It is hardly doubtful that things would have fallen out better this way – they could hardly have fallen out worse – than by fighting relentlessly on till absolute victory was won. And then what? Cromwell himself found in the end that that was no solution, and after the death of the great man things came back to what they had been before – except for all the ruin and destruction and waste of life.

> When civil fury first grew high,
> And men fell out they knew not why . . .

and proceeded to conduct the argument, not settle it, by

> The holy text of pike and gun
> Decide all controversies by
> Infallible artillery,
> And prove their doctrine orthodox
> By Apostolic blows and knocks,
> Call Fire and Sword and Desolation
> A Godly – Thorough – Reformation.

175

Many people early saw through the fatuity of it all, but it is always dangerous to try to act upon reason and sense when people are swept away by gusts of unreason.

Sir John Hotham, the Parliamentarian Governor of Hull, was a not very nice Yorkshireman, though intelligently self-seeking – as may be seen from his marrying five wives, each of whom brought an increase to his estate. He had no sympathy with the religious aims – if that is the word for it – of the Puritans (what they were out for was power, to impose themselves upon other people), but he had no objection to profiting from the livings they sequestered. A reflective man, if somewhat uncouth in the Northern manner, he wrote to Speaker Lenthall after Edgehill, 'If the sword were once drawn, it would be with us as it was with the Romans in the time of Caesar and Pompey: when 'twas said, whoever had the better the Roman liberty was sure to have the worst.' This was much to the point, and so it turned out.

In such a frame of mind the Governor was prepared to listen to those who thought similarly on the other side – and perhaps to surrender Hull, for a consideration. He was propelled into action by his son, a tough customer and a cynic – such as such times encourage – who excused his depredations upon both sides by saying that since 'he fought for liberty he expected it in all things'. This ruffian opened his mouth too wide – he had the excuse that so far he had made only three marriages, each with an increment to his estate. While he delayed action, for a viscounty for his father, a barony and £20,000 for himself, the negotiations were discovered and the Hothams brought to book, i.e. the Tower. Sir John was a Member of Parliament, and this was awkward; the Presbyterians there tried to save his life, but the whole-hoggers, led by Cromwell, were determined to execute. Sir John had the benefit, on the scaffold, of the ministrations of Hugh Peters.

It was another Cornishman who got into similar trouble about the same time: Sir Alexander Carew, Governor of Plymouth. He was the only son of Richard Carew, the delightful antiquary of the Elizabethan *Survey of Cornwall*. At the time of Strafford's attainder, Carew's friend Sir Bevil Grenville besought him to oppose it. Carew replied, 'If I were sure to be the next man that should suffer upon the same scaffold with the same axe, I would give my consent to the passing of it.' Little can he have expected to meet the same fate. When, in 1643, the King's army swept the West and Plymouth was surrounded, Carew's estates on the Tamar were endangered, and he began to have second thoughts. He opened negotiations with the Royalists at Exeter to surrender

Left: Sir John Hotham, the Parliamentarian Governor of Hull, who was executed for his plot to betray the city to the Royalists. *Right:* Edmund Waller, the poet and Parliamentarian, who was imprisoned for his intrigue to go over to the King

Plymouth. Betrayed by a servant, he was carried off to the Tower by sea. His wife pleaded that his mind was distracted. No doubt. On Tower Hill he arranged that his signal to the executioner should be, pathetically, 'the last words that ever my mother spoke when she died'.

Carew had the good looks of his family, and was only thirty-four; Grenville had the more charming personality, and was fifty when he was killed at Lansdown. Their lives were both thrown away.

A more congenial case is that of the poet Edmund Waller. A man of genius, he was a moderate, not a good party man; but he was a cousin of John Hampden and a connection of Cromwell and this inclined him to the side of Parliament, until it took the path of revolution under Pym. In 1643 he was one of the commissioners to treat with the King at Oxford; on his return he made himself the channel of communication with the moderates in London seeking an agreed peace. There was a plot on the part of the peace-party to secure the City, seize the Tower and liberate the Earl of Bath as leader. Of course the plot was betrayed, and Waller fetched up within its walls. No doubt whatever about his guilt, but, since he was a Member of Parliament, there was a disinclination to proceed by martial law. At his trial he made a brilliant speech, based on the plea that he 'made not this business [the plot] but found it'. It is likely that the intervention of Cromwell was more effective in saving Waller's life – was he not a relation? Waller had to pay the enormous fine of £10,000 and was banished the realm. And so a famous poet's life was saved for England. But it had been 'the nearest run thing'. Waller lived to become the most admired speaker in Parliament after the Restoration; no one followed him, however, for he saw through both sides.

Another middle-of-the-road man, a moderate, straight and honourable, was one of the ablest soldiers of the lot: the Devonshireman George Monk. He was a professional soldier who had done good service for the King in Ireland – and would have done better, if that man had known how to be served. On returning to England, he found his old regiment given away and himself fought at the head of it as a volunteer at Nantwich, where he was captured and taken to the Tower as a traitor. There he remained in dire necessity for two years, 1644–6, attempting to live on a pittance of seven shillings a week, for he had no means of his own. In the stress of war his Royalist brother scraped together fifty pounds to help him; eventually the King, who was not ungenerous (where only money was concerned), sent him a hundred pounds, for which Monk was eternally grateful.

His fellow West Countryman Pym had been anxious to recruit Monk's professional abilities for Parliament; and, in the end, the soldier consented to serve Parliament in Ireland. He engaged his honour and served Parliament faithfully, always with the saving clause that he was not to serve against the King. The tradition of the Tower is that, on his departure for Ireland, Bishop Wren gave him his blessing on this understanding. Monk proceeded to have a most distinguished career, trusted alike by Parliament and by Cromwell. It is no wonder that, when that episode was over, a Royalist at heart, he negotiated the Restoration of Charles II. It proved a marvel of prudence and political skill. He ended up vastly rich, Duke of Albemarle, hailed by Charles II as Father of his Country – which in a way he was. But he had married a silly woman, and his son was a numbskull, with whom the dukedom expired.

In 1650 there came into the Tower a fellow-poet and friend of Waller, Sir William Davenant. A fascinating and congenial character, some thought he was a by-blow of Shakespeare's on his journeys through Oxford, by the buxom hostess of the Crown inn. Certainly Sir William had much more in common with the dramatist than with mine host, not only genius but in temperament. He had fought bravely on the Royalist side and, an exile, was caught off the French coast transporting help to the Cavaliers in Virginia. Brought in to Cowes Castle, he was sent to the Tower for a couple of years. He was lucky to escape with his life; he certainly seems to have expected to die: it was not mere rhetoric that made him write to his friend Endymion Porter:

> I gave when last I was about to die
> The poets of this isle a legacy

This was his Heroic Poem, *Gondibert*, of which he had written the first two books. Imprisonment gave him the time to write a third: while in the Tower he published the three books of the poem, in 1651. His reprieve from trial and sentencing has been variously attributed, but it was civilised of the Puritan authorities to treat so distinguished an opponent with indulgence and release him. He lived on to become the Laureate of the Restoration, its most admired dramatist before Dryden.

In circumstances of revolution the scum is apt to rise to the surface, as with the Jacobins and the Reign of Terror they exercised in France in 1792–4. So it was – less barbarously, though no less loquaciously – in England with the Levellers. They have been given an adventitious importance in our time, for contemporary political reasons. And also quite anachronistically, for their programme of social and political equality was unworkable, as experienced men like Cromwell and Ireton well understood.

Their most vociferous leader was John Lilburne, 'Honest John' – as if others were not equally honest. Before the war he had been whipped and pilloried by Star Chamber for his violent attacks on the Church and the poor bishops. The Long Parliament made a hero of him, quashed his sentence, promised him a large compensation – and got what they deserved: henceforth he agitated in season and out of season for his reward. An incessant pamphleteer, like Prynne, in 1645 Lilburne attacked Prynne for the intolerance of the Presbyterians harsher, and with less justification (for they were a minority), than that of the Church. Lilburne found, as Milton had, that

> New Presbyter is but old Priest writ large.

Prynne replied with vehemence, and the pot boiled merrily, while the country was at sixes and sevens. Wenceslaus Hollar told Aubrey that when he had first come into England, 'which was a serene time of peace, the people both poor and rich did look cheerfully. But, at his return, he found the countenances of

John Lilburne, leader of the Levellers – whipped and pilloried by the King's government, and imprisoned by Parliament

the people all changed, melancholy, spiteful, as if bewitched.' As indeed they had been, by the nonsense they supposed themselves to think.

Too well treated by Parliament, Lilburne repaid them next year with a blistering attack on their General, the Earl of Manchester. At this the Parliament Lords sentenced Lilburne to seven years in the Tower and to pay a large fine – severer than anything the King's government had allotted him. In 1647 the Army made Fairfax Lieutenant of the Tower, and Lilburne was released. He celebrated by demanding the abolition of the Lords and agitating for the political programme of the Levellers, equality and all that – idiotic in the circumstances of the time. Next year Lilburne was back in the Tower, which must have seemed like home, but was released by Parliament, now at daggers drawn with the Army, which had won their victory for them but which they refused to pay. Lilburne lent himself, his voice and his pen, to the campaign now organised against the Army and Cromwell.

Lilburne attracted around him, as the manner is, a number of restless spirits who would not take even Yes for an answer. There was the printer Overton, who had made an onslaught on the stiff-necked Westminster Assembly of Presbyterian divines, which had given the ungodly to rejoice. Lilburne and Overton issued their programme in *The Agreement of the Free People of England* – the unspoken joke of which was that the Free People of

England were not agreed about anything. This was in 1649, the year of the King's execution which made a rift between the Puritans and the nation at large for ever. When the Army leaders refused to accept the unworkable nonsense of the Levellers as the foundation of the new Jerusalem, William Walwyn let fly with *England's New Chains Discovered*, which these impossible people found to be no better than the old. Actually the 'chains' they meant were no more than the necessary conditions of law and order.

When summoned before the new Council of State, they refused to acknowledge its jurisdiction. The Army leaders were having no nonsense of that kind and sent them off to the Tower. From this eyrie Lilburne, 'whom it was utterly impossible to deprive of ink', deluged London with protests, petitions, pamphlets, tracts. He managed to incite a mutiny in a regiment at Oxford. Summoned to trial, he protested that the Cromwellian judges were 'no more but ciphers to pronounce their verdict'. This was true enough, but such candour is unsettling to government: one of the judges declared it 'a damnable blasphemous heresy'. Banished, Honest John went off to the Netherlands, where he conspired with Cavaliers to overthrow Cromwell. When he came back to try it, he was returned to the Tower in 1653, whence he was transferred to Guernsey. Becoming a Quaker, this quietened him down and Cromwell, placable enough towards enemies on the Left, released him. Of this, or of old age, Lilburne shortly died:

> Is John departed, and is Lilburne gone!
> Farewell to Lilburne, and farewell to John:
> But lay John here, lay Lilburne hereabout,
> For if they ever meet they will fall out.

He was buried appropriately in the churchyard next to Bedlam.

Other oddities turn up in the Tower, besides the normal casualties of civil war – prisoners captured in battle, conspirators, traitors, i.e. those unlucky in the throw of the dice. In some we observe the agreeable process of revolutionaries eating each other up. Christopher Love was a Puritan who, when a boy at Oxford, was accustomed to 'hold out prating for more than an hour' at St Peter-le-Bailey. As army chaplain he took to inflammatory sermons; after the war was over he could not but burn his fingers in intrigues with the Royalists abroad and the Presbyterians in Scotland against the Puritan Army in England. In 1651 he was laid by the heels for treason; and at his trial acknowledged all

the charges, exhibiting all, and more than all, of the unyielding Puritan spirit.
  Clarendon tells us,

it is wonderful what operation this Presbyterian spirit had upon the minds of those who were possessed by it. This poor man, Love . . . when he was upon the scaffold, where he appeared with a marvellous undauntedness, he seemed so much delighted with the memory of all that he had done against his late Majesty and against the bishops, that he could not even then forbear to speak with animosity and bitterness against both. And in this raving fit, he laid his head upon the block with as much courage as the bravest and honestest man could do on the most pious occasion.

Love had published any number of polemical works: we may take as typical *England's Distemper, having Division and Error as its Cause*. After all, this was what poor Archbishop Laud had thought. But only Mr Love knew its cause – no idea that the distemper consisted of people like himself. Parliament settled his hash, as Laud could never have done, on Tower Hill.

  Miles Sindercombe, of a sinister name, was a quartermaster in the Parliamentary horse, who became a Leveller. In 1655 he was the chief agent in a plot to seize Monk and set the Army in Scotland against Cromwell. Next year he engaged himself to assassinate the Puritan dictator: he hired a house at Hammersmith, whence to shoot the Lord Protector on his way to Hampton Court, and lurked about Hyde Park and Whitehall for other opportunities. Missing his chance, he set fire to the chapel at Whitehall, hoping to profit from the confusion; but he and an accomplice were discovered. Condemned to death, and already severely wounded, he contrived to obtain some poison through his sister and died in the Tower. Royalists, of course, said that he had been put out of the way by Colonel Barksted, now Governor: 'Had he lived, his name had been registered with Brutus and Cato, and he had his statues as well as they.'

  Such was the spirit released by civil war.

  The old historian of the Tower, John Bayley, says truly, 'It would be an endless task to notice all the prisoners who were committed to the Tower, by the Parliament and the Army, during that melancholy period which preceded the decapitation of the King.' Or afterwards either, we may add. We may say that, on a conservative estimate, one-third of the peerage passed through its portals, many of them to emerge only on Tower Hill.

  Shortly after the King's death four peers were brought in: the Duke of Hamilton, the Earl of Holland, Lord Capel and the Earl of Norwich. The last escaped death at his trial by the casting vote of Speaker Lenthall, who was under a private obligation to him. Lord Holland had been a Parliament man, but had changed sides; great interest was made for his life by the Presbyterian party, but Cromwell, the whole-hogger, spoke with much animus against a turncoat and got him condemned to death. Lord Capel made a remarkable escape: he let himself down by a cord out of his chamber and thence over the outer wall into the ditch. 'But there, had he not been a head taller than most other men, he must have perished. The water and mud came up to his chin; the distance was great to the opposite side and, had not some friends been there to assist him, his exhausted spirits must have yielded.' They carried him to the Temple for a few days, then found him a lodging in Lambeth Marsh. But one evening a waterman suspected Capel, who was crossing the Thames in his wherry, and delated him. He was returned to the Tower and death; 'His betrayer, though rewarded by the Parliament, became the scorn and contempt of everybody, and lived afterwards in shame and misery.'

Along with the Levellers, in 1651, the Council of State, with military impartiality committed Lords Beauchamp, Bellasis, Chandos, 'upon suspicion of designing new troubles', and Lord Howard of Escrick for electoral bribery. Some time before, the Army leaders had not scrupled to imprison yet another elected Lord Mayor, Sir Abraham Reynardson, and manipulate the government of the City to suit them. In 1652 the Marquis of Worcester, who had spent a fortune on the Royalist cause, returned from exile impoverished. He was apprehended, but spared by Cromwell, and spent the next two years in the Tower agreeably engrossed in his scientific and mechanical studies, for he was a projector and inventor. In the year the Marquis was released the Earl of Oxford took his place, along with a group of Catholic Gerrards plotting to seize the Tower and restore the King. In 1655 Cromwell sent in his colleagues, Generals Penn and Venables, for their failure in the expedition to Jamaica, *pour encourager les autres.*

In the last year of the dictator's life, 1658, and in the prevailing insecurity of the eighteen months before the Restoration, any number of Royalists were confined, from the Duke of Buckingham downwards. In the very last months a few choice restless republicans were gathered in, such as Lambert and Hazlerigg, whom Monk outmanœuvred and then spared their lives. On the whole, the Restoration was effected with surprisingly little effusion of blood, except for the regicides, whom Charles II, easy-going as he was, could not forgive for beheading his father. Prynne, in accordance with his principles, tried to restrict the operation of the Act of Indemnity and except from its provisions a number of the late leaders. Hazlerigg was sent to the Tower, where he died next year. Lambert went back and forth between there and the isle of Guernsey, which gave him the opportunity to introduce the Guernsey lily into England, according to gardening lore.

Confinement in the Tower and later at Portsea Castle had a different effect upon the doctrinaire Republican of *Oceana*, James Harington: it turned his wits. According to Aubrey,

his durance in these prisons – he being a gentleman of a high spirit and hot head – was the procacatrique cause of his deliration or madness. Which was not outrageous, for he would discourse rationally enough and be very facetious company. But he grew to have a fancy that his perspiration turned to flies, and sometimes to bees, etc. 'Twas the strangest sort of madness that ever I found in anyone: talk of anything else, his discourse would be very ingenious and pleasant.

Along with the regicides who were captured, confined in the Tower, and killed off, the turn of two singular figures came who had not, strictly speaking, been regicides. No one had any sympathy for Sir Henry Vane. His dubious evidence had sworn Strafford's life away. He was an arrogant intellectual whom ordinary people found incomprehensible and daunting. He could probably have saved himself by submission, but that was not in his nature. Charles II wrote down,

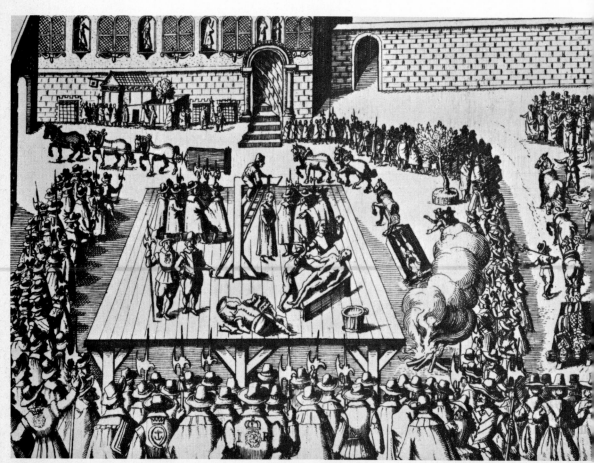

'Sir Henry Vane's carriage was so insolent as to justify all he had done. . . . Certainly he is too dangerous to let live, if we can honestly put him out of the way.' The intellectual went to his death with a courage people had not expected.

Hugh Peters, too, was afraid that he might not display courage when his turn came. He was unjustly condemned, for he had been no regicide, though – like Milton – he had defended it. Peters had done many good deeds in the day of his power, but no one defended him now: he suffered the revilings and cat-calls of the people as cruelly as Laud had done. Even on the scaffold at Charing Cross, he was taunted by an inhuman – or all too human – bystander, up-braiding him with Charles I's death, calling on him to repent. 'Friend,' said Peters mildly, 'You do not well to trample on a dying man. You are greatly mistaken: I had nothing to do in the death of the King.' In the Tower he preached his last sermon to his fellow-prisoners – he had been a famous preacher in his day. He took for his text the passage from the Psalms: 'I will say unto the God of my strength, why hast thou forgotten me: why go I thus heavily, while the enemy oppresseth me?'

It is a question that many of these people, dying for their convictions, might well ask.

Left: Hanging, drawing and quartering the regicides

A contemporary engraving of Hugh Peters' last sermon which he preached in the Tower to his fellow prisoners

30 Iuni 1679. R.P. ANTONIUS TURNER PRIESTER DER SOCIETEIT IESV GEHANGEN EN GEVIERENDEELT BUYTEN LONDEN.

30 Iuni 1679. R.P. IOANNES FENWICK PRIESTER DER SOCIETEYT IESV GEHANGEN EN GEVIERENDEELT BUYTEN LONDE.

den 30 Iuni 1679. R.P. IOANNES ... IESV GEHANGEN EN GEVIERENDEELT BUYTEN LONDEN.

30 Iuni 1679. R.P. GULIELMUS WARING VANDE SOCIETEYT IESV GEHANGEN EN GEVIERENDEELT BUYTEN LONDEN.

den 30 Iuni 1679 R.P. THOMAS ... IESV GEHANGEN EN GEVIERENDEELT BUYTEN LONDEN.

6 Sept 1679 R.P. CAROLUS BAKER PRIESTER DER SOCIETEYT IESV GEHANGEN EN GEVIERENDEELT BUYTEN LONDEN.

1 Aug 1679 R.P. PHILIPPUS ... IESV GEHANGEN EN GEVIERENDEELT BUYTEN LONDE.

TITUS OATES OP VOLLE BLYCKINGHE
OVERWONNEN VAN VALSCHE GHETUYGHEN

TITUS OATES

TITUS OATES WORT OP DEFERENTE PLSEN VPEREL...

II

The Restoration: Whig and Tory Antics

As the Restoration approached, the Tower loomed up as a decisive strongpoint of which to make sure. Of all people John Evelyn – by no means an unquiet spirit, but a submissive conservative, loyal to Church and King – tried to get it surrendered to Charles II before even the time was ripe or Monk had declared for him. How can Evelyn have so dangerously engaged himself? The answer is that the Lieutenant of the Tower had been at school with him at Westminster. The Old School Tie has been, and is, more important in English history and literature than people admit.

As early as 10 December 1659, Evelyn writes, 'I treated privately with Colonel Morley – then Lieutenant of the Tower and in great trust and power – concerning delivering it to the King and the bringing of him in, to the great hazard of my life. But the Colonel had been my schoolfellow and I knew would not betray me.' A few days later Evelyn made another attempt to seduce the Colonel. Next month Evelyn went to the Tower Chapel to press Morley to declare for the King, but he was doubtful and did not believe that Monk intended to bring in the King. It shows how prudent and politic Monk was, in waiting till the country was ready for the move. When the King was restored, he nominated Evelyn to be a Knight of the Bath at the coronation; but he declined the honour, regarding plain John Evelyn more honourable – as we do.

Charles II's coronation procession, in the manner customary through the centuries, was the last to take place. The ceremonies were conducted with meticulous care for precedent and particular splendour to bridge over the abyss that had opened up since the last one, and make people forget. It was extraordinary how quickly they did – people were glad to be quit of the canting Puritans with their nasal whine. Laud's friend Hyde, now an elderly Lord Chancellor, was head of the commission to arrange the coronation; with his historic sense nothing was omitted to make it memorable and expunge the past.

A Dutch print of Titus Oates in the stocks surrounded by the
victims of the Popish Plot which he claimed to have discovered

The coronation was fixed for St George's Day, 23 April 1661, to give plenty of time to repair damage of every kind from the late deplorable events. The day before, the King went by water down to the Tower, now safely under the command of a faithful Royalist, Sir John Robinson – Laud's nephew and heir. An immense number of Knights of the Bath had been created to fill up gaps, sixty-eight in all; so too with the peerage, six earls and ten barons: the social order was being repaired. Hyde was made Earl of Clarendon for his services to the monarchy; Sir Bevil Grenville's son became Earl of Bath; Pepys's master, the Cromwellian Montagu – a complete cynic who had taken advantage of every turn of tide – blossomed forth as Earl of Sandwich. Even strait-laced Puritans like Denzil Holles and Lord Robartes, who had rejected the father, consented to take honours at the hand of the son. Not that they had seen the error of their ways, but simply what happened when the people were given their head.

The mob viewed the spectacle of the procession on 22 April with as much enthusiasm as a grand execution. All the officers of state and of the royal household, along with the nobility and principal gentry were there to greet the King and accompany him through the City to Westminster – where he was to be crowned by Juxon, Laud's colleague, whom Charles I on the scaffold had adjured to 'Remember!' Behind the new King rode the new Duke of Albemarle (former Monk), who had managed things so well. The Lieutenant of the Tower commanded the horse and foot at the tail-end.

The crowds were amazed at the exhibition of splendour,

... almost inconceivable. And much wonder it caused to outlandish persons, who were acquainted with our late troubles and confusions, how it was possible for the English to appear in so rich and stately a manner. It is incredible to think what costly clothes were worn that day: the cloaks could hardly be seen what silk or satin they were made of, for the gold and silver laces and embroidery that were laid upon them. Besides the inestimable value and treasures of diamonds, pearls and other jewels worn upon their backs and in their hats: to omit the sumptuous and rich liveries of their pages and footmen.

People must have been glad of the colour and display, after the drab rule of the Saints. But it serves to underline the historical consideration that, in spite of everything, the real wealth of the country was increasing.

We cannot call on Pepys and Evelyn to describe the procession for us – they were waiting for it at Westminster. In the course of Charles II's reign they were both in and out of the Tower a good deal, Pepys as a hard-working official of

Charles II's Coronation procession

the Admiralty, Evelyn as a gentlemanly amateur, a Commissioner of the Mint; later on, it must have surprised the former to find himself a prisoner for a while, visited by the latter. In June 1661, Pepys had to go down there to bespeak ammunition for his master, Sandwich's ships and, curious as always, 'with much pleasure walked quite around the Tower, which I never did before'. In November he viewed the reception of the Russian ambassador on Tower Hill, appropriately in unwonted snow and fur caps. Next May he was dining with Lady Sandwich and taking all the children to see the lions. Later on, a Moroccan ambassador presented the King with a couple more lions and thirty ostriches for the Tower zoo.

Now Lord Sandwich is all worked up about a rumour of the treasure hidden by the Cromwellian Governor, Barksted – supposed to be £7000, to be shared with the King, if found. That autumn Pepys made three searches in a cellar and, digging away, bursts out, 'Lord, what a young simple fantastique cockscomb is made Deputy-Governor!' A Tower woman deposed that she and Barksted had concealed the money in butter-firkins; it turned out to be a mare's nest. Then Pepys accompanied the King and the Duke of York to see the real Dunkirk money at the Tower – in exchange for its surrender to France. None of

The two famous diarists of the Restoration, John Evelyn (*left*) and Samuel Pepys (*right*). The latter was himself imprisoned in the Tower for a short time during the Popish Plot hysteria

them had ever seen so much cash. It was accompanied by a good deal of 'frothy discourse', on the part of the royals, about the large codpieces provided on the armours – talk of which Mr Pepys, with his Puritan upbringing, disapproved: he preferred to look at the stamps for the new coinage.

Meanwhile John Evelyn was serving on the committee to regulate the Mint; in March 1664 he signalises a specimen of a fine new milled coin. In the summer of 1666 he was sitting there with the Commissioners of Ordnance concerning saltpetre; and in September notes that it was only the demolitions around the Tower, with the change of wind, that saved it from destruction in the Great Fire. Later on, in 1679, he returns to try a metal at the Mint, and watches the 'incomparable graver' Rotier at work, who was emulating the ancients in metal and stone. Certainly the coins and medals of the Restoration, in which Evelyn was so much interested, have never been surpassed. It is through the eyes of Mr Pepys that we have the best view of the Great Fire that devastated the City in the first days of September 1666. Here we can go into it only so far as it affected the Tower. The Fire broke out in the night of Saturday, 1 September, with a high wind blowing. Early on Sunday morning Pepys was called up by the maids to take a view of it some distance away by London Bridge.

So I made myself ready presently and walked to the Tower, and there got up upon one of the high places, Sir John Robinson's little son going up with me. And there I did see that end of the Bridge all on fire, and an infinite great fire on this and the other side the end of the Bridge. So down, with my heart full of trouble to the Lieutenant of the Tower, who tells me that it began this morning in the King's Baker's house in Pudding Lane, and that it hath burned St Magnus's Church and most part of Fish Street already.

Pepys got down to the water side and off up the river to Whitehall to inform the King and the Duke of York of what he had seen, 'and that unless his Majesty did command houses to be pulled down nothing could stop the Fire'.

The Fire burned all Sunday, Monday and Tuesday, engulfing the City westward as far as Blackfriars, lapping along the river bank, then northwards. People piled their goods on the open space of Tower Hill, Pepys among them. On the fourth day he loaded the rest of his goods on a lighter, and dug a pit in his garden to lay in his Navy Office papers, his wine and Parmesan cheese. Distracted but, consumed with the curiosity that in him amounted to genius, he took Sir William Penn along with him to Tower Street and 'there met the Fire . . . people working from one end to the other, the Fire coming on in that narrow street, on both sides, with infinite fury'.

The Great Fire of London painted by Jan Wyck.
The fire burned right up to the Tower moat

The grave danger to the Tower was that, at that time – it was in the midst of the Dutch War – the White Tower was packed with stores of gunpowder for the Navy. Evelyn was terrified by the thought of what might happen if the flames leaped across the houses that encroached upon the walls. If the magazine had exploded 'it would not only have beaten down and destroyed all the Bridge, but sunk and torn all the vessels in the river, and rendered the demolition beyond all expression for several miles about the country'.

By this time the resolution was taken to blow up houses with gunpowder, in the path of the Fire, and around the Tower. Mr Pepys, 4 September: 'I after supper walked in the dark down to Tower Street and there saw it all on fire, at the Trinity House on that side, and the Dolphin tavern on this side, which was very near us; and the Fire with extraordinary vehemence. Now begins the practice of blowing up of houses in Tower Street, those next the Tower – which did frighten the people more than anything.' The poor people thought that its cannon were being fired to bring down the houses and clear a safe space around it. 'But it stopped the fire where it was done, it bringing down the houses to the ground in the same places they stood.'

This, according to a newsletter reporting into the country, saved the Tower. The Fire had 'burned down to the very moat. They were fearful of the Tower, carried out all the gunpowder, and brought out all the goldsmiths' money – which was at first carried thither – to Whitehall, above £1,200,000' in bullion.

On the fifth day, when the Fire ceased, the whole City lay waste; and the King came, and saw that it was bad.

The official narrative assured the nation that the catastrophe was not the work of its enemies, but that of Providence, 'the heavy hand of God upon us for our sins'. Also, it was 'by the blessing of God' that on Thursday it was beat down and extinguished. Scores of thousands were ruined. But 'about the Tower the seasonable orders for plucking down houses, to secure the magazines of powder, was more especially successful, that part being up the wind. Notwithstanding which it came almost to the very gates of it, so as by this early provision the several stores of war lodged in the Tower were entirely saved.' And for saving the stores for war they were 'particularly to give God thanks'.

Mr Pepys had more varied avocations. On Ordnance business one day, he was at dinner with the Lieutenant when they were disturbed by the King's arrival to inspect the new Storehouse that had been built: a 'noble sight'. In December 1666 there was a quarrel in the House of Lords between the Duke of Buckingham and the Marquis of Dorchester; blows were struck and both were committed to the Tower. The Lieutenant took Pepys thither to dinner,

. . . where I dined at the head of his table, next his lady, who is comely and seeming sober and stately, but very proud and very cunning, or I am mistaken, and wanton, too. This day's work will bring the Lieutenant of the Tower £350. But a strange, conceited, vain man he is that ever I met withal, in his own praise. Thence home, and upon Tower Hill saw three or four hundred seamen get together; one, standing upon a pile of bricks, made his sign with his handkercher upon his stick, and called all the rest to him, and several shouts they gave. This made me afeared, so I got home as fast as I could.

Perhaps Pepys had not far to go, for while his house was preparing he had lodgings on the Hill, at the Angel Tavern. In March 1669 we find him visiting Sir William Coventry, who was temporarily confined for challenging the crazy Duke of Buckingham. We notice at this time how frequently hot-blooded and hot-headed peers were sent there for duelling or sending challenges. Coventry was a good House of Commons man and had much support against the ministers constituting the Cabal. Many of his friends came to pay their respects. Mr Pepys 'walked and talked with him an hour alone, from one good thing to another'. They exchanged political gossip, and then 'walked down to the Stone Walk, which is called my Lord of Northumberland's Walk, being paved by someone of that title that was prisoner there [Mr Pepys was no historian]. At the end of it there is a piece of iron upon the wall, with his arms upon it, and holes to put in a peg for every turn that they make upon that walk.' We learn that Northumberland, in his grand manner, used to hire the Brick Tower as an occasional residence for his son, from the then Master of Ordnance, Lord Carew. (We can see *him* upon his resplendent tomb at Stratford.)

Pepys kept his resolution not to drink whisky, after once drinking 'a cup of strong water' at Tower Gate for his health, against his vow. We find him frequently there on business, walking round the Hill, or taking barge or boat – and so to Greenwich. One Lord's Day in Maytime 1668, he is engaged on the Tower Wharf flirting, and rather more, with pretty Mrs Lowther. It was raining, which gave Pepys the chance to shelter her under his cloak, while he sent for a pair of shoes for her. 'And there I did pull the others off and put them on, elle being peu shy, but do speak con mighty kindness to me that she would desire me pour su mari if it were to be done.'

Shortly a very different character fetched up within the walls. This was the holy William Penn, who wrote a naughty book – quite like old times – called *The Sandy Foundation Shaken*, which called in question the sacred truths of the Creed on the Trinity and Atonement, and on Calvinist Justification. John Evelyn called it 'a blasphemous book', and Penn was committed close prisoner. This gave him the chance to write his best-seller, *No Cross, No Crown*, on the Christian duty of self-sacrifice: this was very popular, especially with those who preferred the idea of vicarious self-sacrifice. Stillingfleet, the eminent divine, was sent to reason (if that is the word) with him. But Penn found that 'the Tower is to me the worst argument in the world. My prison shall be my grave before I will budge a jot.' However, he did budge, and wrote a conciliatory tract affirming at least a larger hope in the deity of Christ, if this were more reasonable of him. Anyway it got him out.

Pepys celebrated St George's Day, 1668, by carrying a bevy of lady-friends to the Tower, 'and showed them all to be seen there, and, among other things, the Crown and Sceptres and rich plate, which I myself never saw before, and indeed is noble, and I mightily pleased with it'. Much of this had been made for Charles II's coronation, the ancient regalia having been broken up by the Commonwealth, thinking to put an end to such nonsense. The next thing was the brazen attempt of Colonel Blood to steal the Crown Jewels.

Blood was a Cromwellian Irish adventurer, who already had several exploits to his discredit. In 1671 he put in practice a bold plan to capture the Crown Jewels, at first introducing himself to the Keeper, Talbot Edwards, 'in the habit of a parson, with a long cloak, cassock and canonical girdle, and brought a woman with him whom he called his wife'. The 'wife' desired to see the crown, and, having seen it, feigned a faint. This gained them admission to the Keeper's private rooms for the lady to rest on a bed. For this civility Blood returned a few days later with a present of gloves for Mrs Edwards, and rapidly improved the acquaintance with the offer of a 'nephew, who hath two or three hundred a year in land, and is at my disposal', for a daughter the Edwardses had to dispose of.

The early morning 'marriage' a few days later provided the opportunity to bring in a number of confederates, who, under their finery, were armed. On pretence of waiting for his wife, Blood prevailed on Edwards to show them the Crown Jewels, to pass the time. When the gullible Keeper entered the room where they were kept, carefully closing the door, he was overwhelmed and gagged. When he tried to call out, he was knocked down with a mallet. One gallant fellow pocketed the sacred orb in his loose breeches; Blood crushed the crown under his parson's cloak; a third was filing the sceptre in two to bag it, when young Edwards returned and the alarm was given. The improbable cry went up, 'Treason, the crown is stolen!' The desperados were captured while making off, the loot on them.

Colonel Blood's summing up of the affair was cool: 'It was a bold attempt, but it was for a crown.' Not the least extraordinary part of it was that he was never punished and an indulgent monarch restored to him his confiscated estate in Ireland. A sense of humour always paid with Charles, and Blood's next move was to refuse to confess anything except to the King himself. The merry monarch, who considered attending debates in the House of Lords as 'good as a stage-play', was agog to hear Blood's own account. In the course of it Charles learned that only the sacredness of his person had saved him from

Colonel Blood and his accomplices making off with the Crown Jewels after knocking out the Keeper with a mallet

being assassinated while bathing at Battersea. The King was charmed, and Blood was often seen about the palace, where he had found a protector in the scandalous Buckingham, who shared the King's sense of humour.

Not so John Evelyn, however, who had none. He met Blood one day, dining at the Treasurer's: 'The man had not only a daring but a villainous unmerciful look; a false countenance, but very well spoken and dangerously insinuating.' Evelyn could not understand why he had been pardoned, but gathered that the real reason was that Blood did the King service as a spy among the sectaries.

And this apparently was the secret of it.

As Charles II's reign went on the political and party struggle became more acute, envenomed and dangerous. Once more it came to concentrate on the issue of the Succession. For Charles II had no legitimate offspring, though any number of bastards, for whom the state had to provide; and his heir, his brother James, Duke of York, was a declared Roman Catholic in a frantically Protestant country. Charles knew well what an obstinate fool his brother was, and gave him only three years of rule, if he succeeded – and this turned out exactly right. Charles was intelligent enough not to declare himself, until on his death-bed. But by the Secret Treaty of Dover, 1672, he pledged himself to make England Catholic and bound her to the chariot of Louis XIV – thus aiding him to achieve the European ascendancy which it took a generation of war to correct – in return for the subsidies Parliament would not grant.

After this there was no trusting Charles: the conflict over and around the monarchy inflamed party spirit with religious venom and hysteria. The supposed discovery of a Popish Plot by Titus Oates in 1678 produced a panic like MacCarthyism in America in our time, with its dreadful trail of persecution of innocent Catholics, beheadings, genuine plots against the Stuart monarchy, and a furious campaign on the part of the Whigs to exclude James from the throne. James's own conduct during his brief period as King proved them to have been right about him, and both Whigs and Tories united in the Revolution of 1688 to get rid of him. After that there remained a party in sympathy with the exiled Stuarts – or, even more, out of sympathy with the charmless Germans who took their place (they had at least more common sense). This, in turn, led to the Rebellions of 1715 and 1745, from the backward Highlands.

All this is faithfully reflected in the story of the Tower.

It is impossible to go in detail into the harassing, and sometimes harrowing, antics of Whig and Tory, the bitter feuds and vendettas, the mutual proscriptions followed by sudden changes of side, the swallowing of 'principles' – nothing easier to eat than words, in politics. To make sense of it all we must remind ourselves that these grandees were in it for power and money – it was a struggle for survival in the snake-pit; some were in it even for fun: they liked it and were conditioned to it. To the appreciative reader, centuries after, we at least have the consolation we have not got today, that it gave rise to masterpieces of literature like the political satires of Dryden, the prose works of Halifax, Locke and Swift.

The leakage of the Secret Treaty of Dover broke the Cabal, some of whom had connived at it, while others had been fooled by it. Charles now found a tough Yorkshire Tory, Danby, to manage Parliament for him and hold the Whigs at bay by an extensive system of bribery which had its effect. Unfortunately there was not enough money to bait the biggest fish, and in the end Charles ruined his minister, as the Stuarts often had done their ablest servants. Danby was a patriot, anxious to resist Louis xiv's rise to domination. Charles used Danby to raise subsidies from Parliament for war against France; the King then used this position to lever Louis into granting him huge subsidies, six million *livres* a year for three years, to make him independent of Parliament. What was worse, Charles made Danby countersign the agreement. Though it was contrary to his principles and policies, Danby did it to hold on to power and the chances of making a fortune that went with it.

Where Charles would never make a stand – except for the rights of monarchy itself, the only thing he believed in – Danby stood up stoutly to a Parliament increasingly dominated by the Whigs, as they were by the genius for publicity and intrigue of Shaftesbury, or 'Little Sincerity', as Charles called him. Dryden called him Achitophel:

> Of these the false Achitophel was first,
> A name to all succeeding ages cursed.
> For close designs and crooked counsels fit,
> Sagacious, bold, and turbulent of wit,
> Restless, unfixed in principles and place,
> In power unpleased, unpatient of disgrace:
> A fiery soul which, working out its way,
> Fretted the pigmy body to decay,
> And o'er-informed the tenement of clay.
> A daring pilot in extremity . . .

Opposite above: A view of the Royal Mint in the Tower
Below: A Victorian print of the fire which destroyed the Armoury in 1841
Overleaf: The Tower and the Mint; a painting by T. Shotter Boys in the mid-nineteenth century

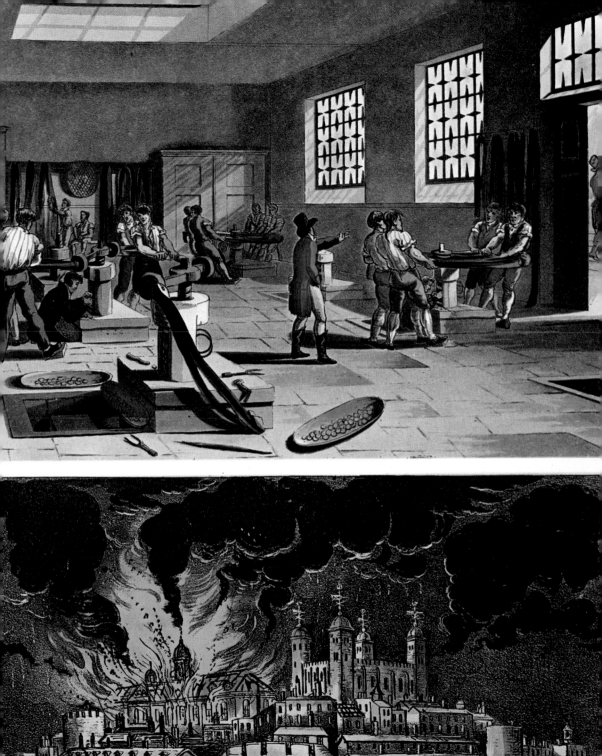

An old Cromwellian, Shaftesbury was certainly an extremist; this was his weakness: he overplayed his hand.

Danby took advantage in 1677 of a constitutional error on the part of the Whig leaders, attacking the legality of a prorogation of Parliament when it didn't suit them, to pop four of them in the Tower: the Duke of Buckingham, and Lords Shaftesbury, Salisbury and Wharton. Shaftesbury and Salisbury made the insulting request that they might have their own cooks with them. Their behaviour was no less unaccommodating: imprisoned separately, they met at chapel where they consulted with each other, talking all through the service. Shaftesbury kept up a barrage of petitions for release, though making no submission or acknowledgment of his error, organised sympathy in the City where his chief support was, and then sued a writ of *habeas corpus* in King's Bench. For a man with an open ulcer in his side, with a silver pipe for its issue, his energy was phenomenal; but it was not only his body that was ulcerated.

He was kept longer in the Tower than the others, and the rest did him good: his health improved. By nature an intellectual he did a great deal of reading and found pleasure in studying the war-maps of Europe brought in to him. He was let out in February 1678. In October there broke upon the country the news of the Popish Plot, with the lying revelations of Titus Oates, corroborated, it seemed, by the murder of the good Protestant J.P. Sir Edmund Berry Godfrey, the mystery of which no one has solved to this day. Panic swept the country, more especially London; Shaftesbury took his opportunity to drive it on to lunatic heights and sacrifice innocent lives.

That same month five unfortunate backwoods peers who happened to be Catholics were seized and taken to the Tower: Lords Arundell of Wardour, Bellasis, Petre, Powis and Stafford. Titus Oates – the MacCarthy of the time – was prepared to swear their lives away; the King could not save them, and James was hampered by the fact that there *had* been a Jesuit *consulta* in his wife's apartments at Whitehall for the furtherance of the Catholic cause. William Howard, Lord Stafford, was singled out for trial for high treason, because weaker than the others and 'less able to labour his own defence'. Again and again he protested that all that he had done was to discuss ways and means of gaining toleration (for Catholics). But he was 'not a man beloved, especially of his own family', and all his kinsmen, except one, voted him guilty. His trial was driven on by a relation, the third Lord Howard of Escrick, who had been a republican, one of Cromwell's lifeguards. He had been in the Tower in 1674 for being in correspondence with the Dutch in war-time, and was to be again in 1681. He ended his career in triumph by bringing the republican Algernon Sidney and Lord Russell to the block. Not a very nice member of that family so much to the fore in these pages!

Lord Stafford was condemned, and carried out to be beheaded on 29 December 1679. Lord Petre remained within, until he died in 1683. Oates swore that Bellasis was to head the Catholic Army of his imagination (but which James II tried within a few years to bring into being): Bellasis remained there till February 1684. Lord Arundell occupied himself with writing inferior religious verse. Lord Powis, of a Catholic branch of the Herberts, was a sensible moderate, but his wife was 'a zealous managing Papist', and she was brought in to accompany him for a supposed share in the 'Meal-Tub Plot'. The air was thick with plots and conspiracies, and collective hysteria such as crowds generate. Nor were peers the only victims; among others brought in were the head of the Tichborne family, and John Carroll of the name to become well known in Maryland.

The Popish Plot achieved Shaftesbury's grand aim of bringing down Danby, who had from the first discredited Titus Oates' lies; the answer to this was to charge him with being a party to the Plot – Danby who, of all things, knew which side his bread was buttered and how absurd it was to be anything but a Protestant in such a world. More to the point were his double-dealings, at Charles's behest, with Louis. Danby thought that he had made all well and purchased a pardon from the King under the Great Seal, by marrying his daughter to Charles's bastard, the Earl of Plymouth. Nothing availed him; like Strafford, he was proceeded against by attainder, and was sent to the

Tower, in April 1679. He pleaded his pardon: this was taken as an admission of the charges. He remained in the Tower for practically five years.

Like that other Yorkshireman again, Danby remained at first a power from his prison. Shaftesbury and the Whigs moved forward from the ground they had won with the Plot to demand the exclusion of James from the throne. This objective was sensible enough, as events proved; but they made the fatal mistake of putting forward as candidate for the throne their own creature, Charles's senior bastard, the Duke of Monmouth. As the agitation for the Exclusion Bill reached its climax and people thought that 1640 and the days of the Long Parliament had returned, Danby kept urging the King to hold firm and outface the Opposition – which eventually he did – and meanwhile to secure the Tower and prepare to meet insurrection.

Like Shaftesbury, Danby did not cease to campaign from within the Tower: he put forth libels and tracts, he went in for a diet of pamphleteering – and, as to the rest, for a milk-diet. For he was ill:

> He is as stiff as any stake,
> And leaner Dick than any rake:
>   Envy is not so pale.
> And though by selling of us all
> He brought himself into Whitehall
>   He looks like bird of gaol.

He conducted his campaign for release with tireless industry and skill, but without effect: he was always, again like Strafford, too unpopular. And Shaftesbury riposted by accusing him of plotting Godfrey's murder. Shaftesbury could always command popularity, and the credulous crowd believed him.

An Irish Catholic intriguer of good birth, Edward Fitzharris, was made use of to incriminate Danby. This man had spent years in Catholic intrigues at Court, through Charles's French mistress, the Duchess of Portsmouth (there was no Duke), and he had in fact had interviews with the King through her channel. He had written a pamphlet advocating the deposition of Charles as well as the exclusion of James, probably intending to palm it off on a Whig, then turn informer. Betrayed by a Catholic accomplice, he was sent to the Tower, where he pretended that he could discover the secret of Godfrey's murder and implicated Danby. The Commons impeached Fitzharris, as it were in inverted commas, not meaning to destroy him but to get at the Court. The Chaplain of the Tower, Francis Hawkins, then took him in hand in the interests of the Court, offering Fitzharris pardon for a bogus confession

A popular broadsheet describing the Popish Plot

Two great political rivals of the reign of Charles II imprisoned in the Tower at the same time: Thomas Osborne, Earl of Danby (*left*) and Anthony Ashley Cooper, Earl of Shaftesbury (*right*)

charging Lord Howard of Escrick with writing the libel against King and Duke. (Lord Howard had befriended Fitzharris.) The informer was thereupon executed; the Chaplain was rewarded with the Deanery of Chichester; the indictment against Lord Howard was withdrawn. Danby received no redress for all the libels now circulating against him – too smeared and unpopular.

We observe that there was a lively reptilian element in the politics of the age.

For Shaftesbury now came to join his great enemy in the Tower – besides the remaining four Popish Lords he had put there, not to mention Lord Howard of Escrick. The climax of the Exclusion agitation had been reached with the Parliament that met that year at Oxford. Charles had had his first stroke – probably with the strain of it all, or from the strain of his dissipated life; but he had now got his subsidies from Louis XIV, could dispense with Parliament for the rest of his reign, and live a (politically) quiet life. Moreover the country was tiring of agitation, with the fuel stoked up by Shaftesbury's bringing over Monmouth, contrary to Charles's order – the nation did not want his bastard for king.

The Restoration: Whig and Tory Antics

The Tory reaction could now foreclose on the Whig leader: Shaftesbury was taken to the Tower by water, 2 July 1681. Tradition says that when someone called out 'God deliver you from your enemies', he replied, 'I have nothing to fear: they have: pray God to deliver them from me.' If true, it is just like his impudence. There were other stories put about this popular figure – to the effect that when one of the Popish Lords asked what brought him there, he replied that he had been ill with ague and was come to take some Jesuits' powder. It at least shows how popular the Jesuits had made themselves by a century of intrigue. It was true that he was ill, and he was permitted to take the air in his coach, with his lady and servants, within the Tower. In the heat of August the Lieutenant moved him to cooler quarters.

Not being brought to trial as he wished, Shaftesbury feared that he might end his feverish life where he was. So he issued instructions for the sale of his stud at St Giles's in Dorset, and offered to exile himself for the rest of his life to Carolina, of which he was Proprietor. Brought to trial, he was acquitted: 'Immediately the people fell ahollaing and shouting; the bells rang, bonfires were made, and such public rejoicing in the City that never such an insolent defiance of authority was seen.' His grand friends celebrated in more respectable style, by striking a fine medal with his bust on one side, the Tower on the other with the sun emerging from a cloud. *Laetamur* – let us rejoice. He did not rejoice for long: the Tory reaction at length removed his basis of support in the City Corporation. Without their protection he thought it prudent to escape – which he did in the appropriate disguise of a Presbyterian minister, and ended his mischievous days in Holland.

The event has come down to us, celebrated in Dryden's splendid satire, *The Medal*, with its comment on the adage *Vox populi vox dei*:

> Almighty Crowd, thou shorten'st all dispute:
> Power is thy essence, wit thy attribute!
> Nor Faith nor Reason make thee at a stay,
> Thou leapst o'er all external truths in thy Pindaric way!
> Crowds err not, though to both extremes they run:
> To kill the father and recall the son –

a reference to Charles's stroke and the Whigs bringing Monmouth back to the country in expectation.

> This side today, and that tomorrow burns,
> So all are God Almighties in their turns.

There follows a brilliant summing up of Shaftesbury's career from Presbyterian humbug to Restoration debauchee :

> He cast himself into the saint-like mould,
> Groaned, sighed, and prayed while godliness was gain,
> The loudest bagpipe of the squeaking train.
> But as 'tis hard to cheat a juggler's eyes,
> His open lewdness he could ne'er disguise.
> Besides, their pace was formal, grave, and slack,
> His nimble pace outran the heavy pack.
> Yet still he found his fortune at a stay,
> Whole droves of blockheads choking up his way.

Excellent as literature, there was political perception in that summing up.

Meanwhile Charles II was not incurring the odium of releasing his servant Danby, who had petitioned the Oxford Parliament for a hearing in vain. Next year, 1682, he appeared in person before King's Bench to ask for bail : it was refused. He was pursued by family troubles, which we need not go into. His wife had access to him, and friends were fairly free to come and go. One of them found him 'pretty well, good company, and temperate in what he said'. In December 1683 Evelyn visited him, and was received with much kindness – were they not both loyal Tories, Church of England men, and good patriots? It was the French influence, exerted through the Duchess of Portsmouth, that kept Danby so long languishing. At length, in the year before he died, Charles exerted himself: 'He said that, if the Judges would not bail you – which he would see and speak with the Judges tomorrow – he would, by God, free you himself.' When Danby appeared at Whitehall to kiss the King's hand, he complained of his long imprisonment; but perhaps the fortune he made for his family in the King's service had made it worth while. It is expedient that one man should be sacrificed for the family.

Along with the great men who were victims of the Popish Plot panic there was one small man who, by the accident of his genius as a diarist, means more to us than any of them: little Mr Pepys. He was also an admirable civil servant, indefatigable in his labours for the Navy. This brought him into close touch with its head, the Duke of York, as Lord High Admiral and Pepys was in consequence one of those exposed by association at the time of the Plot. His efficiency had raised up a number of enemies, headed by William Harbord, a Whig MP who wanted his job. Pepys was accused in Parliament of piracy,

Popery, and treason, the 'evidence' fabricated by a lying adventurer of the Titus Oates breed, Colonel Scott, who fed Shaftesbury with such information. Patently false as it was, and in spite of a most able, factual defence in the Commons, Pepys was sent to the Tower on 22 May 1679, and a weak subordinate, Will Hayter, took over his office. A Tory friend wrote, 'Mr Pepys is to be pulled to pieces.'

But Mr Pepys was nothing daunted: buoyant as a cork, he wrote to the Duke of York in exile, whose fatuity had endangered them all, that it was 'hard for me to tell your Highness which of the two enjoys the greater pleasure: whether Mr Harbord in public from the contemplation of the conquest his malice has obtained over me, or I in private from what my innocence tells me I shall sometime or other – if any justice may be hoped for – obtain against him.' The mishap was financially unfortunate: next day, 10 June, Pepys wrote that it had all been so sudden 'as I have been forced to be beholden to my friends for £100 to pay my fees and defray my expenses here, and will cost more'.

However, Pepys enjoyed visits from kind Mr Houblon, who stood bail for him, and Evelyn who dined with him and took the opportunity to salute Lords Stafford and Petre at the same time. The King himself sent Mr Pepys a fat buck out of Enfield Chase to feed his friends. Shortly Mr Pepys was out of the Tower and into the Marshalsea, under the jurisdiction of the Common Law – and so to rehabilitation and ultimate reinstatement.

Before Shaftesbury's flight, while he lay doggo in the City, he had urged insurrection upon his followers as the only response to the Tory reaction in full flood. The Whig or Country party were now in complete disarray, largely as the result of his extremism. Monmouth, though popular for his extraordinarily handsome looks and his winning manners, was a feather-head politically, and a non-starter for the throne. Sensible Whigs looked to the Protestant succession of Mary and William of Orange – James's elder daughter and her husband – and meanwhile to place constitutional limitations upon James during the interval of his rule. The divisions among the Whigs enabled James to succeed without any check upon him – and so to run straight on to the rocks. Shaftesbury favoured agitation in the City, and in the confusion to seize the Tower, along with insurrection elsewhere. An extremist group plotted to assassinate Charles and James – the Rye House Plot. These plots incriminated other Whig leaders, though they had not given their assent to them but merely talked: the fate that befell them more than bore out Dryden's characterisation of Achitophel.

The uncovering of the Rye House Plot immediately endangered Lord Russell, the Earl of Essex, and Algernon Sidney, who were cast into the Tower on 26 June 1683. Others followed, including Major John Wildman, who had often been there before, an arch-plotter who had lived a lifetime of plotting and always managed to escape, a cat with nine lives. Not so the three aristocrats. Wildman, an inveterate pamphleteer, was a close associate of Algernon Sidney. Sidney was an old Commonwealthman, a doctrinaire intellectual of a republican cast of mind. He was the grandson of the Wizard Earl of Northumberland – his name Algernon came from the Percies – and he inherited his stubborn temper and his arrogance from him, his opposition-mindedness from that family. Brought to trial, he made an extremely able defence of himself – the chief witness against both him and Russell being the turncoat Lord Howard of Escrick, whom the historian, Sir Charles Firth, described as 'a man discredited by his character, his complicity and his contradictory statements'. Both Russell and Sidney were condemned to death; neither was guilty. Sidney refused to make the usual application to the monarch that the family might have the body: it is part of the verbal tradition at Penshurst that he said, 'Let the King have my arse to make him a purse.'

On the morning of Russell's trial, Essex – he was a Capel, not a Devereux – cut his throat in the Tower. The government claimed that this was a confession of guilt; it was nothing of the kind, but a confession of despair. Essex was, in fact, a moderate, who had given both the King and the Whigs good advice all along; he had not even wished to exclude James, but to place constitutional limitations upon him. Now Essex's own party had lost that opportunity through their extremists and their own divisions. Nothing is more sickening than the idiocies of one's own side in politics; Essex saw victory emerging for James, and he was driven to despair.

In the Tower he had been taken to the same apartments as those from which his Royalist father, Lord Capel, had been conducted to execution in 1649. One sees something of the family associations, the inherited affiliations, of the Tower. Essex was heard to commend the action of the Wizard Earl's father in committing suicide to save his estates. Sleepless, he recalled his last interview as a youth of seventeen with his father – and sent for a razor. Charles II, who was not an inhumane man, said: 'My Lord Essex might have tried my mercy: I owe a life to his family.'

There was even more pathos in Lord Russell's case, for he was young, innocent, and very much in love with his remarkable wife, Rachel Wriothesley, grand-daughter of Shakespeare's Southampton. She was the co-heiress through whom the Russells inherited their rich London estate, and Southampton House was a dynastic meeting place of opposition to the Stuarts. In the Tower Russell showed perfect confidence in his innocence and, a virtuous man, spent his time reading his Bible. A charming touch of aristocractic chivalry passed between him and Monmouth, who gracefully offered to take Russell's place and share his fate, an offer which Russell as gracefully declined.

Lord Howard of Escrick agreeably provided the evidence, though Russell had not so much as heard the particular design for complicity in which he was condemned; the witnesses for his defence were of unimpeachable authority. Russell made a solemn protest against the illegality of his condemnation; but Charles II, usually as humane as he was cynical, had been hardened by the exigencies of politics and merely commuted the sentence from hanging to beheading, with 'a sarcastical glance at Lord Stafford's case'. The King had been unable to save Lord Stafford, who was equally innocent on the other side. The Whigs had driven on his death – even Essex had urged it on: it was now a head for a head.

Russell's tragic fate aroused widespread sympathy, and Rachel Russell spent the rest of her long life driving the point home against the Stuarts. People saw the unwisdom of the monarchy making an enemy of so influential a house, closely connected with the Cavendishes: these people brought about the Revolution of 1688. She was an indefatigable correspondent; her Letters and Russell's biography were best-sellers in the eighteenth century – in old second-hand book shops one used frequently to come upon them: they did no good to the memory of the Stuarts among the Wig aristocracy. One still finds Russell and Sidney's names inscribed as Whig heroes, martyrs for liberty, in the dilapidated temples upon what is left of their grounds.

The one who got off scot-free was, of course, Major John Wildman; there is a charm upon him, in both senses – a fascinating rogue. An old-time Leveller and advocate of equality, he at least believed in equality of opportunity – and made a fortune out of speculating in the estates of Royalists confiscated for their convictions. In 1654 he had plotted to combine Levellers with Royalists to overthrow Cromwell. At the moment of his seizure he was dictating a 'Declaration of the Free and Well-affected People of England now in arms against the tyrant Oliver Cromwell'. The tyrant popped him into the Tower for a year, but agreeably released him on the petition of a number of Wildman's fellow-speculators: the affluent Leveller was able to raise security for £10,000.

Shortly after the Restoration Wildman got a severer sentence for his Republican plotting: six years, at first in the Tower; then in the Scilly Islands, which must have been healthy; then in Pendennis Castle, which has a beautiful view. Involved in the Rye House Plot, he was sent to the Tower along with his friend Sidney. Before the end of the year he was bailed, and shortly freed – to encourage Monmouth in his hare-brained schemes against his uncle, James II. Monmouth complained that Wildman 'would govern everybody', and 'liked nothing of anybody's doing but his own'. At any rate the old Leveller had more sense than the Duke, and survived him to become a knight at the Revolution. He died rich enough to have a fine monument in his church, celebrating, with some exaggeration, his having 'spent the best part of his days in prisons, without crimes, being conscious of no offence towards man'. Macaulay refers, with more point, to his 'tender care for his own safety', and Faithorne's engravings of him gives him the motto *Nil Admirari*.

As the result of Whig divisions and the skill with which the great Trimmer, Halifax, exploited them and saved the monarchy, James II came into his own – as Mary Tudor had done – with a large measure of goodwill and without limitations upon his power. The bloody fiasco of Monmouth's insurection

Left: Major John Wildman, ex-Leveller and accomplice of the Duke of Monmouth who survived to be knighted after the Revolution. *Right:* James, Duke of Monmouth, illegitimate son of Charles II, who led an unsuccessful rebellion against his uncle, James II

merely strengthened James's hand and encouraged him to go further – as Wyatt's rebellion had done Mary. (The result was fatal in both instances.) Everything about Monmouth recommended him to the people – his wonderful looks and generosity, his fondness for sport, for women and horses and racing, his open purse and empty head: they were ready to die for him, and hundreds did, both at Sedgemoor and in the terrible revenge exacted upon his Puritan following in the West Country.

So that we cannot condemn his uncle James II for Monmouth's execution, though James exhibited his usual characteristics over it, implacable and vindictive. Monmouth's children had preceded him to the Tower; he was followed there by his faithful wife, to whom he was openly unfaithful, preferring to live with Lady Wentworth. His wife was a great heiress, Countess of Buccleuch in her own right, a match that had been made for him as Charles II's recognised bastard. He was the son of Lucy Walters, who had been placed by Cromwell in the Tower in 1656 with her boy, then about seven, when she arrived in England declaring him to be Charles's. (She had been Robert Sidney's mistress shortly before, and Monmouth was much more like the Sidneys than the Bourbon-looking Charles. Lucy eventually became a prostitute

The execution of the Duke of Monmouth on Tower Hill

and, according to James II, died 'of the disease incident to that profession'. (He and Charles appear to have been similarly, if less seriously, affected.)

Monmouth's end was very swift, for he had already been condemned by attainder: his execution was fixed for the second day after his committal, and his uncle refused even a day's respite for the necessary business he had to transact before his demise. He was allowed a bevy of bishops for the good of his soul, however, and to them he expressed contrition for the bloodshed he had so stupidly caused. He would express no contrition for his connection with Lady Wentworth, which he fancied love excused, and so he was denied the sacrament. His execution next day was horribly bungled by the notorious John Ketch: five strokes 'severed not his head from the body till he cut it off with his knife'.

The susceptible Grammont has, in his *Memoirs*, celebrated 'the astonishing beauty of his outward form', and the furore created by his first appearance at Court. Such looks – what a pity!

James's triumph encouraged him to go forward with his programme – like Mary Tudor before him he was convinced that God was with him: always a dangerous delusion. What precipitated his fall was that he came up against the Church of England in prosecuting the Seven Bishops – a surprise to both parties. The Church had preached the doctrines of the divine right of kings and of passive obedience with assiduity – and the crowned fool believed them. But a Supreme Governor of the Church of England who would not attend its services – when a visiting Archbishop of Rheims found that it did not hurt to do so – was busily engaged in sawing off the bough upon which he sat. He had filled up the cup of grievances against him with his appointments of Catholics to posts in central and local administration, officering his army with Catholics, attacking the rights of the universities, expropriating the Fellows of Magdalen (their return is still annually celebrated).

Now he ordered a Second Declaration of Indulgence to be read in all the churches, which was intended not merely to extend toleration to Catholics and Dissenters, but to attack the established position of the Church to favour Roman Catholics. This was the whole logic of James's policy. The bishops who gathered at Lambeth – with other leading clerics – decided to use their right as peers to approach James with a petition not to have to read it. Obtuse as he was, he was greatly surprised, and railed at the deputation of bishops on their knees before him, 'This is a standard of rebellion.' They were equally

The Seven Bishops on their way down the Thames to the Tower. Their trial united popular opinion against James II surprised: nothing was further from their thought. 'I did not expect this from your Church,' said the royal head of it, 'especially from some of you' – looking angrily at Bishop Trelawny. With the spirit of his family, Trelawny replied that he presumed his Majesty was not of that opinion when he had sent him into the West – at the time of Monmouth's rebellion – and 'was like to have fallen into the enemy's hands'. He added, for good measure, 'If some of my family had proved rebellious to the Crown, I should not have much stood in need of your favour or protection.' James afterwards commented that of all the Bishops, Trelawny was the most 'saucy'.

But someone betrayed the secret of the petition to the press, and overnight it did become, what they never intended, a standard of rebellion. The nation seized on it as a signal that this was where James got off; the whole Church, with few exceptions, went into reverse gear and disobeyed him: they refused to read the Declaration. James's advisers were nonplussed as to what to do: both the cynical Lord Sunderland who simply told James what he wanted to hear, and the Jesuit Father Petre – conceive of the folly of making a Jesuit his adviser in a wildly Protestant country, after all that had happened!

Eventually it was decided to prosecute the Seven Bishops for seditious libel, though they had never committed it or published their humble petition – Father Petre 'made no secret of his delight at the humiliation which the bishops were to undergo'. On 8 June 1688 the famous Seven, headed by their Archbishop, were packed off to the Tower. The crowds around the palace were such that there might have been an attempt at rescue had they been conveyed by coach. So they were sent off down the river – a bargeful of bishops. People crowded the river bank to cheer them, and when they arrived at the Tower wharf people rushed forward to touch them (an atavistic impulse of anthro-

Contemporary portraits of the Seven Bishops

pological interest); even the soldiers at the Tower drank their health. Never before or since have bishops been so popular or regarded with such veneration; but it really was an anti-government demonstration, the greatest since 1641.

On Trinity Sunday, 10 June, the Bishops received communion in the Tower chapel. The Chaplain had received a special order from on high to read the Declaration of Indulgence; he did not, and was dismissed. Crowds of people came to ask the prelates' blessing; the courtyard was thronged with the carriages of the great; even the indulged Dissenters came to express their sympathy. That Sunday a son and heir was born to James; all around him urged a general amnesty, but this vindictive man missed his opportunity.

The attitude of the people, and the facts of the situation, put paid to the doctrine of passive obedience. The prelates were stiff: within the Tower they refused to pay the Lieutenant for their keep, on the ground of wrongful imprisonment. This was Sir Edward Hales, who had turned Catholic to qualify for James's favour, who gave him the key-posts of Lieutenant of Dover Castle and Deputy Warden of the Cinque Ports, Lieutenant of the Tower and Master of the Ordnance – all with obvious intention. When James skedaddled from Whitehall, he went with Hales, disguised as his servant; Hales was recognised and returned to the Tower as a prisoner.

A couple of days before their trial on 15 June, Evelyn, who was very churchy, went to visit his particular friends, the Archbishop, the Bishops of Ely, St Asaph, and Bath and Wells. He found them in good spirits, though Hales had 'used them very surlily'. There was a rumour that he intended a chapel for Popish services in the Tower. On the departure of the Bishops for trial he threatened that if they came into his power again they should feel it. They never did. Once more the crowds swarmed to greet them on their way to Westminster Hall, and on their acquittal there were universal rejoicings in which the soldiers of James's army at Hounslow joined. (He had thought to overawe London with it.) When he heard the cheering, he asked the cause and was told, 'It is nothing: only the soldiers rejoicing at the acquittal of the bishops.' 'Do you call that Nothing?' said James, and left the camp in agitation, repeating in his manner, '*Tant pis pour eux, tant pis pour eux.*' But, of course, it was so much the worse for *him*, half French and wholly un-English as he was.

It needed only the birth of a male heir to serve sentence on him: the nation was not going to stand a Catholic dynasty, and there never has been a Catholic monarch since. Immediately upon that event the invitation was sent from the grandees of both parties for William and Mary to come and take over.

12
Stuart Sequel: the '15 and '45 Rebellions

FTER a revolution there is an inevitable sequel: consequences to be clarified, dubieties cleared up, ministers of the late régime punished or thwarted, supporters rewarded, opposition repressed. In 1688 the nation – or the most powerful elements in it – made its choice. But a number of important people continued to look to the exiled James II, and after him to his son, the Old Pretender – the more because neither Mary nor Anne, who succeeded, had children that lived to inherit the throne. This made for a succession problem again, though Parliament now regulated it by an Act of Succession in 1701, to bring in the Protestant Hanoverians. Those who didn't like them were apt to look to the Stuarts abroad and make trouble. Both Queen Mary and Princess Anne affected to give credence to the lying rumour that their half-brother, James's son, was supposititious, brought in in a warming-pan; but, then, they were not disinterested.

The most detested instrument of the late régime was the Lord Chancellor, 'Judge Jeffreys' of ill fame for the savagery of his treatment of Monmouth's followers in the West Country. Before the King's flight Jeffreys surrendered the Great Seal to him, who threw it into the Thames on his way – a childish action, hoping to impede the process of law and create confusion. Jeffreys disguised himself as a common sailor and hid on board ship at Wapping, hoping to escape overseas. Next morning, unable to hold out – for he was addicted to drink – he imprudently went ashore and while drinking in the Red Cow, in Anchor and Hope Alley, was recognised.

At once a crowd assembled who hooted and pelted him: he might well have been lynched but for the arrival of a trained-band. Carried before the Lord Mayor, who swooned at the spectacle, Jeffreys knew where he would be safest, and requested the Tower with an armed escort to protect him from the fury of the mob. The warrant of committal from the Council had to follow after. Examined by a deputation of Lords, he acknowledged his crimes but pleaded that the severities of the Bloody Assizes had fallen short of James's

Judge Jeffreys, James II's Lord Chancellor, arrested at Wapping while trying to escape disguised as a common sailor demands. Jeffreys was already ill of an internal ulcer, which drink aggravated, and on 18 April he died. He was buried in St Peter-ad-vincula – by that macabre propriety we have observed before – in the grave beside Monmouth.

In May a whole clutch was brought in of persons, great and small, who had lent themselves to James's purposes or curried favour with him by verting to Catholicism. Among them was the unworthy representative of the Hatfield branch of the Cecils, the fourth Earl of Salisbury – we have seen that his father was inside, with Shaftesbury, in 1677; so that the Tower had its quota of Cecils, at last, in this age. Macaulay has a rude description of the fourth Earl as 'foolish to a proverb. His figure was so bloated by sensual indulgence as to be almost incapable of moving. . . . He was represented in popular lampoons as a man made to be duped, as a man who had hitherto been the prey of gamesters and who might as well be the prey of friars.' He was committed as a Popish recusant, but the prosecution was kindly dropped. A couple of years later his name was unkindly forged to a bond to take arms for James and seize William of Orange. Upon this he was inside again, but shortly released.

Another earl in the bag was a more entertaining character, the Earl of Castlemaine, who had been awarded his earldom for the services of his wife, the notorious Barbara, as mistress of Charles II. He was a devout Roman Catholic and, when his wife presented him with Charles's offspring, Charles Fitzroy, the nominal father had the boy baptised by a Catholic priest. Whereupon his wife had the child re-baptised by an Anglican clergyman. This led to ill-feeling between the couple, and the affronted Earl left his wife to travel abroad. On his return, at the time of the Popish Plot he was in the Tower, where, with his ready pen, he wrote a *Compendium* of the sufferings of previous victims of the Plot. At the time of the Meal Tub Plot he was in again, but at his trial turned the tables on informers and prosecutors, and got free.

James II naturally made much of him, and sent him with *éclat* as ambassador to the Pope, who gave him a very cool reception. The intelligent Innocent XI had no opinion of James and less in the forcible conversion of England: he (rightly) put his money on William of Orange. This was provoking for Castlemaine, whom the Pope pointedly reminded that the morning hours were best for travelling in Italy. At James's flight Castlemaine absconded with plate to the value of £2500. Committed to the Tower, he was released on large recognisances, then recommitted on suspicion of complicity in plotting James's return. Allowed to go abroad, in 1695 he was back again, accused of being concerned in the plot for assassinating William, but was released on pain of banishment. So much travel had made a good linguist of him; he was also a mathematician and inventor, and wrote a good deal. In his peculiar family circumstances, it is not surprising that the bulk of his property went not to his wife's children but to his own nephew.

Among other grandees in this haul were the Earls of Peterborough and Arran, Viscount Preston, Lords Montgomery and Forbes. Among the small was old Obadiah Walker, Master of University College, Oxford, of whom Macaulay made such fun. He had lent himself to James's purposes, dedicating a Catholic chapel in his college, licensing Catholic works for publication, and recommending a convert as Dean of Christ Church. In return the young men of the House put up a bogus natural to sing doggerel at the Master's door:

> Oh, old Obadiah,
> Sing Ave Maria,
> But so will not I-a.
> For why-a:
> I had rather be a fool than a knave-a.

Now old Obadiah found himself for a few months in the Tower, nothing worse; deprived of his Mastership, he lived on charity and died in poverty, all for the *beaux yeux* of James II.

The event of the Revolution naturally resulted in confusion in some people's minds as to the proper object of their loyalty: the King to whom they had sworn allegiance, but who had turned out impossible; or his daughter and son-in-law who had stepped into his shoes. Ambivalence spread widely, notably in the Church; it was understandable that more worldly persons sought to reinsure themselves, keeping their rear intact by a privy correspondence with the King in exile.

Lord Preston, a Graham of Netherby, had been a faithful follower of James; but, a Protestant, he had vainly urged moderation upon the infatuated monarch. (He had previously been ordered to inquire into the circumstances of Essex's suicide in the Tower, and to trace Bomeny, the valet who **had** brought him the razor.) After the Revolution Louis XIV entrusted Preston with large sums to make trouble for William – with which he embarked on measures in the North to restore James. Laid by the heels, Preston spent the warm summer of 1689 in the Tower. Allowed out, he was back again in the autumn for accepting a peerage from the King in exile. Leniently treated, Preston carried on his plotting with assiduity, until, on New Year's Day 1691, he and a couple of accomplices were seized as they lay concealed under the hatches of a smack making across Channel. The conspirators failed to drop overboard the treasonable papers they had tied and weighted for the purpose; they also failed incompetently in the attempt to bribe their captors.

Preston was sent back to his old quarters, uncertain of his fate, but was at length condemned to death. His wife, on petitioning Queen Mary, found that his life might be spared if he made a full discovery of the plot. So Preston spent his mornings drawing up confessions, which he proceeded to burn after he found courage in dining and wining. At length he made a clean breast of it, incriminating Clarendon and Dartmouth, one of the Seven Bishops and William Penn – and, for good measure, he added a list of William Penn's acquaintances friendly to James. For this Preston's life was spared; he spent the rest of his life in tranquillity in Yorkshire, in disgrace with his old Jacobite friends.

A sensible choice: wasn't life worth any amount of words?

But Clarendon was inculpated. The brother of James's first wife, his loyalty was such that he had been able to pay kind attentions to disaffected persons like Essex and Monmouth when in the Tower. At the time of Preston's plot Clarendon's niece, Queen Mary, was 'sorrier than it may well be believed' at having to lodge him there – so she reported to her absent husband. (She was a more loyal wife than daughter, but it was impossible to be loyal to such a father.) After Preston's relevations Clarendon was put under lock and key again for a good many months; once again he had his wife with him for company, and was visited by his friend Evelyn. In the high summer he was allowed to go into the country for air, attended by his warder, and shortly was permitted to go into rustication, and keep quiet for good.

The faithful Dartmouth was less lucky. At the beginning of his reign James had made him Governor of the Tower, i.e. Constable, the grander honorific office. At the moment of William's invasion Dartmouth was in command of James's fleet; though loyal himself, the ground – or, rather, the sea – gave way beneath him. The whole fleet, disgusted by James's nonsense, went over to William, and even Dartmouth took the new oath of allegiance. Trying to go back on it, he was committed and charged with conspiring to hand over to the French. There was no evidence to support the allegation (Dartmouth's family name was Legge); and perhaps the shock contributed to the apoplexy of which he died in the Tower.

The fortune of the Churchills had been made by James. Arabella was his *maîtresse en titre* for some years and had by him a number of children whose descendants still shine among Spanish grandees and English peers – Albas, Waldegraves, Falmouths. John Churchill, to become the great Marlborough, began as page, then ensign, and a close dependant of James as Duke of York. But at Salisbury in 1688 he had gone over to William. Marlborough was a secretive man, and he never let on; but the explanation of his conduct is fairly obvious: he hoped to dominate the situation as his fellow West Countryman, Monk, had done at the Restoration and emerge, too, with a dukedom. Actually his treachery might have benefited James, who would at least have remained as nominal King. But the plan failed – Marlborough's dukedom was postponed by a dozen years.★

And the Revolution was dominated by William III – a truly great man, who had saved his own country from Louis XIV, was now saving Britain and posthumously, through Marlborough's military genius, was to save Europe. But, for the present, Marlborough was a disappointed man, a malcontent; an Englishman, he resented the ascendancy of the Dutch around Dutch William; a Churchill, he was resentful that William did not put him in command of the army or make proper use of his powers. He kept up a correspondence with St Germain and fed James with illusory hopes, that unfortunate's favourite diet.

Marlborough's wife, the beautiful Sarah, was the intimate confidant of Princess Anne, who was more than half in love with her – and Queen Mary, neglected by William, was jealous of the emotional attachment. Princess Anne, as heir to the throne – for William and Mary had no children – stood together against 'the Dutch Abortion', as they called the little great man. Already in open opposition, Marlborough was dismissed from all his appointments when a sham plot was framed against him, with his and other signatures forged – including Bishop Sprat of the Royal Society. Off to the Tower they went, in May 1692.

Princess Anne wrote to Sarah, full of tender solicitude:

I hear Lord Marlborough is sent to the Tower; and though I am certain they have nothing against him, yet I was struck when I was told it, for methinks it is a dismal thing to have one's friends sent to that place. . . . But let them do what they please, nothing shall ever vex me so I can have the satisfaction of seeing dear Mrs Freeman [i.e. Sarah]; and I swear I would live on bread and water, between four walls, without repining. For as long as you continue kind, nothing can ever be a real mortification to your faithful Mrs Morley [i.e. Princess Anne].

★I put forward this explanation of his hitherto unexplained conduct in *The Early Churchills*, chap. X.

In June Anne is writing to ask if there were as yet 'any hopes of Lord Marlborough's being soon at liberty. For God's sake have a care of your dear self, and give as little way to melancholy thoughts as you can. I will not fail of being with my dear Mrs Freeman about five or six o'clock, unless you are to go to the Tower.' By then Bishop Sprat, who was not an historical researcher for nothing, had been able to disprove the forged signatures. Marlborough and he applied for bail. At once Princess Anne to Sarah: 'it is a comfort they cannot keep Lord Marlborough in the Tower longer than the end of the term. And I hope, when the Parliament sits, care will be taken that people may not be clapt up for nothing, or else there will be no living in quiet for anybody but insolent Dutch and sneaking mercenary Englishmen.'

In fact Marlborough was in correspondence with James – and everybody was mercenary in that age, including the royal family, particularly the future George I and George II, very keen on the cash. As early as November 1689 Marlborough's brother, George – who was to become active head of the Admiralty, in their heyday under Queen Anne – was sent to the Tower by the House of Commons 'for requiring and taking money for convoys'. After the battle of Blenheim in which the third brother, Charles, ably seconded Marlborough, he was rewarded with the Lieutenancy of the Tower, which he held for a year only, to exchange for the better bargain of Guernsey.

Anyhow, it is pleasant to add the Churchills to all the other great families that have had the hospitality of the Tower.

John Churchill, Duke of Marlborough. The future victor of the Battle of Blenheim spent a short time in the Tower after being framed for plotting against King William III

In the following years two escapes made news, those of Colonel Parker and Lord Clancarty. The latter had been brought to London when barely sixteen to be shown 'the diversions of the town at Christmas time' – the term included dissipations. James rewarded him for changing his religion by giving him a troop of horse. Engaged in James's forlorn hope of regaining the kingdom he had so foolishly lost, now from Ireland as a base, Clancarty was caught at the capitulation of Cork in 1690 and forwarded to the Tower. Pious John Evelyn paid a visit to the Earl's mother 'to condole with her concerning her debauched and dissolute son, who had done so much mischief in Ireland'. After two or three years Clancarty tired of confinement and managed to escape. He dressed up a block with his periwig on its head, and installed it in his bed with the inscription, 'The block must answer for me.'

When Colonel Parker also succeeded in escaping, suspicion fell upon Lord Lucas, then Governor, who was also reprimanded by the Council for his ill-treatment of another prisoner, Major-General Dorrington.

The ambiguous circumstances of the time were propitious to plotters; one of the most persistent was Sir John Fenwick, of Wallington, a Northumbrian grandee of ancient family. His personal animosity against William III is said to have gone back to a rebuff he received from the Prince when serving in Holland. Early in 1689 he was fomenting unrest in the North, and in conse-quence spent summer in the Tower. Released, he continued his activities and in 1695 involved himself in a plot to assassinate William – since it was impossible to defeat him. Lady Fenwick pleaded for him that he had frustrated the plot; it is more likely that William had done so by leaving for Flanders. Next year there was another attempt by Sir George Barclay and Robert Charnock, the Catholic priest who had lent himself to James's designs upon Magdalen College, Oxford. Charnock corroborated Hobbes's view of the deleterious effect of too much reading of the classics, by comparing himself to Mucius Scaevola; while a contemporary gentleman of family commented that, if Charnock had not been of inferior extraction, 'he might have been another Catiline'.

Barclay and Charnock got together a band of braves to kill the King as he was returning from Richmond, in a narrow lane at Turnham Green where his coach-and-six could not turn – which was the way Henri IV had been caught in Paris, and Walter Rathenau in our time in Berlin. However, the plot was revealed, and William remained that day at home. Fenwick was probably cognisant of this plot, as he certainly was of that of the previous year. Back he went to the Tower, while he was proceeded against by attainder. By this time a feeling had grown up against so unjudicial a procedure, and large minorities voted against it in both Houses – Fenwick was very well connected. On his condemnation the Jacobite desired the services of one of the bishops who had sacrificed the sweets of his see out of loyalty to James. These were accorded him through the courtesy of the Whig Bishop Burnet, who wrote that Fenwick died 'very composed, in a much better temper than was to be expected, for his life had been very irregular'. Since he was connected with so many noble families he was given all the honours proper to a peer.

His horse was the famous Sorrel – so celebrated by Jacobites; for it came into William's possession, who met his death by Sorrel's stumbling over a molehill in Kensington Park.

By way of relief from inveterate plotters, perhaps we may turn to an inveterate duellist, Lord Mohun, who was thrice put under restraint for his irresistible propensity. The first time was when he was only seventeen, and played his part in the killing of Mountfort the actor. The actor had the ill taste to dispute the favours of the actress Mrs Bracegirdle with Captain Richard Hill. Hill and Mohun lay in wait in Howard Street for the actor, who reproached the young peer with the ill company he kept – Hill was drunk; Lord Mohun, justly offended, thereupon ran the impertinent actor through. Hill decamped; Mohun, from the Tower, was brought to trial before his peers at Westminster. It was the sensation of the hour on account of his youth; even the great William, with better things to do, could not but attend. The young lord was

Sir Robert Walpole, the first Prime Minister of Great Britain. His six-month imprisonment in the Tower made him a Whig hero

acquitted – there was some doubt about who had provoked whom; though a relative sensibly suggested that he 'should be taken away and whipped'.

Young Mohun progressed to other duels, including one with a fellow-Cornishman, Francis Scobell, who dared to stop him making a brutal assault upon his own coachman. In 1697 he was in at the death of Captain Hill, followed by that of Captain Richard Coote in 1699. Both times he was sent to the Tower, and again acquitted; apparently correctly, for he had not fomented the quarrel or given the offence. For some years he behaved himself – or, at least, attended the House of Lords as a Whig. Then in 1712 he met his end in a duel in Hyde Park with the Duke of Hamilton, in which each killed the other – over a bequest, which they might more reasonably have shared. But it was the end of the peerage, and of that family at Boconnoc, in the beautiful Lerryn valley, in Cornwall.

It had been no disadvantage to Marlborough to have a spell in the Tower: hitherto he had been looked upon as a royal favourite and renegade; after that he was regarded as a patriot, upholder of the rights of Englishmen. Similarly with his *protégé*, Robert Walpole. Towards the end of Queen Anne's reign the Tories came in and the Whigs went out. Walpole was much the ablest Whig leader in the Commons; the incoming, ambivalent Tory, Harley, made flattering overtures to him, telling him that he was worth half his party. When these were rejected and Walpole led the opposition to the Tory peace – which the nation desired – a couple of trumped-up charges were ready to hand to relegate him to the Tower.

He was supposed to have made money on army contracts as Secretary at War; though one would not put this past most eighteenth-century politicians, in fact the money had not come into Walpole's hands. He was of course pronounced guilty by Tory majorities in Parliament and spent six months in the Tower, January to July 1712. This was an unmixed blessing: the peace negotiations went forward unimpeded, and Walpole became the Whig hero. He spent his time composing his defence; he scratched his name on a window as a memorial of his martyrdom for the cause (where his antecedent, the Jesuit Walpole, had been really martyred for his). He was visited in form by all the Whig grandees and leaders, 'his apartments exhibited the appearance of a crowded levee'. It pre-figured the long years when he would hold sole power under George II.

Many years afterwards Horace Walpole remembered that, when his father's power was beginning to decline, the Tory leader in the Commons in 1739, 'Sir William Wyndham, no fool for that time, *laboured* to be sent to the Tower. My father told him in plain terms he knew his meaning and would not indulge him.' Civilised eighteenth century! We observe that commitment to the Tower becomes more and more infrequent – except at peaks of crisis, such as the Jacobite rebellions in 1715 and 1745, and in time of war-scares.

The Tower held no scare for Horace Walpole, who regarded it in rather a comic light, its antique horrors putting it on a level with the Castle of Otranto. In 1741 when his father's majority was sinking (he was now opposing war when before he had been opposing peace), Horace wrote to his friend Horace Mann that the question was becoming

. . . Downing Street or the Tower: will you come and see a body if one should happen to lodge at the latter? There are a thousand pretty things to amuse you: the lions, the Armoury, the Crown, King Harry's cod-piece, and the axe that beheaded Anne Boleyn. I design to make interest for the room where the two Princes were smothered: in the long winter evenings when one wants company, one may sit and scribble verses against Crouch-backed Richard and dirges on the sweet babes.

That was the spirit in which Horace wrote his light-hearted *jeu d'esprit*, his *Historic Doubts on the Life and Reign of Richard III*. It was written half in inverted commas, like so much of what he wrote – he had a lively sense of amusement and loved shocking conventional views. He was put in his place by a great historian, David Hume, and gracefully retired: he had the intelligence to realise when he didn't know what he was talking about.

The Jacobite Rebellion of 1715 – before the Hanoverians got firmly seated – brought a crop of backwoods Scotch and Northern peers in, but also endangered more important figures. After the collapse of the rebellion the Earls of Derwentwater, Nithsdale and Carnwath, Lords Kenmure, Widdrington and Nairn were lodged in the Devereux tower. Three were reprieved, leaving three to be dealt with. Derwentwater aroused much sympathy, for he was young and inexperienced; he had been brought up at St Germain as a companion to Prince James Edward, who inherited the dull stupidity of his father. Derwentwater threw himself on George I's mercy, who had not much in his composition. The young Earl's mother was a bastard daughter of Charles II; so a bevy of these grand connections, the Duke and Duchess of Richmond and the Duchess of Cleveland assaulted George I's bedchamber, while the Countess assailed him in French. £60,000 were offered to save Derwentwater, but Walpole was determined to make an example. He made, in fact, two; but the third escaped him.

The night before the execution of Derwentwater and Kenmure, Nithsdale got out. His Countess had made a difficult journey from the North on his behalf, and succeeded in gaining entrance to St James's Palace, where she threw herself at the Hanoverian's feet for mercy. In vain. Herself a Herbert of Powis, the Countess was not to be defeated. She gained access to the Tower with some women companions, and in the feminine confusion was able to throw a cloak and hood over her husband and get him past the guards. Disguised as a servant of the Venetian ambassador, Nithsdale then crossed the Channel. George I, who had no romantic illusions, commented sensibly on the exploit that 'it was the best thing a man in his position could have done'.

More important figures to come in were these: Sir William Wyndham, the Tory leader in the Commons, the Earl of Powis, and the great Robert Harley, Earl of Oxford. Oxford had remained calmly in England when his Tory colleague, Bolingbroke, fled the country – to be disillusioned with the exiled Stuarts. In 1715 Oxford was impeached and sent to the Tower – and was greeted by one of Swift's magnificent formal salutes. It must have been almost worthwhile being within those portals to receive such stately, if hardly spiritual, consolation.

My Lord, It may look like an idle or officious thing in me to give your Lordship any interruption under your present circumstances. Yet I could never forgive myself if, after having been treated for several years with the greatest kindness and distinction, by a person of your Lordship's virtue and wisdom, I should omit making you at this time the humblest offers of my poor service and attendance . . .

And then, very grandly:

I do not conceive myself obliged to regulate my opinions by the proceedings of a House of Lords or Commons; and therefore, however they may acquit themselves in your Lordship's case, I shall take the liberty of thinking and calling you the ablest and faithfullest minister, and truest lover of your country, that this age hath produced. And I have already taken care that you shall be so represented to posterity, in spite of all the rage and malice of your enemies.

This is Swift speaking as the historian of *The Last Four Years of the Queen*; it is, of course, historians not politicians who have the last word.

Not even his political opponents could convict Oxford of treason, though they let him languish for a couple of years. By that time their venom had subsided, and the impeachment was dismissed. A proposal to proceed against him by attainder could not even find a seconder – a marked contrast with the heyday of such things in the previous century.

The Church continued to be a centre of opposition to the triumphant Whigs, and its most irrepressible spokesman, Atterbury – Dean of Westminster and Bishop of Rochester – was in correspondence with the Stuart Court. Consigned to the Tower in 1722, he was summoned before the Commons to answer to a bill of pains and penalties introduced against him. He declined to do so, with the snub that he was 'content with the opportunity – if the bill went on – to make his defence before another House, of which he had the honour to be a member'. Irrefutable as this was, Atterbury found few friends in the Lords, now packed with Whig nominees; he was compromised by a little spotted dog, which had been sent to him by the Jacobite Secretary of State, and figured frequently in the correspondence as if standing for something other than itself.

Such was the animosity aroused by this too loquacious clerical politician that one peer opined it could be accounted for only on the principle of the 'wild Americans [Indians, of course], who fondly hope to inherit not only the spoils but the abilities of him whom they should destroy'. Sentenced to deprivation and banishment, Atterbury was a hero to the Tory clergy. He was prayed for publicly in the churches under the guise of 'one suffering from the gout', which was true enough; verses were circulated in his honour, and a print of

him looking out through the bars like another Laud. But times had changed, and in the summer of 1723 he was given a fine send-off from the Tower wharf, barges and boats, full of sympathisers, cheering him on the Thames, with a Tory Duke – one of Charles II's progeny – to make him a presentation of a sword, more appropriate for him than a pastoral staff.

As the more civilised eighteenth century proceeds there are far fewer commitments to the Tower, and in those that take place there is a self-conscious assertion of the ceremonial and archaic. When Horace Walpole is describing them, even the execution of the Scottish lords after the '45, there is an element of the comic along with the macabre, as if this kind of thing was out of date. And, as the old historian of the Tower, Bayley, observes, 'their names terminate, it is hoped for ever, the long list of executions of which, for so many ages, this noted spot had been the accustomed scene'.

Horace Walpole reports for us the verses that Lord Lansdowne wrote when in the Tower for eighteen months after the '15. He scratched the following lines on the window of the same room that had been Walpole's father's:

> Good unexpected, evil unforeseen
> Appear by turns as Fortune shifts the scene:
> Some raised aloft come tumbling down amain
> And fall so hard they bound and rise again.

This refers to Walpole's good luck in that his imprisonment had been a step to popularity and power. The haughty Lansdowne took it as a good omen for himself: it turned out not to be.

We observe very well in Walpole's Letters how the Tower was regarded in this age, the mixture of comedy with tragedy, decorum and snobbery, the family pride – for one was nobody if an ancestor or relation had not at least been in the Tower. When Horace published an Opposition tract against the government in war-time, in 1757, Mrs Clive cried out, 'Lord! You will be sent to the Tower.' '"Well," said I coolly, "my father was there before me."' When Marshal Bellisle was captured it was thought of to send him there, 'but that is contrary to the *politesse* of modern war'. 'Peers', said Horace with dignity, 'are generally confined at the Tower, not at Justice Fielding's' – the novelist's brother's. When Dr Cameron, a Jacobite agent, was parting from his wife, at the gates being locked, she fell at his feet in anguish. He said, 'Madam, this was not what you promised me', watched her coach drive away with great coolness, then turned his face to the wall and wept.

Opposite left: Robert Harley, Earl of Oxford, who was impeached and
sent to the Tower for two years in 1715. *Right:* Bishop Atterbury who
was given a fine farewell from the Tower when sent into exile

One sees the eighteenth-century mixture of barbarity and decorum.

Walpole tells us that, in 1745, Kelly escaped who had been in the Tower ever since the Assassination Plot against William III – if so, after half a century. One of the Ratcliffes, who had been concerned in the '15 but escaped, was supposed to be the Pretender's youngest son; 'the mob, persuaded of his being the youngest Pretender, could scarcely be restrained from tearing him to pieces all the way on the road. He said he had heard of English mobs, but could not conceive they were so dreadful, and wished he had been shot at the battle of Dettingen.' The young man's father, Lord Derwentwater, on his entering the gates had 'never expected to arrive there alive'. So much for Stuart silliness! When the Highland lords were brought in, Walpole found himself melted by their bearing. Kilmarnock was tall, slender and handsome; Balmerino, 'the most natural brave old fellow I ever saw. He pressed extremely to have his wife, his pretty Peggy, with him in the Tower. But the instant she came to him he stripped her and went to bed.' When they all were setting out in separate coaches for their trial in Westminster, 'there was some dispute in which the axe must go – old Balmerino cried, "Come, come, put it with me"; and in Westminster Hall, conversing with another he held it between them like a fan.'

Lord Lovat was a ruffianly Highland chieftain who had ruled the Fraser clan like a despot. When he was brought in, he told them that 'if he were not so old and infirm they would find it difficult to keep him there. They told him they had kept much younger. "Yes," said he, "but they were inexperienced: they had not broke so many gaols as I have." His last art was to shift his treason upon his eldest son, whom he had forced into the Rebellion. He told Williamson, the Lieutenant of the Tower, "we will hang my eldest son, and then my second shall marry your niece". He has a sort of ready humour at repartee, not very well adapted to his situation.' The Lieutenant complained that he couldn't sleep, he was so haunted with rats – which old Lovat emended to Ratcliffes, who had been executed. On the way to trial a woman looked into his coach with, 'You ugly old dog, don't you think you will have that frightful head cut off?' He replied, 'You damned ugly old bitch, I believe I shall.'

At their trial the Whig Lady Townshend fell hopelessly in love with young Lord Kilmarnock's sloping shoulders. 'She has been under his window [so had Horace]; sends messages to him; has got his dog and his snuff-box, forswears conversing with the bloody English' – and took to learning French. When it was all over, the infatuated lady picked up a stable-boy in the Tower, whom the warders told her was a natural son of her beau, Kilmarnock. She

Lord Lovat, the Jacobite peer, who was executed after taking part in the '45 Rebellion

promptly adopted him. Meanwhile, Balmerino on his way back from trial had stopped his coach at Charing Cross, in the most natural way in the world, 'to buy honey-blobs, as the Scotch call gooseberries'. When the death-warrant was brought into his room at dinner, his lady fainted. His lordship said, 'Lieutenant, with your damned death-warrant you have spoiled my Lady's stomach.'

At their executions they behaved accordingly: Kilmarnock greeted Balmerino with 'My Lord, I am heartily sorry to have your company in this expedition.' Both peers were concerned only to exonerate Prince Charles Edward from the charge of having given the order of no quarter at the battle of Culloden. Balmerino: 'My Lord Kilmarnock, I am only sorry that I cannot pay this reckoning alone.' Upon which the Earl expressed a wish that Balmerino might have precedence upon the scaffold; but this was contrary not only to order but to orders.

Old Lord Lovat behaved in character. Owing to age and infirmity, he sat in a chair to contemplate the vast concourse gathered to see 'the taking off of an old grey head', and described them justly enough, 'Look, how they are all piled up like rotten oranges.' He put on his spectacles to read the inscription on his coffin, and pronounced it correct. He then drank a bumper to King James and the good old cause for which his family, for ages past, had been engaged: 'If I had a thousand lives, I would lay them all down here in the same cause.' One of his acquaintance was looking dejected, so, putting a hand on his shoulder, 'Cheer up thy heart, man: I am not afraid: why should you?' He was in his eightieth year, so perhaps it did not so much matter to him; but what about the others he had misled?

Horace Walpole reports that 'the foreigners were much struck; Niccolini seemed a great deal shocked, but he comforts himself with the knowledge he thinks he has gained of the English constitution'. The Italians who were present with Horace's gouty friend Chute – Mr Chute of 'The Vine' – were 'more entertained than shocked: Panciatici told me, it was a *"triste spectacle, mais qu'il ne laissait d'être beau"*'. George Selwyn, a bright social butterfly, improved on this with a macabre story Horace thought 'excessive good'. Some ladies reproved him for going to see Lord Lovat's beheading. '"Nay," says he, "if that was such a crime, I am sure I have made amends, for I went to see it sewed on again".' Which he had done – when head and body were together again in the coffin, the young lawyer put on the Lord Chancellor's voice and said, 'My Lord Lovat, your lordship may rise.'

232

Taken in a Highlander of Day before he was taken

13
Georgian Amenities: Eccentrics, Americans, Spies, Traitors

THE fourth Earl Ferrers was more than a little eccentric: he deliberately murdered his steward, locking him in a room for the purpose at his house of Staunton Harold in Leicestershire, across from the fine Laudian church built by his ancestor as a challenge to Cromwell as Protector. Though Ferrers pleaded 'occasional insanity', probably truly enough, he was held capable of managing his estates and therefore responsible. He was in his fortieth year when this happened, in 1760, and was under the necessity of leaving provision for four natural daughters, and their mother, his mistress; to this his will added in recompense £1300 to the daughters of his murdered servant. As a peer the Earl was taken to the Tower, though hanged at Tyburn. All this was wonderful material for the pointed pen of Horace Walpole.

He tells us that the Washingtons, from whom Ferrers was descended, 'were certainly a very frantic race, and I have no doubt of madness in him, but not of a pardonable sort'. He was a sadistic brute, who imputed all his troubles to his marriage, and took against his wife, who separated from him for his beating her. The sainted Selina, Countess of Huntingdon – the 'Saint Teresa of the Methodists' – was his aunt and visited him. Not that the Earl had any mind to be a convert: he admitted her just for company. When she insisted on preaching at him, 'he grew sick of her and complained that she was enough to provoke anybody' – she was lucky to escape without a beating. She then sent her suffragan, preacher Whitefield, who could do nothing with his lordship and reported that my Lord's heart was as stone. The Earl wanted to see only his mistress; but the Governor, Lord Cornwallis, 'as simple an old woman as my Lady Huntingdon herself', consulted her whether he should permit it. 'Oh, by no means, it would be letting him die in adultery!'

'So you see,' wrote Horace, 'the good-natured people of England will not want their favourite amusement, executions.' Elections ran them a close second; a couple of years before, Horace had been able to report on election-night 'the sovereign people can scarce stand upright'. The night before his

Lord George Gordon, whose opposition to the removal of some
Catholic disabilities stirred up mob riots in London in 1780 when
three hundred people were killed

death, the Earl made one of his keepers read *Hamlet* to him in bed. In the morning 'he paid all his bills as if leaving an inn and, half an hour before the sheriffs fetched him, corrected some verses he had written in the Tower in imitation of the Duke of Buckingham's epitaph, *Dubius sed non improbus vixi*'. He dressed himself in his wedding finery, embroidered with silver, saying that this was 'at least as good an occasion of putting them on as that for which they were first made'.

'He set out from the Tower at nine, amidst crowds, thousands . . . in his own landau-and-six, his coachman crying all the way.' A French bookseller, in his robes and in his best mourning, sat as a magistrate beside the Earl, but, as a bookseller, apologised for his presence. 'On the contrary,' said the Earl with eighteenth-century politeness, 'I feared the disagreeableness of the duty might make you depute your under-sheriff. As you are so good as to execute it your-self, I am persuaded the dreadful apparatus will be conducted with more expedition.' To the chaplain, plaguing him to be more contrite for his crime against God and man, the Earl replied that he had done everything he proposed to do with regard to God and man: what he wanted was a drink. This was refused, and he had to content himself with some pigtail tobacco. At Tyburn he tipped the hangman and the chaplain, impartially, five guineas each.

Horace Walpole, the son of Sir Robert Walpole, whose letters are a lively and invaluable record of politics and society during the middle years of the eighteenth century

Walpole frequently refers to the animals in the Tower and evidently found them a useful term of reference for the antics of politicians. This same year 1760 he reports that the big news from India is that Clive has taken the Grand Moghul's grandmother. Horace supposed that she would be brought over and put in the Tower with the Shahgoest, 'the strange beast that Mr Pitt gave to the King this winter'. Apparently this was an exotic kind of lynx given to Clive by Jaffir Ali: it created much interest in the *Gentleman's Magazine*, which called it the 'Siyah-gush'. A favourite lion which everyone knew was called Old Nero: Horace warned a friend that if he didn't cease his factious opposition he would be sent to the Tower and shown as Old Nero. People were apt to give the great Mr Pitt presents – and, as when Churchill was presented with a lion-cub during the last war, he was able to carry on the old joke and respond that at present all was quiet in Downing Street, but one never knew when the lion would come in useful.

In the year of victories, 1759, Horace reports solemnly to his friend Mann that 'it is *not* true that Pitt made the King ride upon one of the cannons to the Tower'. Faction found a dangerous leader in the 1760s with 'that Devil Wilkes', as George III called him; for, through everything, thick and thin, Wilkes remained the idol of the populace. He made the utmost of his privilege

Elephant Armour brought from India by Clive. It was probably a trophy of the Battle of Plassy. It is now in the Armoury

'That Devil Wilkes',
engraved by
William Hogarth

as Member of Parliament in his campaign of scurrilities against government and the Crown itself. An enthusiastic rake, with a talent for obscenity, author of the pornographic *Essay on Woman*, garnished with bogus notes by 'Bishop Warburton' and dedicated to the frail beauty Fanny Murray – 'Awake, my Fanny,' etc. – he succeeded in distracting the government and putting it in the wrong on the issue of imprisonment on a general warrant, instead of on a specific charge. When he was sent to the Tower on one such, in April 1763, he was able to put himself forward as a victim of something like a French *lettre de cachet*, which consigned a man to the Bastille without specifying cause.

Thus Wilkes identified himself with the cause of political, no less than of sexual, liberty and appealed to the instincts of every right-thinking – or, rather, left-thinking – Englishman. Horace Walpole was with the Opposition on both counts, and reports on the ministry sending Wilkes to the Tower, 'Aye, to the Tower, *tout de bon*' – Horace thought it absurd and the Scotch 'Aye' was evidently a laugh at the minister, Lord Bute. When the insufferable Lord Temple was refused admittance to Wilkes, 'I thought this was the Tower,' said Horace, 'but I find it is the Bastille.' This was Whig humbug, of course, but one discerns a note of pride in, almost fondness for, the Tower. Wilkes was only in for a week, but the government never dared to send him there again, though he richly deserved it. In 1768 one finds the Guards from the Tower having to be employed in one of the riots he instigated.

Meanwhile, in 1764, 'of follies, thank the moon! we never have a dearth. For one we are obliged to the Archbishop who, in remembrance, I suppose, of his original profession of midwifery, has ordered some decent alterations to be made in King Henry's figure in the Tower' – an allusion to the enormous codpiece often specified as one of its sights. It was naughty of him to be so snobbish about Archbishop Secker, who had been born of humble Dissenting parents and was originally a medical student. His biographer tells us that when he entered the Church, 'his knowledge of medicine was of great service to his poorer parishioners'; so perhaps Horace was right about the midwifery.

The domestic distractions of the time, the political factionalism, the divisions among the Whigs, enabled Lord North, backed by George III, to hold sway and this coincided with, perhaps encouraged, the revolt of the American Colonies. In the panicky conditions of 1775, on the threshold of the Declaration of Independence and open war, the government seized on a dubious American banker in London, Mr Sayre, and popped him in the Tower. He had been one of Wilkes's supporters as sheriff, so the ministry would believe anything of him. He was supposed to be remitting money to the rebels and sending intelligence; but another American swore on oath that Sayre had offered him £1500 to seize the Tower and steal the King – 'and I suppose send them to New York', said Horace contemptuously. For the stupid Secretary of State, Lord Rochford, had fallen into a mare's nest.

Sayre took advantage of the rights of an Englishman to sue out a writ of *habeas corpus*, which set him at liberty after only five days, 'instead of being,' Horace thought, 'as he ought to be, in Bedlam'. Now Lord Rochford 'will be prosecuted, instead of being shut up for a fool, as he ought to be'. Sayre proceeded to sue the Secretary of State for illegal imprisonment and was awarded £1000 damages. Horace concluded, 'it is not the prisoners in this country that are mad but the ministers'.

It was not only the ministers, however, who were mad. At the height of the American war, in 1779, Lord George Gordon became President of the Protestant Association, formed to oppose the modest removal of some Catholic disabilities. This was, and is, a subject liable to unleash lunatic sentiments and actions. The mob-agitation, encouraged by having an inflammatory lord at its head, passed all bounds in the Gordon Riots in 1780. On 7 June London was given over to a night of horror – which, of course, Gordon was unable to restrain: prisons were burnt down, two thousand criminals joined the mob; among others, the fine house of the tolerant and liberal Lord Chief Justice Mansfield was destroyed, with its magnificent and irreplaceable library. Three hundred persons were killed in this example of mob–rule.

Lord George Gordon was fetched off to the Tower, though Walpole was of the opinion that 'the Tower is much too dignified a prison for *him*'. A few days later, 'the monster that conjured up this tempest is now manacled in the Tower. – But what a nation is Scotland: in every reign engendering traitors to the state, and false and pernicious to the kings that favour it the most.' This is a reference not only to the Stuarts but to George III's partiality for Lord Bute and Lord Mansfield. 'Black Wednesday was the most horrible night that ever I beheld' – nothing can have been like that night of fire and terror, until we come to our own civilised era, with the German blitzes on London.

Walpole tells us that 'one project of the diabolical incendiaries was to let loose the lions in the Tower and the lunatics in Bedlam. The latter might be from a fellow-feeling in Lord George, but cannibals do not invite wild beasts to their banquets.' When Lord George was brought to trial, he was acquitted, owing largely to the eloquence of his Scottish counsel, Erskine, and the absence of any proof that he had approved the riots. After eight months in the Tower he was freed to pursue his divagatory course, becoming a Jew, penetrating Newgate for converts, libelling the Queen of France and British justice. The last had been too kind to him, but at length laid him by the heels in Newgate, where he had a good time, entertaining largely, giving a ball every fortnight and conforming strictly to Jewish rites. There were not wanting Leftist newspapers to lament his being kept in durance; it was in fact a protective measure, today Soviet Russia would keep him in a lunatic asylum. Walpole had no sympathy with the outcry at his being in confinement. 'So are the tigers and hyena in the Tower, and I hope his lordship will not find bail before they do.'

In the autumn of 1780 there was captured off Newfoundland Henry Laurens, the wealthy South Carolina leader of colonial opposition to Britain, who had been President of the second Continental Congress in 1777–8. His papers were found to contain the project of a treaty between the revolting colonies and Holland, with a prospective loan. This had the importance that it led to war with Holland and the ex-President's residence in the Tower. The *Dictionary of American Biography* informs us that 'his diplomatic activity was hampered by his tendency to be self-righteous and over-sensitive'. No doubt. He thought he was being treated harshly: no idea that the Tower was an honour, usually reserved for peers. To the authorities he was, of course, a rebel; he insisted that he was an ambassador, and filled friendly ears with his plaints.

On his arrival he was greeted cheerfully by the warders singing 'Yankee Doodle', which only aroused his 'sublime contempt' – he had *no* sense of humour. He was lodged comfortably in the house of one of them, and left a legacy to the wife, while entertaining a *tendresse* for the daughter. Less agreeably, he was visited by the inevitable Selina, Countess of Huntingdon, and her girl-friend, Lady Ann Erskine. One day on his walk round the grounds he was saluted by Lord George Gordon, who invited him to join him: the rebel-ambassador at once fled to his own quarters. 'Wealthy merchants and nobles poured in delicacies almost daily, with which he made happy the kind subordinates about him.' The Lieutenant, General Vernon, was courtesy itself. He permitted a number of prominent pro-Americans to visit Laurens; whose reluctant residence enabled him to welcome his son, being educated in England, whom he had not seen for six years.

Such time as he could spare from drawing up protests and conducting pro-American propaganda, he spent in copying out long extracts from Gibbon's *Decline and Fall of the Roman Empire*, pointing out the parallels with the Decline and Fall of Britain, of which Gibbon himself was conscious. Burke took up Laurens' case and got him released on parole to go down to Bath to take the waters for his health. Ultimately he was exchanged for Lord Cornwallis, unfortunate at Yorktown, who was in fact Constable of the Tower.

When the apostle of liberty got back to his slave-owning plantations, his neighbours called him 'Tower' Laurens, with a note of distinction and pride in his war-time experience.

France's joining in the war brought out a spy, in the person of Francis de la

Henry Laurens, an American Revolutionary leader, sent Ambassador to Holland, who was captured and imprisoned in the Tower

Motte, in 1781. He had procured 'the most authentic intelligence respecting our naval operations'; this on the evidence given by one Lutterloh, to whom he had paid fifty guineas a month. De la Motte was aged fifty and 'of a comely countenance; his deportment was exceedingly genteel'. Found guilty, he showed becoming firmness and fortitude in the coach: 'He only expressed the same wish as he had to the sheriffs, that his dissolution might be immediate by striking off his head, if his Majesty would graciously grant him that indulgence.'

He was evidently a gentleman; I do not know if he had that indulgence.

The French Revolution gave rise to fond hopes in liberal breasts: Charles James Fox welcomed the Fall of the Bastille as 'the best news since [the disaster to his country at] Saratoga'. Charles Fox might be indulged as an aristocrat and a descendant of the Stuarts, for whom he was named. But the Jacobin Reign of Terror from 1792 frightened the governing class, and they were not amused when Corresponding Societies were formed across the country to propagate radical reform. Towards the end of the Reign of Terror the government of the younger Pitt – who himself had been a reformer – in a panic pounced on a group of harmless Radicals.

Among them was the amusing rascal Horne Tooke, who had been thick as thieves with Wilkes and then, of course, they bitterly quarrelled. An inveterate pamphleteer, Horne Tooke was always in and out of the courts for libel. His father, a poulterer, had been owed thousands by Frederick, Prince of Wales, which were never paid – enough to make anyone a Radical, and father had insisted on son undergoing what the latter described as 'the infectious hand of a bishop' – in other words, take orders – for a livelihood. In 1794 Horne Tooke was playing a more dangerous game of making a sham confession to a spy; the government absurdly took this to refer to a rising and brought the Corresponding Society leaders – Thomas Hardy, who had started these societies, John Thelwall, Horne Tooke and others – into the security of the Tower.

After four months in prison the men were brought to trial in October, Hardy first. This lasted eight days; the government case completely broke down, and Erskine had another forensic triumph. On his acquittal Hardy was drawn through the cheering crowds of London in a coach. The government foolishly persisted with Horne Tooke's case; tried with conspicuous fairness, a verdict of 'not guilty' was instantly returned. In December came Thelwall's turn. He handed a note saying he wished to plead his own case. 'If you do, you will be hanged,' said Erskine. 'Then I'll be hanged if I do,' replied Thelwall, and was acquitted. Soon after he published his *Poems written in Close Confinement in the Tower and Newgate*. The acquittal of all the prisoners, a dozen in all from both sanctuaries, was a blow to the government and to 'Billy Pitt – damn his eyes' – as I have heard a great liberal historian, G. M. Trevelyan, say as if he were contemporary with the event.

In different vein there came in 1803 the appointment of Samuel Lysons as Keeper of the Records, who takes his place among the most eminent of those who have been concerned with them, Lambarde, Selden, Prynne. For Lysons' tenure marked a new epoch in their administration and bringing them before the public. He increased the staff from one to six, and, as the *Annual Register* sums up, 'under his direction this office soon became one of a very important nature. Many interesting documents have been discovered among confused heaps of unknown records, which had lain mouldering for ages. These have been carefully examined, sorted and arranged in complete order.'

Lysons was a favourite with George III, who liked scholars and did his best to promote the arts. The antiquary was an artist of some skill, who occasionally exhibited views of old buildings at the Royal Academy. He made his reputation with several works on the antiquities of his native Gloucestershire; then followed his splendid production, on which he laboured for over twenty years and spent £6000, chiefly on some 150 beautifully coloured plates, *Reliquiae Britannico-Romanae*, illustrating Roman antiquities in England. For twenty

Radicals in conclave – John Glynn, John Wilkes
and Horne Tooke, painted by R. Houston in about 1768

years he aided his brother, Daniel, with the vast undertaking *Magna Britannia*, of which six volumes appeared. Samuel provided the topography, geology, and dealt with the scenery, himself making many of the drawings and etchings. Daniel had already produced his superb *Environs of London* in five volumes, with another of Corrections and Additions. The major undertaking was beyond their joint capacities to complete, but an immense collection of materials and correspondence relating to it, in the British Museum, attests their industry.

Meanwhile Keeper Samuel Lysons continued to publish Roman antiquities newly brought to light, and also to direct the Society of Antiquaries. Made a Fellow of the Royal Society, he became its Vice-President and Treasurer in 1810. He then initiated a scheme for publishing a series of royal letters from the archives in his care and some of the earliest proceedings in Chancery – the latter published posthumously. For he was only in his fifties when he died in 1819 – perhaps from too much research. John Bayley, who acknowledges his indebtedness to Lysons in undertaking his big History of the Tower, tells us that Lysons' originating mind had formed many more projects he did not live to carry out. On the other hand it was probably his celibate state that enabled him to achieve so much.

Lysons' chief clerk of the Records was one Robert Lemon, the first of three generations of archivists. He trained up his son, another Robert, who then became assistant to his father for a short period before graduating to the State Paper Office, where he initiated the arrangements of the state papers for eventual publication. An Act of 1838 brought the public records under the jurisdiction of the Master of the Rolls and paved the way for their ultimate concentration in one Record Office. From the Middle Ages the Tower had been one of the chief repositories – mainly of Chancery rolls – along with Westminster, where the Exchequer resided.

Samuel Lysons,
Keeper of the
Records

So the Tower became one of the parents of the Public Record Office about the same time as of the Zoo.

In 1810 there supervened the comic episode of the brief incarceration of Sir Francis Burdett – a characteristic Regency farce. A pupil of Horne Tooke, Burdett's marriage to the heiress of the banker Coutts multiplied his resources for reform and making trouble. At last the unreformed House of Commons caught him for a breach of their precious privileges, and off he went to the Tower. Burdett, being not only radical but rich, refused to go and barricaded himself in his Piccadilly mansion, defended by the mob – after all, a wealthy baronet was almost as good as a lord. When the horrid soldiery broke into the house, they found Sir Francis striking a Regency attitude making his son translate Magna Carta aloud. The mob retaliated in customary fashion by breaking the windows of Tory peers, and thousands of soldiers were found necessary to defend the Tower.

From that eyrie Sir Francis indited a 'saucy' letter to the Speaker and proceeded to sue him at law as well as Lord Moira – the Regent's favourite – Constable of the Tower, for wrongful detention. Sir Francis was abundantly consoled for his heroic sufferings in the cause by the addresses from different parts of the kingdom for his liberation. The House of Commons, inundated by these, was only too glad to let the matter drop, and Sir Francis out, with the end of the session.

His mob of supporters prepared him a splendid triumph. A vast procession wound through the City to escort the conquering hero, all wearing blue cockades, his colour. Most of the ladies wore the Garter-blue ribbon. Bands were playing, blue silk banners flying with improving mottoes – 'Magna Carta', 'The Constitution', 'Trial by Jury', etc. The Radical celebrity Major Cartwright, who devoted a mis-spent life to the cause of votes for everybody, trumpeted on a pure white horse, flourishing an oak baton to signify Liberty.

They all arrived at the Tower to find that their hero had absconded. They would not believe it, until the placard was posted: 'Sir Francis Burdett left the Tower by water at half past three o'clock.' It was too bad. 'The news excited not only surprise but indignation in many. For some time considerable confusion prevailed, and discontent appeared in every countenance.' At last, convinced that the news was only too true, the procession wound its sorry length along back to Piccadilly, dragging an empty car. Next day a deputation of sadder, if not wiser, men waited on the baronet to protest that at least he might have let them know – before they made such fools of themselves. The celebrated wire-puller Francis Place, who had wire-pulled it all, never spoke to the baronet again, and it is doubtful if Sir Francis's number was ever the same among the stern unbending Left.

A few years later there followed the real thing: the Cato Street Conspiracy, formed to assassinate the leading members of the government at a Cabinet dinner, in 1820. The inspirer of this was Arthur Thistlewood, who had spent his adult life in conspiracy and agitation; he had already been in the Tower once. He in turn had been inspired in youth by the superficial rationalism of Tom Paine, who thought that the French Revolution would usher in the Earthly Jerusalem, not the military dictatorship that the historical prescience of Edmund Burke foresaw.

Young Thistlewood, tall and slender, soldierly in appearance, was able to marry a fortune; but his wife died young, her fortune went back to her family, and he took to gambling. Political gambling was more dangerous: he became infected with the naïve revolutionary ideas of Thomas Spence. In December 1816 Thistlewood and his confederates in these societies organised a vast demonstration in Spa Fields, to take advantage of the prevailing distress to launch their revolution. First, the Tower and the Bank of England were to be seized. For months before, Thistlewood had been agitating in guard-rooms and barracks and, with the fatuous optimism of such types, he fully believed that the Tower Guard would throw open the gates to the mob. The government was well informed of the plans, through its spies among the agitators. Thistlewood and his fellow-conspirator the younger Watson went into hiding; the latter got away to America, but Thistlewood was taken in time on board the ship on which he had booked his passage. He and the elder Watson found themselves within the walls they had fancied would capitulate to them.

Such was the repressive reaction of the Tory government that, when Thistlewood and Watson were put on trial, it decided to submit no evidence and all got off. This liberal leniency had no effect on Thistlewood, who immediately resumed his contacts with the reforming and revolutionary groups. He broke with the moderate reformers for their ineffectiveness, and himself favoured the assassination of the Prince Regent or the Privy Council on the occasion of a public dinner. In and out of gaol once more, he formed a secret knot of thirteen – quite like old Elizabethan times. The state of distress in the country in 1819 – unemployment, high prices, scarcity, widespread suffering among the poorer classes – gave him hope. From December 1819 to February 1820 he was anxiously awaiting his chance, to attack the ministers at a public dinner, set fire to public buildings, and seize the Mansion House and the Tower.

George III's death in 1820 was thought a propitious moment – the Regent was most unpopular – and a cabinet dinner at Lord Harrowby's the occasion. Thistlewood's closest confidant, however, was a government spy; the conspirators were caught as they were arming themselves for Lord Harrowby's party. Thistlewood killed the police-officer and escaped in the *mêlée*. Next day he was captured and on 3 March, with seven of his companions, carried to the Tower. This time there was no mistaken leniency: he and four of his desperados were hanged, two transported for life, the eighth turned king's evidence. Thistlewood remained defiant to the last: 'Albion is still in the chains of slavery. I quit it without regret. My only sorrow is that the soil should be a theatre for slaves, for cowards, for despots.'

It is the same spirit of fanaticism that we have seen at work again and again in the course of this book – one of the most deplorable elements in the fabric of human history, more productive of misery and suffering than perhaps any other. More scepticism, a little more sense of humour, less faith and fanaticism, and human history would not be so tragic. However, with this expression of it, perhaps we may close the record.

14
Victoriana – Epilogue

APPY is the land that has no history, it has been said, though somewhat questionably, for it depends on whether its history has on the whole been happy – as England's has been, rather exceptionally. Even the history of the Tower, as we have seen, is not all gloom: there have been comic episodes and ludicrous characters as well as the pathetic, the tragic and the heroic; stately and ceremonial occasions, coronation as well as funeral processions; births and christenings to register with deaths and executions. If the murder of the Princes and the poisoning of Sir Thomas Overbury are the most sensational events, there have been amusing escapes to record. Above all, we have been able to bring out, as never before, what a nursing mother of literature the Tower has been – from the poems of Charles d'Orléans to the devotional works of Sir Thomas More and on to the poetry of Chidiock Tichborne, Robert Southwell and Ralegh. Then there are Ralegh's *History of the World* and the political treatises of Sir John Eliot, not to mention the tracts of the politicians, religious works like those of William Penn, the rich contributions of the Keepers of the Records to history and scholarship.

After the immediate post–Waterloo troubles, the political side to the Tower, so prominent in all its history, fell into inactivity, almost desuetude. Here again it reflects the long Victorian security and peace that Waterloo won for the nation. Where politics ceases history begins. Five years after the Cato Street conspirators had been sent off to Newgate for sentencing, John Bayley in 1825 produced his fine standard *History and Antiquities of the Tower of London*, in two sumptuous folio volumes, splendidly illustrated with numerous plates bringing its familiar features and less familiar recesses to the view. In 1840 Harrison Ainsworth published his famous 'historical romance', *The Tower of London*, with its hardly less famous illustrations by George Cruikshank. Inspired by the works of Walter Scott, and perhaps even more closely by Victor Hugo's *Notre Dame de Paris* only a few years before – for the hero of the

249

Tower Bridge, built in 1875

book is the building itself, rather than any one character – the work came out in monthly parts, printed by the Queen's own printer, Bentley, all through 1840. It is probable that it was this work that formed the impression of the Tower in most people's minds throughout the Victorian Age, as it did mine as a school-boy in remote Cornwall early this century.

In his Preface Ainsworth tells us that 'it has been, for years, the cherished wish of the writer to make the Tower of London – the proudest monument of antiquity, considered with reference to its historical associations, which this country or any other possesses – the groundwork of a Romance'. One aim was to introduce every feature of the old pile, to design his story so as to bring them in, and have them illustrated by 'the inimitable Artist'. Another aim was to introduce the public to the many parts at that time closed: he saw no reason why admission should not be given to St John's Chapel, the Council Chamber, and turrets; nor to the Beauchamp Tower with its wealth of inscriptions, then used as a mess-room. He had the further aim of alerting the public to the state of the buildings, arresting demolition, and restoring them. He had the Victorian dislike of an un-Gothic building such as the Restoration Storehouse, of which Mr Pepys was so proud: Ainsworth called it an 'ugly and incongruous structure'. He pleaded for the cleaning of the walls of St John's Chapel and the Beauchamp Tower, and ended, with Victorian sycophancy, with a pious tribute to Queen Victoria, 'its ever precious jewel', and the infant Princess, who became – we remember – mother of the deplorable German Kaiser.

The year after Ainsworth's best-seller a big fire drew further attention to the Tower and re-inforced what he had said about its state of neglect. The con-flagration broke out, 30 October 1841, in the great Armoury which was completely gutted. The exciting part of it all was the rescue of the Crown Jewels, in the threatened Martin Tower: they had undergone no such adventure since Colonel Blood's attempt on them. It is described in Cruikshank's *Omnibus*, who devoted one of his best etchings to the subject.

There stood the Keeper himself, his wife at his side, partaking the peril, and the warders whom he had summoned to the rescue. We cannot portray the stifling heat and smoke, the clamour of the soldiers outside the closed portal, which the fires of the Armoury were striving to reach; nor the roar of the flames, the hissing of the water-pipes, the voices of the multitude. They are beyond the pencil. . . . The Keeper bided his time – the crowbars were raised in a dozen hands. The first blow since the days of King Charles II descended on the iron fence, and Queen Victoria's crown safely deposited in its case and – sheltered from smoke and flame and the common gaze – was removed to the Governor's house.

Left: A Cruikshank drawing of the Crown Jewels being rescued during the fire on the night of 30 October 1841

Below: The Tower in Victorian days. A view from the Thames

The Duke of Wellington laying the first stone of the Waterloo Barracks
on the site of the old Armoury which had been destroyed by fire

The rest of the Regalia followed – orb, sceptre, diadems, chalices – 'in the care of many a sturdy warder'. But the baptismal font, 'soon to be called into use for the Prince of Wales' (the sacred figure of Edward VII), got stuck and more crowbars were necessary to fork it out. This exploit, when the room was now filling with smoke and heat, was performed by a gallant Metropolitan police-officer and commemorated by Cruikshank. At length, though the cloth upon which the Regalia had rested was charred, they were safely away, leaving the room as empty as Colonel Blood had meant to make it.

The damage caused by the fire was very considerable, the loss estimated at £200,000. The Armoury was destroyed – we have only the sculpted, baroque pediment left. For, four years later, the Waterloo Barracks were built upon its site, opened in state by the Iron Duke himself, then Constable, in 1845. More important, the event set in motion the immense programme of repairs and rebuilding that went on through much of the rest of the century.

Victoriana – Epilogue

A famous American writer, Nathaniel Hawthorne, paid two or three visits during his residence in England in the 1850s. He corroborates for us how little of the Tower was as yet open to the public – mainly only the White Tower and the Beauchamp Tower – and that parties were hustled round so quickly that there was little time to take in what they saw. He paid his first visit on a September day in 1855 and was at once impressed by the Tudor Yeomen of the Guard looking like kings in a pack of cards – he had never seen anything like that before; and indeed the figures in a pack of cards do wear Tudor dress.

Hawthorne was no less impressed by the armour – Henry VIII's, his brother-in-law the Duke of Suffolk's, and Charles I's. He saw the cloak in which General Wolfe died on the Heights of Abraham, 'a coarse, faded, threadbare, light-coloured garment', and glimpsed many other objects of interest, 'had there been time to look at them'. They were shown the headsman's block, 'not that on which Ralegh was beheaded, which I would have given gold to see, but the one that was used for the three Scotch lords, Kilmarnock, Lovat, and Balmerino'.

They were shown the Crown Jewels – Hawthorne could not believe his eyes that they were the real thing – Ralegh's room and the Beauchamp Tower, but there was no time to read the inscriptions. And so to cakes and buns in the refreshment room, and out across the moat, which had been drained 'within a few years'.

On 11 November, two years later, Hawthorne brought his family and went the same round again. There follows another description of the scene dominated by the great White Tower, 'which is now more black than white', and everything giving the impression of venerable decay. The novelist thought of it all as 'really a town within itself, with streets, avenues, and all that pertains to human life', soldiers going through their exercises in the open space, a great many cannon lying about. A few days later he was there again, but handed his family party over to 'one of the Trump Cards' and himself walked all round the exterior to get views from different angles, and watched 'the nursery maids giving children their airings. Probably these may have been the privileged inhabitants of the Tower, which certainly might contain the population of a large village.'

With the recession of politics, the disappearance of treason, we enter the world of building-restoration, archaeology, uncovering and titivating the past; with much of the interior of the Tower mysterious and hardly known to the public then, we begin to see the first indications of the world of tourism that is the feature of today. From 1842 Salvin was called in and continued his work for years; recognised as the leading authority on medieval military architecture, he became the Victorians' favourite restorer and builder, sometimes rebuilder, of castles and fortresses all over the country. It is a glaring default, on the part of architectural historians, that there is no biography of this important figure. At the Tower, the Beauchamp Tower, St Thomas's Tower, Traitors' Gate, the Saltery and the great Keep, the White Tower itself, all received his attention; though one can often recognise the Victorian stonework, one can hardly say, as of so much nineteenth-century restoration in France, *Violé-par-le-Duc*.

In the high Victorian Age news of the Tower is mainly military: otherwise all quiet. In the 1860s – when Disraeli was thinking up his *mot*, 'Sanitas sanitatum, all is sanitation' – the sanitary condition of the Barracks was giving concern. An occasional military concert was held, the armour re-arranged, a new Constable installed. The office was now joined with that of Governor and Lord Lieutenant of the Tower Hamlets, and distinguished retired soldiers were appointed by the Crown. A couple of days before Christmas 1871 Field-Marshal Sir G. Pollock was installed, in a dense Victorian fog as black as if at midnight, with a few lamps and torches and 'a sort of shadowy impressiveness', said *The Times*, 'not out of harmony with the traditions of the place'. It is the world of Charles Dickens.

In the 1870s work and repairs went forward, discoveries were made. In 1876 repairs to St Peter-ad-vincula exposed the coffins of the grandest Tudor victims – Victorians were alerted, for Macaulay's salute to the 'saddest spot in Christendom' was itself already famous. When a 'woman of excessively delicate proportions' was revealed, the Victorians thought it was Anne Boleyn; then there was the large frame of the Duke of Northumberland, and that of an aged lady, the Countess of Salisbury. The year before, 1875, the Tower had its first free opening to the public, two days a week. In the years following, along with improvements to the surroundings, the environment of the Tower received a revolutionary change, such as it had never had in all the centuries before: the erection of that most Victorian structure, Tower Bridge.

On 24 January 1885 occurred three explosions which portend our own enlightened age – they were the work of Irish Fenians. Two were at the Houses of Parliament, the third at the White Tower. It was on a Saturday when the Banqueting Hall was well filled with visitors, and there might have been considerable loss of life. Actually, though the force of the dynamite-charge was alarming, the damage was inconsiderable – chiefly to windows and casements, though the room was set on fire. Since the big fire in 1841, however, fire equipment had been greatly improved – all part of the campaign for bringing the Tower up to date – and the damage was soon repaired.

In our own time, with the two wars that the Germans forced upon Europe, the Tower has emerged from being something of a backdrop to Victorian London, and some characteristic events have taken place there – some spies have received their deserts, and Rudolf Hess, Hitler's close friend and deputy, was briefly there in 1941. In the first German war, 1914–18, little if any damage was done, and some parts remained open to the public. After the war was over, the whole was re-opened, and Dominion Trophies were added to the constantly growing collections – an appropriate symbol of what Britain owed, and was to owe again, to the Dominions for her survival. From between the wars there is a typical story, now part of the folklore of the Tower. The unfriendly ravens that haunt there are a reminder of the old days of the royal zoo, and the folklore goes that, if they come to an end, that will be the end of the British Empire. In the 1930s a Nazi official, on tour, commented – with typical mixture of bombast and inferiority-complex: 'Oh, in our land we have eagles.' One of the ravens heard him, and at once bit him.

One of the Tower ravens

Treasures of the Tower today: the Regalia

In the second war the Germans brought upon Europe, 1939–45, there fell within the Tower precincts fifteen direct hits from high explosives, three V-bombs and innumerable incendiaries. Twenty-three people were killed, besides two ravens; but no vital damage was done to any of the medieval building, only a northern bastion (modern) destroyed. A certain amount of Tudor building was damaged, and a great deal of old glass. Yet, in the course of the war, thousands of Allied troops visited the place, and over seventy-five per cent of all the American troops in the country. The moment the war was over, in 1945, the White Tower was reopened to the public, and in 1947 the Wakefield Tower. The Crown Jewels – a chief magnet of the popular gaze – were refurbished and re-exhibited. There followed the discovery of the missing legs of Henry VIII's armour, which has several times featured in this book, at Scrivelsby, the home of the Dymokes, Kings' Champions for a mere seven hundred years. This has gone along with the extensions to the collection of armours, culminating in the refashioning of the New Armouries in 1957.

Eminent soldiers continued to be installed as Constables: Field-Marshal Wavell in 1948, Field-Marshal Alanbrooke in 1950; today Field-Marshal Sir

Bomb damage at the Tower during the Second World War

The Tower of London

Richard Hull. Beating the bounds of the parish, on Ascension Day every third year, was resumed; the Easter Sunday parade of the Yeomen Warders; the ceremony of 'Beating Retreat'. The Ceremony of the Keys, locking up the Tower every night at 10 o'clock, has been going continuously for the last seven hundred years, with the Chief Warder (formerly Yeoman Porter) carrying a candle-lantern in one hand, the Queen's Keys in the other – one thinks of poor Queen Jane sending for the keys to her apartment in the vanished palace. Still the salutes are fired from the Tower Wharf for coronations, royal births and – a lesser affair – the opening and dissolving of Parliaments.

The chief feature of the age, however, is the astonishing growth of tourism, the hundreds of thousands that now pour in and out of the Tower, and from all countries. How now to describe the functions it performs, with which we began? Like so much in our age, they are fossil-functions, especially those that are archaic and ceremonial; no doubt they serve some purpose to the imagination, for those that have any. The main function, however, must be education and entertainment: the Tower has become a vast and varied, most idiosyncratic, Museum, unique in the world and suitably displayed, with all the resources of modern technology in these last years, by *Son et Lumière*.

The purpose of this book is to be a history, not a guide; rather, a mirror in which one may see the story of the nation reflected, from Conquest to Welfare State and Permissive Society. As such, the reflective historian – revisiting those haunts after the lapse of years, sniffing the Thames smells as so many occupants and visitors before him, as evening descends upon those grey walls and the river mists rise in wraiths about them – is more aware of the past than of the present. The ghosts come flocking into mind: bustling Mr Pepys, not at all out of countenance at finding himself there with his betters – it ministers to self-importance after all; the absurd Seven Bishops, caught out on a limb, heroes in spite of themselves; handsome Monmouth, as silly as he was beautiful, and crazy Lord George Gordon; the stiff and pompous Laurens, along with urbane Oxford receiving Swift's magnificent letter. And so back to the first Elizabeth, young and unstrung, but playing to the gallery as ever; Sir Thomas More playing to the inner gallery of his conscience – for the Tower, with its shifting lights, catches them at their most revealing moments. At last to the poor young Princes, and their uncle Clarence, of Shakespeare's 'fearful dream' –alike victims of their own family; as also was poor, pitiful Henry VI, with the white lilies and roses laid there every year that keep him in fragrant remembrance.

An evening view looking towards the Byward Tower

Chronology

WILLIAM I (1066–87)	1066 Norman Conquest (Battle of Hastings) 1075 Barons' rebellion 1086–7 Domesday Book compiled
WILLIAM II (1087–1100)	1097 Archbishop Anselm exiled
HENRY I (1100–35)	1106 Battle of Tinchebrai 1120 Wreck of *White Ship*
STEPHEN (1135–54)	1135–1153 Intermittent civil war
HENRY II (1154–89)	1164 Constitutions of Clarendon 1170 Becket murdered 1171 Invasion of Ireland 1173 Barons' rebellion
RICHARD I (1189–99)	1189 Richard's departure for Crusade
JOHN (1199–1216)	1203 Death of Prince Arthur 1204–5 Loss of Normandy 1209 Imposition of papal Interdict 1215 Magna Carta Barons' rebellion
HENRY III (1216–72)	1227 Henry takes personal rule 1256 Welsh revolt 1258 Barons' rebellion 1262 Barons' rebellion 1265 Battle of Evesham
EDWARD I (1272–1307)	1295 Campaigns to conquer Scotland Model Parliament

EDWARD II (1307–22)   1314 Defeat of Bannockburn
                       1322 Murder of Edward II

EDWARD III (1322–77)   1338 Beginning of Hundred Years' War
                       1346 Battle of Crecy
                       1346–7 Black Death
                       1356 Battle of Poitiers
                       1376 Good Parliament

RICHARD II (1377–99)   1381 Peasants' Revolt
                       1399 Richard II deposed by Henry of Lancaster

HENRY IV (1399–1413)   1400 Richard II murdered
                       1400–15 Owen Glendower leads Welsh resistance
                       1403 Percys' rebellion

HENRY V (1413–22)   1415 Battle of Agincourt
                       1420 Treaty of Troyes

HENRY VI   1450 Cade's Rebellion
(1422–60, 1470–1)   1454 Loss of French possessions, except Calais
                       1455 Beginning of Wars of the Roses

EDWARD IV (1460–83)   1471 Warwick the Kingmaker killed

EDWARD V (1483)   1483 Edward V deposed
                             Murder of the Princes in the Tower

RICHARD III (1483–5)   1485 Battle of Bosworth Field

HENRY VII (1485–1509) 1487 Battle of Stoke
                       1496 Cabot sails for America
                       1497 Cornish rebellion
                       1502 Death of Arthur, Prince of Wales

HENRY VIII (1509–47)   1513 Battles of the Spurs and Flodden Field
                       1520 Field of the Cloth of Gold
                       1529 Disgrace of Cardinal Wolsey
                       1531 Submission of Clergy
                       1534 Henry VIII proclaimed Head of the Church
                       1534–9 Series of Parliamentary Acts for reformation of
                               Church
                       1536 Death of Catherine of Aragon
                             Execution of Anne Boleyn
                             Dissolution of the Monasteries begun

	1542	Execution of Catherine Howard
	1547	War with Scotland
EDWARD VI (1547–53)	1549	First Prayer Book
	1552	Execution of Protector Seymour
		Second Prayer Book
MARY I (1553–8)	1553	Brief reign of Lady Jane Grey
	1554	Wyatt rebellion
		Execution of Lady Jane Grey
		Mary I marries Philip II of Spain
	1557	Loss of Calais
ELIZABETH I (1558–1603)	1559	Acts of Uniformity and Supremacy
		Peace of Cateau-Cambrésis
	1560	Treaty of Edinburgh
	1570	Papal Bull of Excommunication
	1587	Execution of Mary Queen of Scots
	1588	Spanish Armada
	1600	East India Company founded
	1601	Essex's rebellion
JAMES I (1603–25)	1604	Peace with Spain
	1605	Gunpowder Plot
	1607	Plantation of Ulster
	1618	Execution of Ralegh
	1620	*Mayflower* sails for America
CHARLES I (1625–49)	1629–40	Charles's personal rule
	1638	Scots Covenant signed
	1639	Scots War
	1640	Short and Long Parliaments
	1641	Execution of Strafford
		Irish rebellion begins
		Grand Remonstrance
	1642	Civil War begins
	1648	Second Civil War
	1649	Execution of Charles I
COMMONWEALTH (1649–60)	1650	Battle of Dunbar
	1652–4	War with Netherlands
	1653	Oliver Cromwell Lord Protector
	1656–9	War with Spain

	1658	Oliver Cromwell dies
	1659	Long Parliament restored
CHARLES II (1649–85)	1660	Monarchy restored
	1661–5	Clarendon Code
	1665	Great Plague
	1665–7	War with Netherlands
	1666	Great Fire of London
	1679	Popish Plot
		Habeas Corpus Act
James II (1685–8)	1685	Monmouth's rebellion
	1687	Declaration of Indulgence
	1688	Trial of the Seven Bishops
		'Glorious Revolution'
WILLIAM III (1688–1702)	1690	Battle of the Boyne
and MARY II (1688–94)	1690–7	War with France
	1697	Treaty of Ryswick
	1701–13	War of the Spanish Succession
ANNE (1702–14)	1707	Act of Union with Scotland
	1713	Treaty of Utrecht
GEORGE I (1714–27)	1715	Jacobite rebellion
	1720	South Sea Bubble
GEORGE II (1727–60)	1745	Jacobite rebellion
	1746	Battle of Culloden
	1756–63	Seven Years' War
	1759	Wolfe takes Quebec; conquest of Canada
GEORGE III (1760–1820)	1763	Peace of Paris
	1775–83	American War of Independence
	1793–1802	War with revolutionary France
	1801	Act of Union (with Ireland)
	1802	Treaty of Amiens
	1803–14, and 1815	Napoleonic Wars
	1805	Battle of Trafalgar
	1812–14	War with USA
	1815	Battle of Waterloo
GEORGE IV (1820–30)	1829	Catholic Emancipation Act

WILLIAM IV (1830–7)   1832 Reform Act

VICTORIA (1837–1901)   1846 Repeal of Corn Laws
                           1854–6 Crimean War
                           1867 Second Reform Act
                           1899–1902 Boer War

EDWARD VII (1901–10)   1904 *Entente Cordiale*
                           1905 Anglo-Japanese alliance

GEORGE V (1910–36)   1911 Parliament Act
                           1914–8 First World War
                           1921–3 Irish Civil War

EDWARD VIII (1936)   1936 Abdication of Edward VIII

GEORGE VI (1936–52)   1939–45 Second World War

Plan of the Tower of London

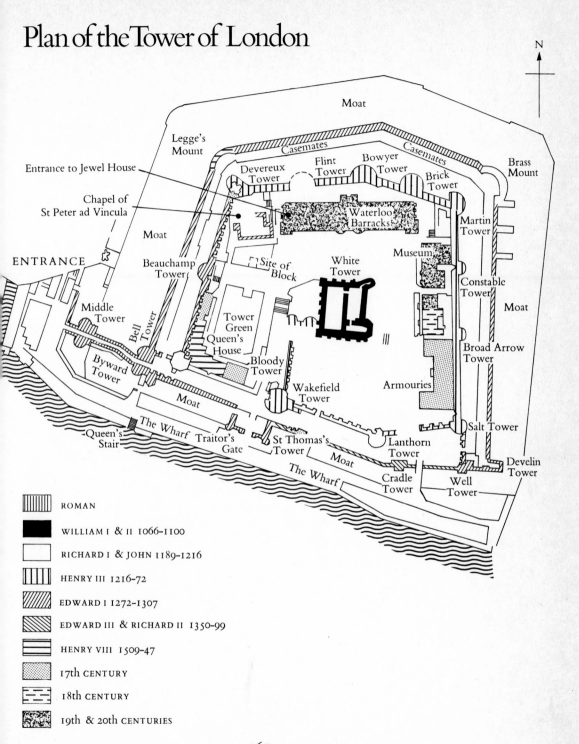

N

Moat

Legge's
Mount

Entrance to Jewel House

Devereux
Tower

Flint
Tower

Bowyer
Tower

Casemates

Casemates

Brass
Mount

Chapel of
St Peter ad Vincula

Moat

Beauchamp
Tower

Brick
Tower

Waterloo
Barracks

Martin
Tower

ENTRANCE

Site of
Block

White
Tower

Museum

Constable
Tower

Moat

Middle
Tower

Bell
Tower

Tower
Green
Queen's
House

Broad Arrow
Tower

Byward
Tower

Bloody
Tower

Armouries

The Wharf

Queen's
Stair

Traitor's
Gate

St Thomas's
Tower

Wakefield
Tower

Lanthorn
Tower

Salt Tower

Develin
Tower

Moat

Moat

The Wharf

Cradle
Tower

Well
Tower

	ROMAN
	WILLIAM I & II 1066–1100
	RICHARD I & JOHN 1189–1216
	HENRY III 1216–72
	EDWARD I 1272–1307
	EDWARD III & RICHARD II 1350–99
	HENRY VIII 1509–47
	17th CENTURY
	18th CENTURY
	19th & 20th CENTURIES

The Normans and Plantagenets

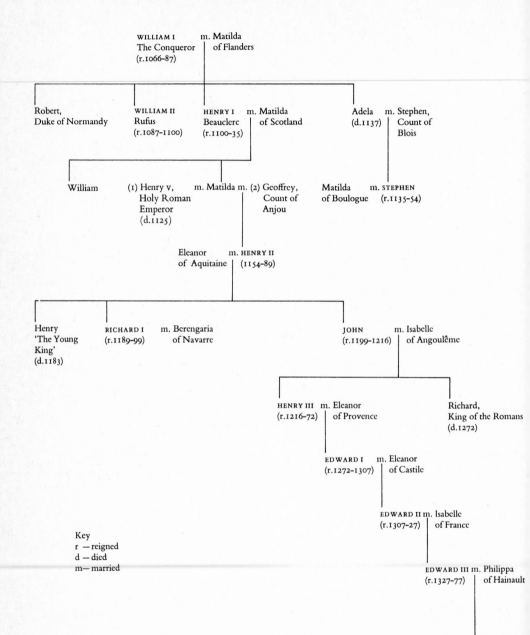

WILLIAM I   m. Matilda
The Conqueror   of Flanders
(r.1066–87)

Robert,   WILLIAM II   HENRY I   m. Matilda   Adela   m. Stephen,
Duke of Normandy   Rufus   Beauclerc   of Scotland   (d.1137)   Count of
     (r.1087–1100)   (r.1100–35)   Blois

William   (1) Henry v,   m. Matilda m. (2) Geoffrey,   Matilda   m. STEPHEN
     Holy Roman   Count of   of Boulogne   (r.1135–54)
     Emperor   Anjou
     (d.1125)

Eleanor   m. HENRY II
of Aquitaine   (1154–89)

Henry   RICHARD I   m. Berengaria   JOHN   m. Isabelle
'The Young   (r.1189–99)   of Navarre   (r.1199–1216)   of Angoulême
King'
(d.1183)

HENRY III   m. Eleanor   Richard,
(r.1216–72)   of Provence   King of the Romans
     (d.1272)

EDWARD I   m. Eleanor
(r.1272–1307)   of Castile

EDWARD II m. Isabelle
(r.1307–27)   of France

EDWARD III m. Philippa
(r.1327–77)   of Hainault

Key
r — reigned
d — died
m— married

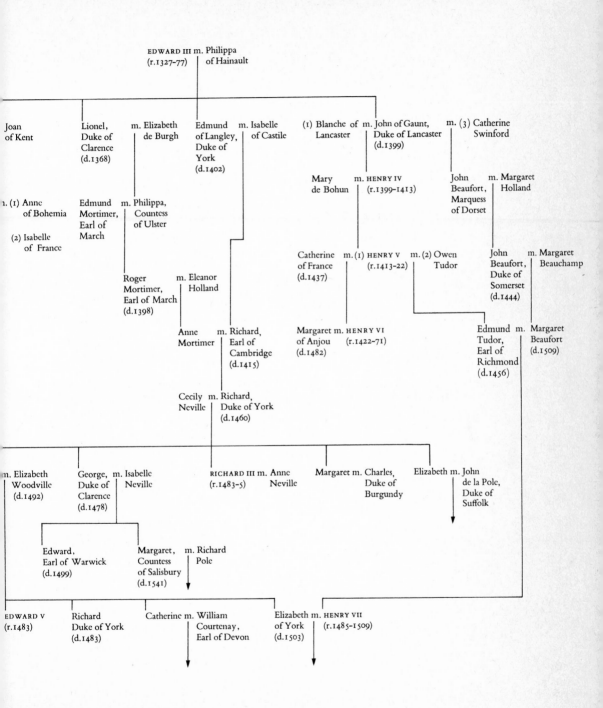

EDWARD III m. Philippa
(r.1327-77) | of Hainault

Joan
of Kent

Lionel,
Duke of
Clarence
(d.1368)

m. Elizabeth
de Burgh

Edmund
of Langley,
Duke of
York
(d.1402)

m. Isabelle
of Castile

(1) Blanche
Lancaster

m. John of Gaunt,
Duke of Lancaster
(d.1399)

m. (3) Catherine
Swinford

Mary
de Bohun

m. HENRY IV
(r.1399-1413)

John
Beaufort,
Marquess
of Dorset

m. Margaret
Holland

m. (1) Anne
of Bohemia

(2) Isabelle
of France

Edmund
Mortimer,
Earl of
March

m. Philippa,
Countess
of Ulster

Catherine
of France
(d.1437)

m. (1) HENRY V
(r.1413-22)

m. (2) Owen
Tudor

John
Beaufort,
Duke of
Somerset
(d.1444)

m. Margaret
Beauchamp

Roger
Mortimer,
Earl of March
(d.1398)

m. Eleanor
Holland

Anne
Mortimer

m. Richard,
Earl of
Cambridge
(d.1415)

Margaret
of Anjou
(d.1482)

m. HENRY VI
(r.1422-71)

Edmund
Tudor,
Earl of
Richmond
(d.1456)

m. Margaret
Beaufort
(d.1509)

Cecily
Neville

m. Richard,
Duke of York
(d.1460)

m. Elizabeth
Woodville
(d.1492)

George,
Duke of
Clarence
(d.1478)

m. Isabelle
Neville

RICHARD III
(r.1483-5)

m. Anne
Neville

Margaret
m. Charles,
Duke of
Burgundy

Elizabeth m. John
de la Pole,
Duke of
Suffolk

Edward,
Earl of Warwick
(d.1499)

Margaret,
Countess
of Salisbury
(d.1541)

m. Richard
Pole

EDWARD V
(r.1483)

Richard
Duke of York
(d.1483)

Catherine
m. William
Courtenay,
Earl of Devon

Elizabeth
of York
(d.1503)

m. HENRY VII
(r.1485-1509)

The Houses of Tudor and Stuart

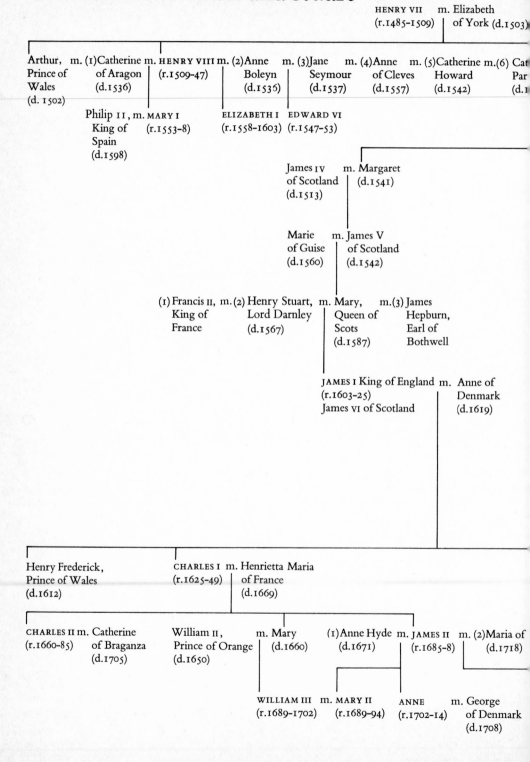

HENRY VII (r.1485-1509) m. Elizabeth of York (d.1503)

Arthur, Prince of Wales (d. 1502) m. (1)Catherine of Aragon (d.1536) m. HENRY VIII (r.1509-47) m. (2)Anne Boleyn (d.1536) m. (3)Jane Seymour (d.1537) m. (4)Anne of Cleves (d.1557) m. (5)Catherine Howard (d.1542) m.(6) Catherine Parr (d.1...)

Philip II, King of Spain (d.1598) m. MARY I (r.1553-8)

ELIZABETH I (r.1558-1603)

EDWARD VI (r.1547-53)

James IV of Scotland (d.1513) m. Margaret (d.1541)

Marie of Guise (d.1560) m. James V of Scotland (d.1542)

(1) Francis II, King of France m. (2) Henry Stuart, Lord Darnley (d.1567) m. Mary, Queen of Scots (d.1587) m.(3) James Hepburn, Earl of Bothwell

JAMES I King of England (r.1603-25) James VI of Scotland m. Anne of Denmark (d.1619)

Henry Frederick, Prince of Wales (d.1612)

CHARLES I (r.1625-49) m. Henrietta Maria of France (d.1669)

CHARLES II (r.1660-85) m. Catherine of Braganza (d.1705)

William II, Prince of Orange (d.1650) m. Mary (d.1660)

(1)Anne Hyde (d.1671) m. JAMES II (r.1685-8) m. (2)Maria of ... (d.1718)

WILLIAM III (r.1689-1702) m. MARY II (r.1689-94)

ANNE (r.1702-14) m. George of Denmark (d.1708)

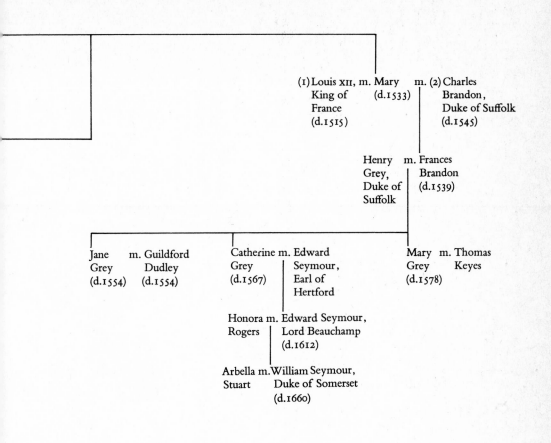

(1) Louis XII, m. Mary   m. (2) Charles
   King of   (d.1533)   Brandon,
   France   Duke of Suffolk
   (d.1515)   (d.1545)

Henry   m. Frances
Grey,   Brandon
Duke of   (d.1539)
Suffolk

Jane   m. Guildford   Catherine m. Edward   Mary   m. Thomas
Grey   Dudley   Grey   Seymour,   Grey   Keyes
(d.1554)   (d.1554)   (d.1567)   Earl of   (d.1578)
                                 Hertford

Honora m. Edward Seymour,
Rogers   Lord Beauchamp
        (d.1612)

Arbella m. William Seymour,
Stuart   Duke of Somerset
       (d.1660)

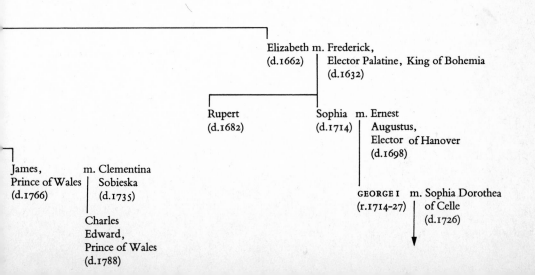

Elizabeth m. Frederick,
(d.1662)   Elector Palatine, King of Bohemia
           (d.1632)

Rupert   Sophia   m. Ernest
(d.1682)   (d.1714)   Augustus,
                          Elector of Hanover
                          (d.1698)

James,   m. Clementina
Prince of Wales   Sobieska
(d.1766)   (d.1735)   GEORGE I   m. Sophia Dorothea
                                      (r.1714-27)   of Celle
   Charles   (d.1726)
   Edward,
   Prince of Wales
   (d.1788)

The Houses of Hanover and Windsor

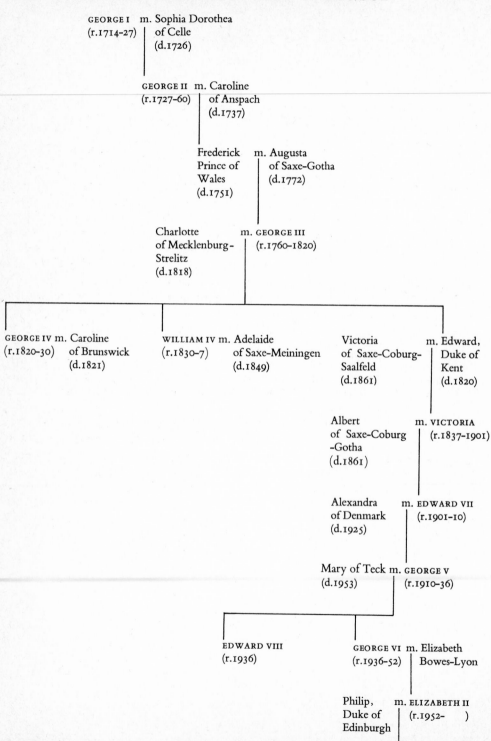

GEORGE I m. Sophia Dorothea
(r.1714-27) of Celle
(d.1726)

GEORGE II m. Caroline
(r.1727-60) of Anspach
(d.1737)

Frederick m. Augusta
Prince of of Saxe-Gotha
Wales (d.1772)
(d.1751)

Charlotte m. GEORGE III
of Mecklenburg- (r.1760-1820)
Strelitz
(d.1818)

GEORGE IV m. Caroline   WILLIAM IV m. Adelaide   Victoria   m. Edward,
(r.1820-30) of Brunswick   (r.1830-7) of Saxe-Meiningen   of Saxe-Coburg-   Duke of
(d.1821)   (d.1849)   Saalfeld   Kent
(d.1861)   (d.1820)

Albert   m. VICTORIA
of Saxe-Coburg   (r.1837-1901)
-Gotha
(d.1861)

Alexandra   m. EDWARD VII
of Denmark   (r.1901-10)
(d.1925)

Mary of Teck m. GEORGE V
(d.1953)   (r.1910-36)

EDWARD VIII   GEORGE VI m. Elizabeth
(r.1936)   (r.1936-52) Bowes-Lyon

Philip,   m. ELIZABETH II
Duke of   (r.1952-   )
Edinburgh

Acknowledgments

The photographs on the following pages were specially commissioned for this book and were taken by Robert Harding: 2, 13, 43, 55, 75, 97, 101, 102–3, 121, 122, 129, 139, *164*, 248, 259.

Photographs and illustrations were supplied or are reproduced by kind permission of the following. The pictures on pages 18, 44, 47, 73, are reproduced by gracious permission of H.M. the Queen; on page 61 by courtesy of the Duke of Norfolk, Arundel Castle; on pages 79 and 133, by kind permission of the Duke of Northumberland; on page 106 by kind permission of the Duke of Bedford, from the Woburn Abbey Collection; on page *117* by kind permission of the Duke of Buccleuch and Queensberry; on page 236 by kind permission of the Marquess of Cholmondeley; on page *161* by kind permission of Lord Brooke, Warwick Castle; on page 36 by kind permission of Baron Thyssen; on page 28 by courtesy of the Dean and Chapter of Canterbury Cathedral; on pages 15/2 and 31 by courtesy of the Dean and Chapter of Westminster Abbey; on page 23 by kind permission of the Warden and Fellows of All Souls College, Oxford. BPC: 171/2; Bodleian Library: 149, 228/2; British Museum: 33, 34, 81, 122, 159, 167, 202; Coleman and Rye Library, Norwich: 175; Henry Cooper: *117*; Country Life: 79; Courtauld Institute of Art: 238; Department of the Environment: *162–3*, 255; Edinburgh University Library: *136*; Entwhistle Photographic Services: 28; R.B. Fleming: *32*, *118*; Fox Photos: 257; John Freeman: 159, 202; Copyright The Frick Collection, New York: 56; John Gay: 255; Guildhall Library: 197/1, 197/2, *198–9*, 211, 213, 233/1, 233/2; Guildhall Library, after survey in Society of Antiquaries: 111; Hardwick Hall, National Trust: 142; HMSO (Crown Copyright): 256; Isabella Stewart Gardner Museum: 67; Lambeth Palace Library: 21/2; London Museum: *118*, 191; Lord St Oswald's Collection: 46; Mansell Collection: 21/1, 60, 76, 126/1, 126/2, 185, 186, 194, 216, 234, 241, 247; Mary Evans: 95, 210/1; National Portrait Gallery: 41/1, 41/2, 51, 52, *135*, 145, 153, 172, 177/1, 177/2, 189/1, 189/2, 204, 210/2, 214, 222, 224, 228, 231, 243; Paul Mellon Foundation for British Art: 106; Pitkin Pictorial: *200/1*, *200/2*; Private Collection, England: 154; Radio Times Hulton Picture Library: 180; Society of Antiquaries: 63; D.M. Smith: 133; Tower of London (Crown Copyright): 105, 122, 237.

Numbers in italic indicate colour illustrations.

Picture research by Jasmine Davies.

Index

Abbot, George, Archbishop, 147, 150, 151
Agincourt, battle, 17
Ainsworth, Harrison, novelist, 249–50
America, 246; American Revolution, 239–42
Andrewes, Lancelot, Bishop, 147
Anne, Queen, 217, 221–2
Anne of Denmark, James I's Queen, 137, 138
Antonio, Don, Portuguese Pretender, 112
Apsley, Sir Allen, Lieutenant, 156
Arden, John, 86, 93–4
Armada, Spanish, 83
Artillery, 12, 65, 71, 101, 121
Arundel, Henry Fitzalan, Earl of, 66, 67; ——,
    Philip Howard, Earl of, 82–4, 88
Arundell of Wardour, Henry, Lord, 201–2
Ashton, Abdy, Puritan preacher, 114
Askew, Anne, Protestant martyr, 59–60
Atterbury, Francis, Bishop, 228–9
Aubrey, John, 145, 171, 184

Babington, Anthony, conspirator, 86
Bailly, Charles, 98
Balfour, Sir William, Lieutenant, 165
Ballard, John, conspirator, 86
Balmerino, Arthur Elphinstone, Lord, 230–2
Barksted, John, Cromwellian Governor, 182, 189
Barnet, battle, 22
Bastille, 238, 242
Bath, 132, 241; ——, Knights of the, 20, 37, 40,
    187, 188
Becket, St Thomas, 12
Bellisle, Marshal, 229
Blenheim, battle, 222
Blood, Colonel Thomas and the Crown Jewels,
    193–5
Blount, Sir Christopher, 114–5; ——, Sir
    Michael, Lieutenant, 83, 91, 100; ——, Mount-
    joy, Earl of Newport, Constable, 100, 165,
    167–8
Boleyn, Queen Anne, 40–2, 47

Bolingbroke, v. Henry IV
Books written in the Tower, 49–50, 68, 83, 91,
    99, 123, 132–3, 155, 170–1
Bosworth, battle, 25, 26, 30
Boulogne, 104
Bracegirdle, Anne, actress, 224
Brackenbury, Sir Robert, Constable, 29
Brooke, George, conspirator, 123
Buckingham, Edward Stafford, Duke of, 61,
    100; ——, George Villiers, 1st Duke of, 132,
    151, 152, 155; ——, George Villiers, 2nd Duke
    of, 183, 192
Burdett, Sir Francis, Radical reformer, 245–6
Burke, Edmund, 241, 246
Burnet, Gilbert, Bishop, 224
Butler, Samuel ('Hudibras'), 175

Cadiz, 104
Caesar, Julius, 9, 10
Calais, 59, 144
Cambridge, 24, 67, 144
Camden, William, historian, 85
Cameron, Doctor Archibald, Jacobite, 229
Campion, Edmund, Jesuit; 85, 87–8; ——, Dr
    Thomas, 147
Capel, Arthur, Lord, 183
Carew, Sir Alexander, 176; ——, Sir Nicholas,
    39
Carlisle, Lucy Hay, Countess of, 132, 160
Carolina, 205, 240
Carr, Robert, Earl of Somerset, 134–7, 141,
    145–52
Carthusians imprisoned, 48
Cartwright, Major John, Radical reformer, 245
Castlehaven, Mervyn Touchet, Earl of, 157–8
Castlemaine, Roger Palmer, Earl of, 218–9
Catesby, Robert, Gunpowder plotter, 125–7, 130
Catherine of Aragon, Henry VIII's Queen, 32,
    35–6
Cato Street Conspiracy, 246–7

Cecil, Sir Robert, 109, 111, 113, 114, 115, 116, and as Earl of Salisbury, 127, 134, 139, 145; ——, Sir William, 79–80, 115

Chaplains of the Tower, 203–4, 215

Charles I, 14, 100, 155, 157, 158–67, 188; —— II, 10, 156, 174, 175, 184–5, 187–90, 192, 193, 194–6, 201–4, 206–8, 209, 226, 229; —— V, Emperor, 57, 74

Charnock, Robert, conspirator, 223

Cholmondeley, Sir Richard, Lieutenant, 100

Churchill, General Charles, Lieutenant, 222; ——, George, Admiral, 222; ——, Sir Winston, 237; and v. Marlborough

Civil War, the, 168, 173–81

Clancarty, Donough MacCarthy, Earl of, 223

Clarence, George, Duke of, 22, 24–5, 30, 40

Clarendon, Edward Hyde, 1st Earl of, 165, 182; ——, Henry Hyde, 2nd Earl of, 220

Clark, Thomas, 98

Cleves, Anne of, 43, 57–8

Clink prison, 91

Clive, Robert, Lord, 237

Cobham, Henry Brooke, Lord, 123–4

Coke, Sir Edward, Attorney-General, 151

Constables of the Tower, 29, 42, 53, 74, 100, 114, 165, 167–8, 220, 235, 241, 252, 254, 256–7

Cornwall, 156, 157, 170–1, 225

Cornwallis, Charles, Marquis, 235, 241

Coronation Processions, 10, 14, 15, 20, 32, 40, 63, 71, 77–8

Courtenay, Edward, Earl of Devon, 38–9, 67, 71, 74, 75; and v. Exeter

Cranmer, Thomas, Archbishop, 42, 43, 45, 59, 68, 69, 70–1

Cromwell, Oliver, 141, 166, 174, 176, 177–8, 179, 182–3; ——, Sir Richard, 45; ——, Thomas, 38, 48, 57–8, 70

Crown Jewels, 193–5, 250–2, 253, 256

Cruikshank, George, artist, 249, 250

Cuffe, Henry, 114–5

Danby, Thomas Osborne, Earl of, 196–204, 206

Danvers, Sir Charles, 114, 119

Dartmouth, George Legge, Lord, 220

Davenant, Sir William, dramatist, 178–9

Derwentwater, Charles Ratcliffe, Earl of, 230

Digby, Sir Everard Digby, Gunpowder plotter, 125, 127

Donne, John, poet, 87

Dover, 17; ——, Secret Treaty of, 195–6

Draper, Hugh, astrologer, 99–100

Dryden, John, 196, 205–6, 207

Dublin, 107

Dudley, Edmund, 37; ——, Lord Guildford, 66; and v. Leicester, Northumberland, Warwick; —— Inscription, 98

Dunbar, William, poet, 9

Dunkirk, 189

Dutch War, 192, 201

Edward I, 12; —— IV, 19–25, 26, 35, 59; —— V, 25–30; —— VI, 60, 63, 65–6, 67; —— VII, 252

Edwards, Talbot, Keeper of the Crown Jewels, 193–4

Eliot, Sir John, Parliamentarian leader, 35, 155–7

Elizabeth I, 40, 63, 64, 65, 71, 72, 74–5, 77–80, 82, 85, 86, 90, 99, 104, 107–8, 108–12, 112–9, 120, 147

Elizabeth Woodville, Edward IV's Queen, 31–2

Elizabeth of York, Henry VII's Queen, 31–2

Elwes, Sir Gervase, Lieutenant, 147–8

Erskine, Thomas, Lord Chancellor, 240, 242

Escapes from the Tower, 93–4, 174, 183, 223

Essex, Arthur Capel, Earl of, 208, 219; ——, Robert Devereux, 112–3, 147

Eton College, 24

Evelyn, John, 187, 188–9, 190–1, 195, 206, 207, 215, 223

Exeter, Henry Courtenay, Marquis of, 39

Fenians, Irish, 254–5

Fenwick, Sir John, conspirator, 223–4

Ferrers, Laurence Shirley, Earl, 235–6

Fire of London, 190–2

Fisher, John, Bishop, 47–8

Fitzharris, Edward, informer, 203–4

Flanders, 99

Ford, John, dramatist, 152

Forman, Simon, 146, 147

Fotheringhay, 75, 86

Fox, Charles James, 242

Foxe, John, martyrologist, 82

France, 17, 22, 27, 179, 189, 242; French Revolution, 242

Gardiner, Stephen, Bishop, 43, 57, 64, 67–71, 74, 75

Garnet, Henry, Jesuit, 92, 93, 125–30

Gaunt, John of, Duke of Lancaster, 14, 15

George I, 222, 226–7, —— III, 237, 239, 243; —— IV as Regent, 246, 247

Gerard, John, Jesuit, 91–4

Germans, the, 14, 96, 255, 256

Gibbon, Edward, historian, 241

Index

Gifford, Gilbert, Catholic informer, 86
Gordon, Lord George, Protestant fanatic, 239–40
Greenwich, 40, 42
Grenville, Sir Bevil, 156, 176–7, 188
Grey, Lady Catherine, 78–9, 91; —— Lady Jane, 65–7, 96, 257; ——, Lady Mary, 79
Griffith, Welsh Prince, 12
Guernsey, isle of, 181, 184, 222
Guiana, 134, 141
Gundulf, Bishop, builder of the Tower, 10
Gunpowder Plot, 125–31

Hales, Sir Edward, Lieutenant, 215
Hall, Arthur, translator, 90
Hamilton, James Douglas, Duke of, 225
Hampden, John, Parliamentarian leader, 155–7
Hardwick, Bess of, Countess of Shrewsbury, 143
Hardy, Thomas, Radical politician, 242
Harington, James, political philosopher, 184
Hastings, William, Lord, 26, 27–9
Hatton, Sir Christopher, Lord Chancellor, 107–8
Hawthorne, Nathaniel, 253
Hay, James, Earl of Carlisle, 132, 152
Hazlerigg, Sir Arthur, 183–4
Henrietta Maria, Charles I's Queen, 159, 165
Henry III, 12, 78; —— IV, 15, 16, 19; —— VI, 19–24, 257; —— VII, 25, 30–2, 35, 37; —— VIII, 9, 12, 32, 35–54, 57–63, 66, 78, 104, 107, 239, 256; ——, Prince, James I's son, 137, 138–40
Hertford, Edward Seymour, Earl of, 78–9; ——, William, Seymour Earl of, 143–4; and v. Somerset
Hess, Rudolf, 255
Hobbes, Thomas, philosopher, 156, 223
Holland, 223, 240
Hollar, Wenceslaus, artist, 179–80
Hooper, John, Bishop, 68
Hopton, Sir Owen, Lieutenant, 79, 82, 87, 107
Hoskins, John, lawyer, 140–1
Hotham, Sir John, Governor of Hull, 176
Howard, Catherine, Henry VIII's Queen, 43–4, 57; —— of Escrick, Edward, Lord, 183, 201–2, 204, 208–9; and v. Norfolk, Northampton
Hull, 176
Huntingdon, Selina, Countess of, 235–6, 241
Hutchinson, Lucy, 156

India, 237
Inscriptions in the Tower, 84, 96–100
Ireland, 15, 30, 107–8, 159, 174, 223

James I, 95, 119, 123, 124, 127, 130, 132, 134, 140, 143, 145, 150–2; —— II, 189–90, 195, 203, 206–7, 210–5, 217, 218–9, 220, 223
Jeffreys, George, Lord Chancellor, 217–8
Jersey, isle of, 123–4
Jews, expulsion of, 12
Jonson, Ben, dramatist, 140

Keepers of the Crown Jewels, 193–4, 250
Keepers of the Records, 65, 157, 171, 243–4
Kent, 111, 120
Keys, Thomas, Serjeant Porter, 79
Kilmarnock, William Boyd, Earl of, 230–2
Kingston, Sir William, Constable, 42

Lambarde, William, Keeper of the Records, 65
Lambert, John, General, 183–4
Lambeth Palace, 42, 114, 168, 212
Lansdowne, George Granville, Lord, 229
Latimer, Hugh, Bishop, 69
Laud, William, Archbishop, 155, 158, 159, 160, 167, 168–70, 188
Laurens, Henry ('Tower'), American Revolutionary leader, 240–1
Lee, Sir Henry, Master of the Ordnance, 120
Leicester, Robert Dudley, Earl of, 77, 79, 80, 86, 87, 108
Lemon, Robert, archivist, 244
Lennox, Margaret Douglas, Countess of, 143
Levellers, the, 179–80, 182, 183, 209–10
Lieutenants of the Tower, 45, 54, 65, 69, 72, 79, 82, 83, 87, 91, 92–3, 96, 100, 107, 124–5, 128, 131, 134, 146–50, 151, 165, 166, 167–8, 173, 180, 182, 187, 188, 189, 192, 205, 215, 222, 230, 241
Lilburne, John, Leveller, 179–81
Lisle, Arthur Plantagenet, Lord, 59
London, 9, 12, 19, 20, 71, 81, 124, 166, 205; —— Bridge, 71, 74, 81
Lopez, Dr Rodrigo, 112–3
Louis XIV, 195, 196, 219
Lovat, Simon Fraser, Lord, 230–2
Love, Christopher, Puritan fanatic, 181–2
Lysons, Daniel, 244; ——, Samuel, Keeper of the Records, 243–4

Machyn, Henry, chronicler, 64, 65
Madre de Dios, carrack, 108
Mancini, D., chronicler, 29
Margaret of Anjou, Henry VI's Queen, 19, 22; Lady —— Beaufort, 27, 31–2, 35, 47; —— of York, Duchess of Burgundy, 24, 31, 32

Marlborough, John Churchill, Duke of, 220–2
Mary I, 39, 41, 65–75; —— II, 207, 217, 220, 221
Mason, Sir John, Secretary of State, 58
Massey, Sir Edward, General, 174
Mayors, Lord, 14, 20, 40, 100, 173, 183
Middleton, John, Earl of, 174
Milton, John, 141, 179
Mint, the, 10, 65, 189, 190
Mohun, Charles, Lord, duellist, 224–5
Mompelgart, Count, tourist, 104
Monk, George, General, Duke of Albemarle, 178, 183, 187, 188, 221
Monmouth, James Scott, Duke of, 203, 205, 210–2
Monson, Sir Thomas, Master of the Armoury, 146–7, 151
Montagu, Edward, Lord, 173
Monuments in the Tower, 100
More, Sir Thomas, 26–30, 32, 38, 45–54, 123
Morley, Herbert, Colonel, Lieutenant, 187
Morton, John, Archbishop and Cardinal, 26, 27–8
Motte, Francis de la, spy, 241–2
Mountfort, William, actor, 224
Mountjoy, Charles Blount, Lord, 114

Netherlands, the, 22
Neville, Edmund, 94; ——, Sir Henry, 114
Newgate prison, 240, 249
New York, 239
Nithsdale, William Maxwell, Earl of, 226–7
Norfolk, Thomas Howard, 3rd Duke of, 38, 43, 57, 60–2, 84; ——, Thomas Howard, 4th Duke of, 80–2
Normans, the, 9–10
Northampton, Henry Howard, Earl of, 30, 84, 130, 146–51
Northumberland, John Dudley, Duke of, 61, 63, 64, 65–72; ——, Henry Percy, 8th Earl of, 84–5; ——, Henry Percy, 9th Earl of, 130–4, 137, 152, 192–3; ——, Thomas Percy, 7th Earl of, 84

Oates, Titus, 195, 201, 202
Ordnance, Masters of, 120–1, 215
Orléans, Charles, Duke of, poet, 17
Overbury, Sir Thomas, poisoning of, 141, 145–52
Oxford, 30, 53, 69, 88, 177, 181, 204, 219, 223; ——, Robert Harley, Earl of, 225, 227–8

Painter, William, Elizabethan writer, 120–1
Parliament, 19, 25, 30, 90, 139, 155, 158–65, 167–70, 173–4, 176, 177, 178, 179–83, 196, 206

Paris, 113, 174
Parry, William, conspirator, 85
Parsons, Robert, Jesuit, 85, 87, 94, 128
Peasants' Revolt, the, 14
Penn, William Quaker, 193, 220
Pepys, Samuel, diarist, 188, 189, 190–3, 206–7
Percy, Thomas, Gunpowder plotter, 127, 130, 131
Perrot, Sir John, 107–8
Peters, Hugh, Puritan preacher, 169, 176, 185
Petre, Edward, Jesuit, 213
Philip II, 71, 83, 85, 86
Pitt, William, the elder, 237; —— ——, the younger, 242–3
Place, Francis, Radical wire-puller, 246
Platter, Thomas, tourist, 104
Plots, 84–7, 123–4, 125–31, 182, 183, 195, 201–5, 207–8, 210, 218, 223–4, 230, 246–7
Plymouth, 176–7
Poems written in the Tower, 50, 87, 89–90, 109–10, 137, 138, 179, 243
Pole, Reginald, Cardinal, 38–9; —— Inscriptions, 98; —— de la, Lord William, 37–8; and v. Suffolk
Pontefract Castle, 17, 27
Pope, Sir Thomas, 53–4
Popish Plot scare, 195, 201–4
Portsmouth, Louise Kéroualle, Duchess of, 203, 206
Preston, Richard Graham, Lord, 219–20
Princes, murder of the, 10, 25–30
Prynne, William, Keeper of the Records, 158–9, 169–71, 174, 179, 183
Pym, John, Parliamentarian leader, 160, 177, 178

Quakers, 181, 193

Radcliffe, Egremont, 98–9
Ralegh, Sir Walter, 108–12, 115, 116, 123–41, 151, 155
Rebellions, 14, 19, 38, 64, 65, 71, 80, 84, 94, 226, 230
Rich, Richard, Lord Chancellor, 50, 53, 60
Richard Coeur-de-lion, 10; —— II, 14–6, 19; —— III, 24, 25–30, 226
Ridley, Nicholas, Bishop, 66, 71
Robinson, Sir John, Lieutenant, 188
Rochford, George Boleyn, Lord, and Lady, 42, 43–4; ——, William Henry Zuylestein, Earl of, anti-American Secretary of State, 239
Romans, the, 9–10

Index

Rome, 10–11, 69, 169, 218
Roper, Margaret, 45–7, 53–4
Russell, William, Lord, 208–9

St John's Chapel, 12, 70, 78, 88
St Loe, Sir William, 72–3, 99
St Peter-ad-vincula Chapel, 12, 72, 82, 91, 100, 134, 148, 254
Salisbury, Margaret Plantagenet, Countess of, 40; ——, James, Earl of, 218
Salvin, Anthony, architect, 254
Sandwich, Edward Montagu, Earl of, 188, 189
Say, James Fiennes, Lord, 19
Sayre, Stephen, American financial agent, 239
Scobell, Francis, 225
Scotland, 19, 181, 226, 229, 230, 240
Secker, Thomas, Archbishop, 239
Selden, John, Keeper of the Records, 157
Selwyn, George, wit and man about town, 232
Seven Bishops, the, 212–5
Seymour, Thomas, Lord Admiral, 61, 63–4; and v. Hertford, Somerset
Shaftesbury, Anthony Ashley Cooper, Earl of, 196–206
Shakespeare, William, 10, 16, 90, 113, 116, 128, 236
Shelley, William, Catholic agent, 84
Sherborne Castle, 134–7, 140
Shrewsbury, Mary Talbot, Countess of, 143–5
Sidney, Algernon, republican, 208
Simnel, Lambert, impostor, 30–1
Simpson, Cuthbert, Protestant martyr, 96
Sindercombe, Miles, Leveller and conspirator, 182
Somerset, Edward Seymour, Duke of, 58, 59, 60, 63–4, 69, 78; and v. Hertford, Seymour
Somerville, John, conspirator and madman, 86
Southampton, Henry Wriothesley, Earl of, 114, 116–9
Southwark, 65, 71
Southwell, Sir Richard, Master of the Ordnance, 50, 89; ——, Robert, Jesuit poet, 89–90
Spain, 83, 87, 96, 99, 112
Spies, 241–2
Sprat, Thomas, Bishop, 221, 222
Stafford, William Howard, Lord, 201–2, 207
Stanley, Thomas, Lord, 27, 28
Stoke, battle, 31
Story, Dr John, 98
Stow, John, chronicler, 100–1, 104
Strafford, Thomas Wentworth, Earl of, 159–67, 173

Stuart, Lady Arbella, 91, 143–4; ——, Mary, Queen of Scots, 80–2, 84, 86
Suffolk, Henry Grey, Duke of, 66, 67, 71, 72; ——, Thomas Howard, Earl of, 150, 152; ——, Edmund de la Pole, Earl of, 37
Surrey, Henry Howard, Earl of, 61–2; and v. Norfolk
Sussex, Thomas Radcliffe, Earl of, 74–5, 77
Swift, Jonathan, Dean, 227

Tewkesbury, battle, 22, 25
Thistlewood, Arthur, conspirator, 246–7
Thomas, William, conspirator, 72
Throckmorton, Elizabeth, Lady Ralegh, 108–12; ——, Job, Puritan, 90; ——, Sir Nicholas, 74, 80; —— his Lady, 67
Tichborne, Chidiock, conspirator, 87
Tooke, Horne, Radical reformer, 242
Topcliffe, Richard, persecutor, 89
Torture, 75, 84, 87, 88, 89, 92, 96
Tournaments, 14–5, 42
Townshend, Lady, 230
Towton, battle, 19
Trelawny, Jonathan, Bishop, 213
Tremayne, Edmund, 75
Turner, Anne, poisoner, 147–8
Tyburn, 32, 88, 235, 236
Tyrrell, Sir James, 29–30

Usk, Adam of, chronicler, 15–6
Ussher, James, Archbishop, 166

Vane, Sir Henry, 160, 184–5
Vernon, Elizabeth, Lady Southampton, 119
Victoria, Queen, 250

Wade, Sir William, Lieutenant, 124–5, 128, 146–7, 151
Walker, Obadiah, Oxford Romanist, 219
Waller, Edmund, poet, 177–8
Walpole, Henry, Jesuit, 88, 92; ——, Horace, 226, 229, 232, 235–7, 238–9, 240; ——, Sir Robert, 225–6, 227
Walters, Lucy, Monmouth's mother, 211
Walworth, Sir William, Lord Mayor, 14
Walwyn, William, Leveller, 181
Warbeck, Perkin, impostor, 32
Warwick, 29; ——, Ambrose Dudley, Earl of, 120–1; ——, Edward Plantagenet, Earl of, 30–1, 32; ——, Richard Neville, Earl of, 'the Kingmaker', 22
Watson, William, conspirator, 123

279

Index

Waynflete, William, Bishop, 22

Wellington, Arthur Wellesley, Duke of, 252

Wentworth, Peter, Parliamentary oppositionist, 90–1

Weston, Richard, poisoner, 147–8; ——, William, Jesuit, 94

Westminster, 10, 169; —— Abbey, 27, 30; —— Gatehouse, 89; —— Hall, 50, 81, 100, 230; —— School, 187

Whitehall, 166, 190, 191

Whitefield, George, preacher, 235

Wildman, Major John, Leveller, 209–10

Wilkes, John, Radical rabble-rouser, 237–8, 242

William I, the Conqueror, 9, 10; —— III, 218, 219, 220–4

Williams, John, Archbishop, 168

Winchester, William, Marquis of, 66, 74, 77, 124

Windsor Castle, 17, 24

Winter, Thomas, Gunpowder plotter, 125

Winwood, Sir Ralph, Secretary of State, 151

Wolfe, James, General, 253

Wolsey, Thomas, Cardinal, 38, 61, 100

Worcester, battle, 174; ——, Edward Somerset, Marquis of, 183

Wren, Sir Christopher, architect, 30; ——, Matthew, Bishop, 174–5

Wriothesley, Thomas, Lord Chancellor, 58, 59, 60

Wyatt Rebellion, 65, 71; ——, Sir Thomas, 75

Wyndham, Sir William, 226, 227

York, 88

Zoo at the Tower, 10, 104, 189, 245